COLONIAL
GEORGIA

A HISTORY

A HISTORY OF THE AMERICAN COLONIES
IN THIRTEEN VOLUMES

GENERAL EDITORS:
MILTON M. KLEIN & JACOB E. COOKE

KENNETH COLEMAN

COLONIAL GEORGIA

A HISTORY

CHARLES SCRIBNER'S SONS, NEW YORK

Library of Congress Cataloging in Publication Data

Coleman, Kenneth.
  Colonial Georgia : a history.
  (A History of the American colonies)
  Bibliography: p. 308
  Includes index.
    1. Georgia—History—Colonial period, ca. 1600–
  1775. 2. Georgia—History—Revolution, 1775-1783.
  I. Title. II. Series.
  F289.C64   975.8'02   75-37534
  ISBN 0-684-14555-3

Page 196, Courtesy, Georgia Department
of Archives and History.

All pictures except the one on page 196 courtesy
The University of Georgia Libraries.

FOR ELLIS MERTON COULTER
SCHOLAR, TEACHER, FRIEND

CONTENTS

ILLUSTRATIONS

EDITORS' INTRODUCTION

The American colonies have not lacked their Boswells. Almost from the time of their founding, the English settlements in the New World became the subjects of historical narratives by promoters, politicians, and clergymen. Some, like John Smith's *General History of Virginia*, sought to stir interest in New World colonization. Others, such as Cotton Mather's *Magnalia Christi Americana*, used New England's past as an object lesson to guide its next generation. And others still, like William Smith's *History of the Province of New-York*, aimed at enhancing the colony's reputation in England by explaining its failures and emphasizing its accomplishments. All of these early chroniclers had their shortcomings but no more so than every generation of historians which essayed the same task thereafter. For it is both the strength and the challenge of the historical guild that in each age its practitioners should readdress themselves to the same subjects of inquiry as their predecessors. If the past is prologue, it must be constantly reenacted. The human drama is unchanging, but the audience is always new: its expectations of the past are different, its mood uniquely its own.

The tercentenary of John Smith's history is almost coterminous with the bicentenary of the end of the American colonial era. It is more than appropriate that the two occasions should be observed by a fresh retelling of the story of the colonization of English America not, as in the case of the earliest histories, in self-justification, national exaltation, or moral purgation but as a plain effort to reexamine the past through the lenses of the present.

Apart from the national observance of the bicentennial of American independence, there is ample justification in the era of the 1970s for a modern history of each of the original thirteen colonies. For many of them, there exists no single-volume narrative published in the present century and, for some, none written since those undertaken by contemporaries in the eighteenth century. The standard multivolume histories of the colonial period—those of Herbert L. Osgood, Charles M. Andrews, and Lawrence H. Gipson—are too comprehensive to provide adequate treatment of individual colonies, too political and institutional in emphasis to deal adequately with social, economic, and cultural developments, and too intercolonial and Anglo-American in focus to permit intensive examination of a single colony's distinctive evolution. The most recent of these comprehensive accounts, that of Gipson, was begun as far back as 1936; since then a considerable body of new scholarship has been produced.

The present series, *A History of the American Colonies*, of which *Colonial Georgia* is part, seeks to synthesize the new research, to treat social, economic, and cultural as well as political developments, and to delineate the broad outlines of each colony's history during the years before independence. No uniformity of organization has been imposed on the authors, although each volume attempts to give some attention to every aspect of the colony's historical development. Each author is a specialist in his own field and has shaped his material to the configuration of the colony about which he writes. While the Revolutionary Era is the terminal point of each volume, the authors have not read the history of the colony backward, as mere preludes to the inevitable movement toward independence and statehood.

Despite their local orientation, the individual volumes, taken together, will provide a collective account that should help us understand the broad foundation on which the future history of the colonies in the new nation was to rest and, at the same time, help clarify that still not completely explained melodrama of

1776 which saw, in John Adams's words, thirteen clocks somewhat amazingly strike as one. In larger perspective, *A History of the American Colonies* seeks to remind today's generation of Americans of its earliest heritage as a contribution to an understanding of its contemporary purpose. The link between past and present is as certain as it is at times indiscernible, for as Michael Kammen has so aptly observed: "The historian is the memory of civilization. A civilization without history ceases to be civilized. A civilization without history ceases to have identity. Without identity there is no purpose; without purpose civilization will wither." *

Georgia's colonial history is a case study in the persistence of historical mythology. Popular accounts and textbook treatments stress the province's uniqueness as an illustration of English humanitarianism and utopian idealism. In fact, as Kenneth Coleman's researches in this volume demonstrate, Georgia was never really a haven for debtors, and few debtors actually came to the colony. Even during the ill-fated Trusteeship, Georgia was peopled largely by the English "worthy poor" and indentured servants, continental Europeans, and immigrants from the Carolinas. The colony's history under the Trusteeship was dominated less by philanthropic strivings than by practical efforts at defense, the improvement of Indian relations, the promotion of the fur trade, and experiments in silk production and viticulture. Even before the Trustees surrendered their charter, a year early, the colony had begun to take on the conventional appearance of a southern frontier settlement, and its economic and social configuration began to approximate that of its neighbor to the north, South Carolina. During the next quarter-century, Georgia became a land of small farmers, frontiersmen, and planters; slavery spread; rice plantations were established; and social distinctions emerged.

What Coleman's perceptive study reveals is the distinctiveness given to Georgia's history by the brevity of its history as an

---

* Michael Kammen, *People of Paradox* (New York, 1972), p. 13.

English colony. It is somewhat shocking to realize that Georgia's founder, James Oglethorpe, and its last royal governor, James Wright, were contemporaries—only twenty years apart in age—and both died in the same year! During a brief twenty-five-year period under the crown, Georgia experienced much of the history of all the mainland colonies in microcosm: growing demographic heterogeneity, rapid economic development, increasing religious liberality, and the emergence of a political elite which employed the Assembly as the forum for expressing those principles of self-government that by 1776 were the common property of all the colonies. Georgians, nevertheless, had ample reasons for approaching independence cautiously: they were young, isolated, and defenseless. They chose to follow their northern brethren not so much out of material interest as out of the conviction that they were more American than British. To understand how they reached this decision, in ways similar to yet different from their fellow colonials, is to begin to comprehend the mystery of the events of 1776. Georgia's colonial history, viewed in conjunction with the histories of the other twelve colonies, clarifies the meaning of a revolution whose inception, however fortuitous, produced consequences so momentous that they live with us still.

MILTON M. KLEIN
JACOB E. COOKE

PREFACE

Serious scholars have long known that Georgia was not settled by debtors, but the tradition persists. The interest in debtors ceased once the Trustees for Founding the Colony of Georgia came into existence in 1732. The period during which these Trustees controlled Georgia (1733–1752) was unique and has been overemphasized in studies of the state's colonial history. Nevertheless, the "Plan" of the Trustees, which was not in reality well thought out, has fascinated people since the eighteenth century. Many historians have written about this period from the Trustees' London viewpoint, without sufficient appreciation of the degree to which events in Georgia differed from the instructions sent from London. After his first year in Georgia, Oglethorpe, the only Trustee who ever came to the colony, was more concerned with defense than with carrying out the Trustees' large ideas. Secretary William Stephens, the most loyal servant the Trustees ever had in Georgia, soon came to agree with the colonists that many instructions from London were impractical and might best be overlooked. Hence he sometimes slanted his reports to satisfy the Trustees rather than to record what actually happened. I have made an effort to emphasize what occurred in Georgia without ignoring what they hoped would occur. If a clearer picture of events in Georgia emerges, it is because of my conscious efforts in this direction and the increased availability of manuscript sources and specialized studies.

The Trustee period has often been considered a failure, and

indeed much of what the Trustees sought was not achieved. Yet their efforts resulted in the formation of a colony that survived as an English settlement in a region that had been claimed by the English and the Spanish since the founding of Carolina in 1670. Who can say what country would have acquired this territory if Georgia had not been founded? Certainly the slowness of Georgia's development in its first twenty years was not entirely the result of the "impractical" ideas of the Trustees; part of it was the result of the newness of the colony and its frontier environment.

The Trustee period is the most interesting part of Georgia's colonial history, but the royal period (1752–1775) is in many ways more important. It was during these years that Georgia began the type of development which would continue long after it became a state in the American Union. Georgia was in these two later decades a rather typical southern frontier area, rather than the unique colony of the Trustee period. Political events for these years are already well known, and I have tried to supply a fuller economic and social picture. I agree with W. W. Abbot's suggestion that the brevity of Georgia's colonial history makes it in many ways the place in which colonial problems can be seen in telescoped fashion and sometimes with more clarity as a result.

My treatment of the Revolutionary Era has followed my earlier and more detailed study of this period, *The American Revolution in Georgia*. Certainly Georgia, a small and poor state adjoining British East Florida, could not contribute personnel and materiel to the military effort proportional to its needs. The effects of the war and separation from Britain were considerable in Georgia, especially in that these events helped to extend political power to the up-country and in general, to expand political, economic, and social democracy.

Anyone who writes a general history on any subject must depend to a considerable extent on earlier writings. I have used the works of many earlier historians which are noted in the bibliography. Others have helped in different ways. I have been inspired over a long period of work in Georgia history by my old teacher and friend E. Merton Coulter, emeritus professor at the

University of Georgia. Of more immediate help in this study has been a former student, Milton Ready, of the University of North Carolina at Asheville. His studies in the economic history of colonial Georgia have supplied much information for this account, and he has read the entire manuscript and made numerous suggestions. Several colleagues at the University of Georgia have helped, most notably Phinizy Spalding and Richard K. Murdoch. The editors of this series, especially Milton M. Klein with whom I have worked most closely, have made numerous helpful suggestions. So has the editorial staff at Charles Scribner's Sons.

Personnel at the University of Georgia Library have been most helpful, especially Porter W. Kellam, the director emeritus, John W. Bonner, the special collections librarian, and Mrs. Susan B. Tate of the special collections department. Personnel at the British Public Records Office provided guidance with the hundreds of manuscript volumes which I consulted during the summer of 1968. Colonel M. E. S. Laws, of Bank Top Cottage in Kent, supplied additional material from London. Librarians and archivists at other depositories noted in the bibliography have been helpful.

Financial assistance, especially for travel, was made possible by Director Emeritus Porter W. Kellam of the University of Georgia Libraries, a grant from the American Philosophical Society, and a grant from the National Society of the Colonial Dames of America in the State of Georgia.

My sincere thanks go to all those named above, as well as to others who have helped at various phases with the preparation of this book. It is my hope that their money and efforts were well spent.

Summer 1975
Athens, Georgia   KENNETH COLEMAN

COLONIAL GEORGIA

A HISTORY

1

BACKGROUND OF SETTLEMENT: DONS AND FRONTIER DEFENSE

Georgia, the last British colony in America which was founded by settlers coming direct from Europe, was located in territory long known to whites. In fact the area had European settlers forty years before the English colony of Jamestown was founded. The Spanish were the first European colonizers in America and likewise the first to occupy the Georgia coast—arriving more than a century and a half before James Edward Oglethorpe and his colonists landed at Yamacraw Bluff in 1733.

The first Europeans known to have set foot in Georgia were Hernando de Soto and his followers in 1540. That spring de Soto's expedition came from Florida into Georgia arriving at the southwestern border of the present state and generally traveling in a northeasterly direction through the coastal plain and piedmont region. In the northern part of the present state the Spaniards turned west into what is now Alabama. This expedition aroused interest in the entire southeastern part of North America and was important for the later exploration and settlement it inspired.

After de Soto's explorations the next Europeans to show interest in the Georgia area were French Huguenots under the leadership of Admiral Gaspard de Coligny. They arrived on the Florida coast early in 1562 and sailed northward until they finally attempted a colony at Port Royal, near where Beaufort,

South Carolina, is now located. Here settlers under Jean Ribaut built Charles Fort. Religious wars in France prevented any aid to Charles Fort, and the approximately thirty men who comprised the expedition eventually built a boat and set sail for France. Two years later Coligny sent out another colony of Huguenots who landed at the mouth of the St. Johns River, near present-day Jacksonville, Florida, where they built Fort Caroline.

Pedro Menendez de Aviles, a Spanish conquistador, was also interested in making a settlement in Florida for the glory of God, king, and Menendez. He was fitting out an expedition when he heard of the new French Huguenot settlement. Accordingly, in August of 1565, he settled St. Augustine, below Fort Caroline, and put the French heretics to the sword. This new settlement, the first permanent European settlement in the area of the present United States, became the nucleus of Spanish Florida.

The next spring Menendez set out to explore the coast above St. Augustine. He stopped at an island where the chieftain was named Guale (pronounced Wallie). The Spaniards applied this name to the island (later called Santa Catalina, now St. Catherines) and eventually Guale came to include the entire upper coast of Florida. Upon his return to St. Augustine, Menendez left a garrison of thirty men on Guale, the first Spanish post in the future Georgia.

In Guale the Spanish followed their dual colonizing policy of founding presidios and missions close to each other. In 1566 Jesuit friars arrived in Florida and began laboring for the Lord in this new vineyard. Missions were established on Santa Catalina and San Pedro (now Cumberland) islands which became centers of Spanish influence. The Jesuits did not prosper, however, because of the small number of priests, inadequate missionary methods, and Indian objections. A few Franciscans arrived in Florida in 1573, but are not known to have operated in Guale on a regular basis until 1596. Soon thereafter five or six Franciscans conducted services at the mission stations in Guale.

For two years the Franciscans seemed to be having great success creating more mission stations, holding services, and baptizing Indians. The missions were fed and supported by

Indian labor. Then in September of 1597 Father Pedro Corpa was murdered by Indians in his church at Tolomato and a revolt of the mission Indians began, apparently because Father Corpa objected to allowing an Indian named Juanillo (or Juan) to become head chieftain of Guale. Juanillo was not a model chief in the missionaries' viewpoint, because he would not give up his pagan ideas. He told the Indians that the missionaries were only a forerunner of increased numbers of Europeans who would eventually deprive the natives of their land and liberty, and he urged that all friars be killed before it was too late. Four more missionaries were killed, and one was captured, but several were protected by friendly Indians. The revolt spread over the entire area of Guale, before Governor Gonzalo Mendez Canzo in St. Augustine began to collect military support to suppress it. Canzo set out at the head of a hundred and fifty soldiers to subdue the Indians and sent smaller expeditions to several places. After a lengthy investigation, an Indian boy, implicated as being present at the death of one of the missionaries, was executed. Governor Canzo ordered the enslavement of all the Guale Indians who had been captured, but this edict was disallowed in Madrid. Eventually many Guale Indians went to St. Augustine and made their submission to the governor. Juanillo was killed while fighting with other Indians in the interior. By 1600 most of the submissions had been made, the troubles were over, and Indian-white relations returned to "normal."

Governor Canzo made a visit or "progress" along the Guale coast in 1603 to try and impress the Indians, take the submission of chieftains, rebuild destroyed or damaged churches, and set the missions on the course they had been following before the revolt. His visit seemed a complete success, but far more impressive was the first episcopal visitation to Guale in the spring of 1606 by Bishop Fray de las Cabezas Altamirano of Santiago. The bishop spent Holy Week and Easter in St. Augustine and then began his journey among the missions. In the Guale area he confirmed over one thousand Indians, including many important chiefs. The visit was thus both a religious and an imperial success.

During the first quarter of the seventeenth century additional friars were sent, new missions were opened, and the missions prospered. Although there has been considerable argument and misunderstanding about the locations of the missions and the material from which they were constructed, it is now agreed that they were made of wood. Generally located in principal Indian villages, most missions were located on islands, with San Pedro on Cumberland Island, San Buenaventura on St. Simons Island, San Jose on Sapelo Island, and Santa Catalina on St. Catherines Island. Santo Domingo, located at Talaje on the mainland at the mouth of the Altamaha River near the present town of Darien, is the only mission which has been positively located by modern archaeologists.

Life for the conscientious friars, usually no more than two per mission, was very full. They had to be architects and contractors, though actual building labor came from the Indians. Agriculture had to be encouraged so that the missions would be self-sustaining and hopefully produce a surplus to be sent to St. Augustine. The children were instructed and the sick visited and treated, daily masses said and special services conducted, Indians advised and led along the way prescribed by the friars and secular officials. Missionaries were also the best link the Spanish government had with the Indians and were expected to report any valuable information received from them. There were accordingly long reports of religious and secular nature to write and to send to superiors in St. Augustine, Cuba, and Spain.

Beginning in the second quarter of the seventeenth century, missions grew up in the interior among the Apalache Indians, reaching their high point in the last quarter of the century. Starting at the Gulf of Mexico on the Apalachicola River, these missions continued up the Chattahoochee River perhaps as far as the present city of Columbus and were especially prized by the Spaniards because they supplied more food to Florida than those on the coast.

After the mission growth of the first half of the seventeenth century, gradual decline set in. This was partly owing to the normal slowing or tiring of the friars and the Spanish authorities, but it was also a result of the Carolina settlement by the English.

In 1663 Charles II granted to the lords proprietors the Carolina territory and two years later he extended it to below St. Augustine, grants which made the Georgia coast English so far as the authorities in London were concerned.

With the English settlement of Charles Town in 1670, the territory between it and St. Augustine became a region of contention between England and Spain. This conflict over the "debatable land" would last until 1763 and have considerable effect upon the development of this area. The decline of the Spanish missions in Guale and Apalache was a part of this fight. Also in 1670, the English and the Spanish agreed through the Treaty of Madrid that Britain might hold forever the areas in America and the West Indies which she then held. This was interpreted as allowing the English to hold lands as far south as Port Royal in Carolina.

Though Spain sent an expedition to destroy Charles Town, storms disrupted the Spanish plans and nothing else was done except to put a garrison on Santa Catalina in Guale in 1673 and to begin a stone fort at St. Augustine the same year, a fort which was largely finished by 1687.

The retreat southward by the Spanish really began in the 1680s. Yuchi, Creek, and Cherokee Indians became allied with the English and attacked Guale missions. Since the Spaniards did not feel that they had sufficient troops to garrison Guale, they began a gradual withdrawal. Pirates attacked the islands and missions at about the same time, and by 1686 all Guale missions had been abandoned. The garrisons were withdrawn and an attempt was made to persuade the Indians to move closer to St. Augustine, but many of them refused to do so and went over to the English instead. At about the same time Indians, under the leadership of the Englishman Dr. Henry Woodward, attacked the missions on the Apalachicola and the Chattahoochee, and they were soon abandoned or declined greatly. Thus by 1690 the Spanish frontier was effectively at the St. Marys River and by 1702 at the St. Johns, even though Spain continued to claim the old Guale territory.

With the Spanish retreating down the coast to St. Augustine,

Carolinians had a brief encounter with the Scots, who made a settlement at Stuart Town on Port Royal Island in 1684. Once located there, the settlers made overtures to the neighboring Indians for trade purposes. This aroused Charles Town Indian traders so that Carolinians gave no help to the Scots when the Spanish destroyed Stuart Town in 1686.

During Queen Anne's War (1702–1713), South Carolinians under Governor James Moore invaded Florida in 1702 and captured St. Augustine but were unable to seize the fort, having little to show for their effort except the pushing back of the Spanish frontier from the St. Marys to the St. Johns rivers. Two years later Moore led an expedition against the Apalache missions and effectively destroyed them, a move which would help the Carolina Indian trade in the interior.

Beginning about 1700 the race between France, England, and Spain for control of the northern coast of the Gulf of Mexico increased the concern of Carolinians for their security. As the English secured no territory on the Gulf of Mexico, their entry would have to be through the land south of the Savannah River. It was fear of Spanish or French control of this territory that excited Carolinians during the first quarter of the eighteenth century, not fear that Carolina settlements would be overrun by the Spanish.

There were several suggestions for English settlements near the mouth of the Mississippi, inspired by the desire to establish links between the Atlantic coast and the Indian country. In 1708 Thomas Nairne, a Carolina Indian agent and leading exponent of western development, proposed such a settlement. In 1713 Hughes Pryce, a Welsh gentleman who had traveled from Carolina to the Mississippi, suggested a new English colony near the mouth of the Mississippi to be settled by poor Welshmen. Both of these colonies were envisioned as means of securing the territory, Indian friendship, and Indian trade before the French moved in; but neither proposal was acted upon despite the fact that the French on the Mississippi greatly worried Carolina Indian traders.

After the destructive Yamassee War of 1715–16 and the deaths

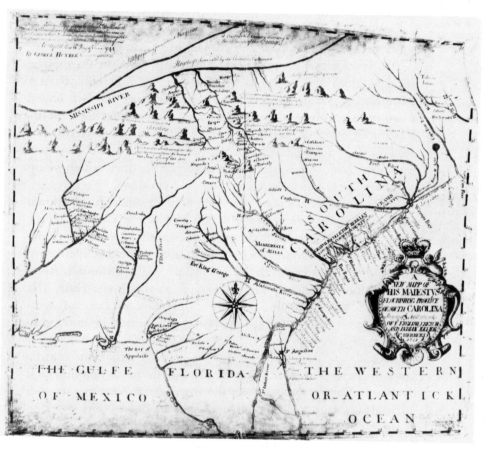

John Herbert's map of Georgia in 1725.

which it caused on the Carolina frontier, Carolinians showed an increased desire to control the land south of the Savannah River, claimed by both Carolina and Florida but occupied by neither. Carolinians thought the only way to have real security for their colony and the Indian trade was to settle this land by citizen-soldiers capable of fighting off Indian and Spanish raids.

If new settlers were necessary, what better way could they be secured than by a proposal made in 1717 by Sir Robert Montgomery, a Scottish baronet, to the lords proprietors of Carolina that he be allowed to settle a new colony between the Savannah and Altamaha rivers? Sir Robert would create this settlement, to be known as the Margravate of Azilia, as a separate colony with himself as governor for life, but the land rights of the Carolina proprietors would continue. The proposed colony would, Sir Robert argued, prevent Spanish or Indian invasions of Carolina. It could also produce silk, wine, olives, raisins, almonds, and currants—items imported by England from the Mediterranean area. The colony could also be extended to the Gulf of Mexico or the River Apalachia via the Altamaha River, thus preventing French expansion along the Gulf. The Carolina proprietors and royal authorities in London were favorable to the settlement. Sir Robert published in London in 1717 *A Discourse Concerning the Design'd Establishment of a New Colony to the South of Carolina, in the Most Delightful Country of the Universe* and in 1720 *A Description of the Golden Islands* as promotional booklets. However, neither Sir Robert nor the Carolina proprietors possessed funds for the colony, so it was never settled.

The importance of Azilia to Georgia lies in those suggestions of Sir Robert which were later applied in the actual settlement of Georgia: the idea of a buffer colony between the Savannah and Altamaha rivers; the compact township settlement plan, with settlers living in a town surrounded by contiguous farm lots; citizen-soldiers recruited from among the poor of Britain who were to fight as needed and to cultivate the land for their support. The suggested agricultural products were those later advocated by the Georgia Trustees. The marvels of the climate and the economic possibilities of the colony later advertised by the Trustees sound remarkably like "The Most Delightful Country of the Universe." The approval of Azilia by royal authorities made it clear that the London government by 1720 was willing to push settlement south of the Savannah River into the debatable land.

The next proposed settlement on the Carolina frontier was that of Jean Pierre Purry of Switzerland. Purry, born in 1675, was a Swiss wine merchant before he went to Batavia as a planter in 1713. In 1717 he proposed to the Dutch East India Company to settle a colony in South Australia and in South Africa. Both locations fit his theory that the ideal climate for human development was near latitude 33° in both hemispheres. Having gotten no support for his proposed colonies from either Holland or France, in 1724 Purry suggested a British settlement in his ideal latitude in North America. Now he wanted to settle six hundred poor Swiss as soldier-workers, with himself as colonel and judge, south or west of the existing Carolina settlements in an area to be called Georgia. This settlement would, hopefully, extend far enough west to create an English wedge between French Louisiana and Quebec. The Board of Trade was interested, and the Carolina proprietors agreed to the idea, but it failed for lack of financing. In 1730, after South Carolina became a royal colony, Purry did make a settlement on the northern side of the Savannah River, called Purrysburg. The location proved a bad one for a town, and Purry himself died in 1736. The town declined and even the name disappeared in the locality.

In January of 1720, the Carolina Assembly made a long and detailed report on the defense of the colony which became the basis of action in England and Carolina. This plan suggested that Port Royal be made into a port and magazine from which to supply outlying forts. The two most important forts suggested should be at Savannah Town at the falls of the Savannah River, and a new settlement at the mouth of the Altamaha River, important in any defense against the Spanish. These locations were declared excellent for Indian trade—Savannah Town had already proved this—and both were surrounded by excellent land capable of supporting agriculture.

Besides these two key forts, several posts in the Alabama-Mississippi country were suggested to cut the French contacts between the lower Mississippi River and Quebec. This fear of the French and their interference with Carolina Indian trade, which extended well into the Mississippi country, was undoubtedly sparked by the founding of New Orleans (1718) and of Fort Toulouse (1717) at the juncture of the Coosa and Tallapoosa rivers in the heart of Creek country. A French post at such a location could not be overlooked by Carolina Indian traders. The best way to man these garrisons, as the report pointed out, was to settle citizen-soldiers there.

The Board of Trade agreed generally with the report and chose the mouth of the Altamaha as the place to erect the first fort, favoring the north bank of the river rather than St. Simons Island. A town should be laid out contiguous to the fort with farm lots to be granted to settlers who would act as soldiers when needed. Clearly the Board of Trade thought it was time to settle the debatable land south of the Savannah River.

An independent company of one hundred "invalids" arrived in Charles Town from England in May of 1721, but the men who were to build the fort on the Altamaha were too ill, and the engineer expected to design it did not arrive. Governor Francis Nicholson therefore sent Colonel John Barnwell to the Altamaha to erect a temporary fort at colonial expense.

South Carolinians were certain that their frontiers could never be safe under the proprietors, who would never spend enough money nor attract enough settlers. In fact the Carolina land office had been closed since 1719 and would remain closed until 1731 to the great discouragement of new settlers. Thus the entire matter of Carolina frontier defense became entangled with the fight to have South Carolina made into a royal province, an effort which was not successful until 1730.

The Spanish immediately protested that the fort at the mouth of the Altamaha, Fort King George, was on their territory and cited the 1670 Treaty of Madrid as proof of its illegality. Carolinians replied, incorrectly, that the Altamaha territory had never belonged to the Spanish and had always been considered a part of Carolina. Carolinians may not have known in 1723 that a Spanish mission had once been located upon the same spot as Fort King George, but they surely knew that the territory had once been Spanish. The government in London authorized direct negotiations between the governors of South Carolina and Florida to determine the common frontier, but nothing was ever done. Carolinians stressed the importance of the Altamaha for contact with Creeks and were sure that if the English did not maintain control of this new fort that the Spanish would build a fort there, a very doubtful probability, in fact.

Fort King George, always unpopular with its garrison, burned at the end of 1725. The Carolina Assembly agreed to rebuild the fort, but Council President Arthur Middleton thought it should be on St. Simons Island, where he said it would be of more value. Governor Francis Nicholson, of South Carolina, in England favored the original site. When Robert Johnson was appointed the first royal governor of South Carolina in 1730 he was instructed to have the fort reconstructed on its original site, but it was never rebuilt.

South Carolina's new royal governor had been her proprietary governor from 1717 to 1719 and was both acquainted with the needs of and concerned about the welfare of his colony. In 1729 and 1730 he submitted to the Board of Trade detailed suggestions for the defense and settling of the colony. Johnson advocated the creation of ten townships on the frontiers with a town at the center of each, surrounded by farm lots for the support of the settlers. These townships were to be at regular intervals on the frontier, three being located on the Savannah River.

Johnson's plan was enthusiastically endorsed by the Board of Trade, which made certain significant alterations in it. The Board specified that land should be granted on the basis of the settlers' ability to cultivate it—fifty acres for each member of the family—but with no grants large enough to interfere with the compactness so essential to defense. Township lands could be granted only to new settlers, in order to increase the white population of South Carolina and make it capable of defending the colony. The Board of Trade specified that two of the townships must be located on the Altamaha, the first specific requirement in England that land this far south should be settled. Clearly the government in London was ready to enter into a contest with Spain and France for the debatable land.

The desired new settlers from Carolina could come from two main sources, Scotch-Irish from Ulster and German Protestants fleeing from Roman Catholic rulers. Both of these groups were coming to America in large numbers by 1730. Leading Carolinians and English merchants trading to Carolina advocated that poor settlers be encouraged to come to the colony by being given aid in transportation and settlement. Governor Johnson was instructed to see that aid was provided to encourage poor but desirable settlers, and the Carolina Assembly in 1731 passed a law to provide such assistance.

By 1730 the settlement of the area south of the Savannah River had become the primary imperial problem of the British and the Carolinians. In fact, most ideas about a new colony since the founding of Pennsylvania in 1680 had envisoned settlement south of the Savannah. It seems fairly safe to say that by 1730 English settlement of this area would soon take place. Certainly this was the biggest problem of South Carolinians, who were more worried about French interference with the Indian trade in the Alabama country than about Spanish advance north from St. Augustine. The Spanish had been receding to the south since the founding of Carolina sixty years before, and there was no reason to suppose they would reverse this trend. But the French were a newer and more aggressive menace, and it was impossible in the 1720s to tell what they would be able to accomplish. It probably is correct to say that the Carolinians did not fully separate French and Spanish dangers. Both Catholic powers interfered with hoped-for Carolina expansion and increased Indian trade south of the Savannah. Both Charles Town and London knew that something had to be done to protect the Carolina frontier.

2

FOUNDING A COLONY:
IDEALISM AND IMPERIALISM

The founding of Georgia stemmed from two divergent movements that initially had no connection but which were merged by
time and place so that each reinforced the other. Thus South
Carolina's need for additional frontier settlers was merged in
London with the desire of James Edward Oglethorpe and his
philanthropic friends to resettle in America poor and unfortunates from London and other English cities.

Oglethorpe was born on December 22, 1696, the son of
Jacobite Colonel Theophilus Oglethorpe. At about the age of
twenty, James Edward saw service with Prince Eugene of Savoy
against the Turks and spent a little time at the Jacobite court of
James III in France. However he returned to England by 1719
and took up residence at the family estate of Westbrook, at
Godalming in Surrey, not far from London. In 1722 he was
elected to the House of Commons from the nearby borough of
Haslemere, a seat which he maintained until 1743. In the House
for six years Oglethorpe pursued an uneventful career of
committee work and other routine activities. In the summer of
1728 a friend, Robert Castell, an architect, was committed to
Fleet Prison in London for debt. Since Castell was not able to
pay special fees to the warden for better treatment, he was
confined in a part of the prison where smallpox was prevalent
and died of the disease. Oglethorpe had visited Castell in the

James Oglethorpe.

Fleet and was sure that his treatment there was responsible for his death. Castell's death aroused Oglethorpe to do something about the condition of English jails, where many poor debtors languished. Oglethorpe moved an investigation in Commons and was appointed in February of 1729 as chairman of a committee to inquire into "the State of the Gaols of this Kingdom." The investigations during 1729 and 1730 resulted in several of the most notorious wardens being prosecuted. Parliament freed an estimated ten thousand prisoners, mainly debtors. To celebrate this great and good deed, the Reverend Samuel Wesley, Jr., brother of John and Charles, published a poem, "The Prisons Open'd," in which he exclaimed:

> Yet Britain cease they Captives' Woes to mourn,
> To break their Chains, see Oglethorpe was born!

This activity brought Oglethorpe considerable acclaim, especially in religious and philanthropic circles. Among those with whom he came in contact was Dr. Thomas Bray, a leading philanthropist and founder of the Society for the Propagation of the Gospel in Foreign Parts and the Society for Promoting Christian Knowledge, who was interested in the plight of the poor and unfortunate in England and in the colonies. In 1730, before his prison investigations had been completed, Oglethorpe became concerned about the welfare of the released debtors and began considering a charity colony in America to which some of them could be sent. Dr. Bray seems to have first suggested such a colony shortly before his death in early 1730, and he undoubtedly influenced Oglethorpe's thinking.

Friends of Bray were organized into the Associates of Dr. Bray to carry on his philanthropic work. Oglethorpe suggested that the associates pursue a charity colony, and they authorized him to present a plan for their consideration. The result was a 1730 application from the Bray associates for a charter to settle a charitable colony in that part of South Carolina south of the Savannah River. It is impossible to know who was responsible for the ideas included in the charter. But knowledge of South Carolina's defense needs, of Governor Johnson's township plan,

SEAL OF THE TRUSTEES
FROM 1732 TO 1733
DRAWN BY MARJORIE TILFORD
FEDERAL WRITERS' PROJECTS

FROM A CHART BY WILLIAM S. IRVINE

and of the South Carolina struggle to become a royal province were all current in London at this time. The similarities between the ideas for Carolina's expansion and protection circulating during the past three decades and what was advocated and actually occurred in Georgia make clear the connection between the two.

The Georgia charter was approved by the Privy Council on January 27, 1732, signed by the king on April 21, and passed the privy seal on June 9, the official date of the charter. The document created "the Trustees for Establishing the Colony of Georgia in America . . . to be a Body politick and Corporate in Deed and in name for ever." All territory between the Savannah and Altamaha rivers and westward from their headwaters to the Pacific was taken away from South Carolina and made into "one Independent and separate Province by the name of Georgia." The political power of the Trustees over the colony was to last for twenty-one years, but their control of the land was permanent. After the Trustees' political rule lapsed, Georgia's government was to become whatever the king directed. The government of Georgia was entirely in the hands of the Trustees except that the command of the militia was vested in the governor of South Carolina. Any governor appointed or laws passed by the Trustees must receive royal approval. One strange omission, considering the pattern of colonial governments by 1730, is that there was no requirement that any sort of legislative assembly be created.

According to the charter, philanthropy was the most evident motive for the founding of Georgia. No Trustee could own land, hold any office of profit or trust, or receive any salary or income because of his efforts for the new colony. The Trustees must labor for the welfare of the colony and of the Empire. These provisions made Georgia different from all other proprietary colonies.

The twenty-one Trustees named in the charter were a self-perpetuating body and could increase their number to twenty-four. Historically, the best-known Georgia Trustee was Oglethorpe, who was very important in the affairs of the Trust throughout his stay in Georgia. The two Trustees who worked hardest in London were James Vernon and John Viscount

Percival, who became the Earl of Egmont in 1733. Several others gave long and faithful service, but a majority of the seventy-one Trustees who served during the life of the Trust gave little time or effort to Georgia.

There was to be a Common Council of fifteen Trustees, which would have considerable authority of its own. The Trustees or the Common Council were authorized to make all laws and ordinances necessary for the colony and to inflict reasonable punishments upon offenders through provincial courts. British subjects or foreigners willing to be naturalized might settle in Georgia; and all people born in Georgia were to enjoy the same rights and liberties as free subjects born in Britain. Georgians were guaranteed liberty of conscience, and all but Roman Catholics could have free exercise of their religion.

Since the creation of a proprietary colony as late as 1732 was out of line with the thinking of the British government then, there were certain safeguards for royal authority written into the charter. Foremost was the provision that the political authority of the Trustees should last only twenty-one years. Approval of laws and a governor by the king and Privy Council was a further check. Governors must give security to obey royal instructions and Parliamentary laws. The Trustees must file annual reports of receipts and expenditures with designated crown officials, and all grants of lands must be registered with crown officials for quitrent purposes. In addition, reports of the progress of the colony must be made to the secretary of state and the Board of Trade.

The charter having been issued, the Trustees for Establishing the Colony of Georgia in America organized as a corporate body in their first meeting called by Viscount Percival at their office in Old Palace Yard, Westminster, on July 20, 1732. Only twelve Trustees attended this initial meeting, and poor attendance was to plague the Trustees' meetings hereafter. The Trustees began work at once and received letters of congratulations, ideas about aid to unfortunates, offers to raise money, and gifts. A commission to solicit and receive subscriptions was appointed. Ideas relating to the government, officers, and requirements for

John Percival, Earl of Egmont.

colonists began to be formulated. Notices were inserted in the London papers that the Trustees were ready to receive applications from people who would like to go to Georgia. Frequently thereafter the Trustees' Journal bears the notation "Examined several Persons who Offered themselves to Go to Georgia, and Enter'd their Names for further Consideration."

Although debtors bear considerable credit for the origin of the Georgia movement, once the charter was issued concern for debtors disappeared. The term now became "unfortunate poor" and so it remained in the thinking of the Trustees. Much has been written about the debtors who came to Georgia and what the Trustees did for the debtors; all of it false. There was never a committee of the Trustees to visit the prisons to seek out worthy debtors. If any colonists had formerly been in debtors' prison, that fact seems to have had nothing to do with their selection. Albert B. Saye, the scholar who has searched hardest for debtors among Georgia's earliest colonists, found no mention of debtors in the contemporary press or in the records of the Trustees. In fact, he estimated that no more than a dozen possible debtors ever came to Georgia.*

The charity colonists, those sent to Georgia at the expense of the Trustees, were poor people from the English towns—the "worthy poor"—whom the Trustees so avidly sought. As the Trustees themselves expressed it, they would take "such as were in decayed Circumstances, and thereby disabled from following any Business in England; and who, if in Debt, had Leave from their Creditors to go, and such as were recommended by the Minister, Church-Wardens, and Overseers of their respective Parishes." Most of these were small tradesmen or artisans and many occupations are included in *A List of the Early Settlers of Georgia*, a collection of information about the settlers kept by the Trustees in London. It may appear strange that no soldiers, sailors, husbandmen, or laborers from the country were accepted for a colony which was supposed to fight Indians and Spaniards on its frontiers and support itself by agriculture. Soldiers and

---

* Albert B. Saye, *New Viewpoints in Georgia History* (Athens, 1943), Preface.

Went at the Tr. charge / age	Occupations	When embark'd	when arrived	Lotts in Savannah	Lotts in Frederica	† dead / q. quitted / r. run away / N.º Divisions
1 Weddal (Austin)	Farmer	14 May 1735		230		† Nov. 1738
2 — (Marg:) w.						
3 Welch (John)	Carpenter . . .	14 Oct. 1735	feb. 1735-6			5. S. q. to Carolina 1740 ?.
4 — (Anne) w.						?º
5 — (James) son						?º
6 — (John) son						?º
7 Wellon (Elias Anne) 19	servt. to Joseph Coles	6 Nov. 1732	1 feb. 1732-3			sent back to England
8 Wesley (J.ⁿ) A.M.	Minister at Savannah	14 Oct. 1735	feb. 1735-6			r 2 Dec. 1737
9 — (Cha.) A.B.	his Brother	dº.	dº.			q. July 1736
10 West (John) 33	Smith	6 Nov. 1732	1 feb. 1732-3	31		† 1739
11 — (Eliz.) w. 33	. . . . . .	. . . . . .	. . . . . .			† 1 July 1733
12 — (Ri.) son 5	. . . . . .	. . . . . .	. . . . . .			† 31 July 1733
13 Weston (Willes)	Tanner	14 Oct. 1735	feb. 1735-6	43		N. deserted before April 1740 †
14 Wheeler (Cha.)	Bookbinder . . .	20 Sept. 1733	14 Jan. 1733-4			†
15 — (Eliz.)	servt. to Will. Bradley	20 Oct. 1735	feb. 1735-6			
16 White (Rich.)	Hatter	14 Oct. 1735	feb. 1735-6	35		5 † dec. 1740 Henless
17 Weisseger (Dan.)		31 Oct. 1734	29 Dec. 1734			in his way to Philadelphia
18 Willoughby (Ja.)	Peruke maker . .	15 June 1733	29 aug. 1733			† 17 Oct. 1734
19 — (Hanah) w.		11 Sept. 1733	16 dec. 1733			

1 Treasurer of the Indian Traders Lycence money. In 1737 he belong'd to the Compy. settled at Fort Augusta

2 the River Inmate on lot 222.

3 On the 1. feb. 1738-9 Col. Oglethorp advanc'd him on the Trustees acct. 53.11.0 to set up a Brew house.

4

5

6

7

8

9 Mr. Cha. Wesley took the Oath of Secr. for the Indian Trade, 19 feb. 1735-6: but quitted the Colony & roed to England July 1736

10 appointed 3. Bailif 19 Oct. 1733, which he some years after resign'd. On 7 Oct. 1735 he had a grant of 500 acres, and 11 May 1737 was permitted to alienate this lot. He marry'd Eliz. Little his 2. wife 25 aug. 1733. and Eliz. Hughes his 3rd.

11 wife 29 April 1734. In June 1739 he had leave to sell his Interest and quit the Colony by reason of ill health, but dies of the consumption before he could set out. his wife remarry'd to Will. Kellaway.

12

13 Return'd dead 1740

14 settled at Skidaway

15

16 Storekeeper at Frederica in Oct. 1738. He was on the 14 Oct. 1735 appointed to be a Bailif in case of vacancy.

17

18

19 Imprison'd for marrying Ri: Mellichamp, Will.m Watkins her 1. husband being alive and she with child by him, and then leaving Mellichamp and by his consent bedding a third man who bought her for 2 shilling.

Page from the Egmont Papers. This list of early settlers indicates the kind of information the Trustees kept about the colonists as well as the type of colonists who came to Georgia. John Wesley's name is included on this page.

sailors were often the dregs of society and therefore undesirable in Trustee thinking. Farm workers were not "surplus population" of the sort the Trustees were seeking to help. There was argument in the eighteenth century and since among historians as to the intention of the Trustees about the type of settlers they would send to Georgia. The mercantilistic thinking of the day objected to taking good workers out of England, hence the Trustees emphasized that their settlers were not productive at home and that their going to Georgia would not drain England of needed workers. Thus it seems logical to believe that the Trustees tried to get the best out of the unfortunate poor who presented themselves, hoped not to hurt the labor force of England, and sincerely believed that they would aid the poor they sent to Georgia by giving them a new chance there.

Oglethorpe, who had taken the initiative in the Georgia movement from the beginning, announced by mid-October of 1732 his intention of going to Georgia with the initial embarkation. Apparently this caused the first settlement to be made sooner than some of the Trustees thought desirable. The Trustees had collected less than £2,000, and many thought this insufficient to begin a colony, as indeed it was. Oglethorpe, a bachelor of an adventurous nature, may have thought of going to Georgia earlier, but the death of his mother the previous June evidently reinforced his decision to go. He went to Georgia with no title—certainly not that of governor—and with no clearly defined authority from the Trustees. Never one to quibble over technical details, Oglethorpe supplied the strong leadership necessary to the colony's early years despite his lack of formal authorization.

The people accepted as the original colonists were all "worthy poor" who went to Georgia at the Trustees' expense; "on the charity" was the expression used. The Trustees engaged a two-hundred-ton frigate, the *Ann*, which anchored at Gravesend to receive passengers and supplies, which (according to the *Gentleman's Magazine*) included ten tons of Alderman Parson's best beer "for the service of the colony."

On the last Sunday before sailing, November 12, 1732, the

Reverend Henry Herbert, who had volunteered to serve as minister until the Trustees could afford to pay one, preached to the future colonists their last sermon on English soil. On Thursday, November 16, seven Trustees came to Gravesend where Oglethorpe presided at a meeting on board the *Ann* and the vessel was inspected and described as "being Tight & Strong & well Manned, Tackled and Provided fitt for Merchant Service." The roll of passengers was called, and Captain John Thomas marked down a total of 114 passengers, or 91 heads, children under twelve being counted at less than a head. The Trustees left "the People very well satisfied."

The *Ann* left Gravesend on Friday, November 17, 1732, about nine in the morning. The last sight of English land was lost on November 22, and the vessel was then in the open Atlantic. The passengers were crowded, but that was normal in the eighteenth century. Food was specified in the charter party as beef four days a week, pork two days, and fish one day. Bread, vegetables (especially onions and carrots), butter, vinegar, wine, molasses, and beer were issued in varying amounts on stated days. Most days must have been fairly monotonous on the crowded vessel, but several celebrations stood out when flip was provided along with a better than usual dinner. For the christening of the infant Georgius Marinus Warren on November 23, Oglethorpe stood godfather. Three quarts of flip were issued to every mess of five heads and a "handsome" supper was served. "The people very much refresht this day were mery. Drank ye Trustees health & Success to the Colony." Oglethorpe's birthday was celebrated on December 21 with cudgel played for a pair of shoes in addition to flip and mutton. Finally on Christmas there were prayers and a sermon before a special dinner with pudding and a pint of flip per head. The *Ann* did not stop at the Madeira Islands to take on five tuns of wine, as had been previously announced, so little wine consumption on the voyage is recorded.

All in all the voyage was a successful and healthful one. The only deaths were two infants, reported by Oglethorpe as weak and half starved before they left England. Oglethorpe and Dr. William Cox saw to the needs of everyone. When the sick needed something, Oglethorpe often provided it out of his private stores. When Oglethorpe caught a dolphin, he gave it to pregnant women who were anxious for fresh food. It was on board the *Ann* that Oglethorpe began to be called "father" by the colonists. His kind of leadership was shown when he ordered a pint of rum punch per head to settle an argument among several people. Oglethorpe told the people to drink and be friends again, and apparently they did. On the Atlantic crossing both the settlers and Oglethorpe decided that he was the leader.

Toward the end of the voyage the men were exercised with guns and bayonets as they had been before they left England. Early on the morning of January 13, 1733, land was sighted near Charles Town, South Carolina. But for the colonists it was to be only a sight. Governor Robert Johnson had warned that they should not come ashore, lest they become too enamored of the town to continue to Georgia.

Oglethorpe went ashore, however, and presented a copy of the Georgia charter to Governor Johnson and his Council whose aid and advice he solicited. South Carolina was especially interested in Georgia's founding as a part of the long-projected protection of the Carolina frontier. Food, labor, and advice were the main issues discussed by Oglethorpe and Johnson. The Carolina Assembly soon voted Georgia one hundred head of breeding cattle, five bulls, twenty breeding sows, four boars, and twenty barrels of rice. Scout boats, rangers, and boats for transportation were also provided.

The day after arrival, the *Ann* sailed for Port Royal to the south. Here Oglethorpe and Lieutenant James Watts of the Independent Company fitted out the new barracks for the reception of the colonists who landed to refresh themselves at Port Royal and Beaufort, three miles away, while Oglethorpe went to pick out the place of actual settlement. Oglethorpe returned on January 24, and on Sunday, January 28, at a special service, the colonists gave thanks for their safe arrival and for their present blessings. The Reverend Mr. Lewis Jones, the Beaufort minister, preached; and after the service there was a bountiful meal consisting of four fat hogs, eight turkeys, fowls, English beef, a hogshead of punch, a hogshead of beer, and a large quantity of wine, "and all was disposed in so regular a Manner that no Person was Drunk nor any Disorder happen'd."

On January 30, the colonists embarked in a sloop and five small boats with a scout boat and Captain MacPherson and fifteen South Carolina rangers to ascend the Savannah River to the site selected for settlement. They arrived in the afternoon of February 1 (February 12, new style) at the foot of Yamacraw Bluff seventeen miles up the Savannah from its mouth. Their journey had ended, but the struggle in the founding of a colony had only begun.

Yamacraw Bluff, named for the Indians who lived there, is the first high ground upriver from the Savannah's mouth. The Yamacraws were a small outlawed group of Creeks, slightly more than one hundred in number. They were served by the trading post of John Musgrove, a South Carolina trader with a half-breed wife named Mary. The area was well known to South Carolina Indian traders and cattle drovers. It was high enough to be free of swamps, surrounded by adequate forests for timber and firewood, isolated from the Indians except for the small Yama- craw group, located on the river for transportation, and just across the river from South Carolina. Although the records are silent, Oglethorpe must have been told of the site by Carolinians. There is no documentary evidence that Colonel William Bull, future lieutenant governor of South Carolina, was actually present with Oglethorpe when Yamacraw Bluff was picked, but he undoubtedly knew and approved of the Yamacraw Bluff site, and was there soon afterward giving aid and advice. Given the geography of Georgia and South Carolina, it is hard to see how Oglethorpe could have found a better site for his settlement.

For the first night on Georgia soil, four large tents were erected. The next morning some of the colonists looked over the area and recorded their views of it. Oglethorpe sent a very perceptive description to the Trustees a week after landing.

I fixed upon a healthy Situation, about Ten Miles from the Sea. The River here forms an Half-moon, along the South side of which the

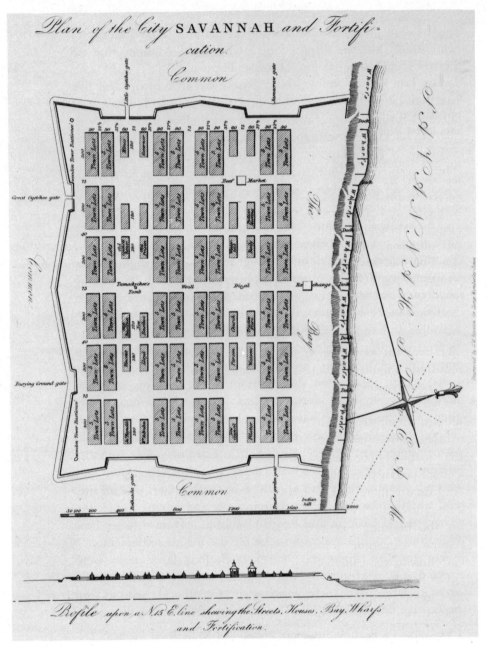

Town plan for Savannah.

Banks are about Forty Feet high, and on the Top a Flat, which they call a Bluff. The plain High ground extends into the Country Five or Six Miles, and along the River-side about a mile. Ships that draw Twelve Feet Water can ride within Ten Yards of the Bank. Upon the River-side, in the Centre of this Plain, I have laid out the Town, opposite to which is an Island of very rich Pasturage, which I think should be kept for the Trustees Cattle. The River is pretty wide, the Water fresh, and from the Key of the Town you see its whole Course to the Sea, with the Island of Tybee, which forms the Mouth of the River, for about Six Miles up into the Country. The Landskip is very agreeable, the Stream being wide, and bordered with high Woods on both sides. . . . I have marked out the Town and Common; half of the former is already cleared, and the first House was begun Yesterday in the Afternoon. A little Indian Nation, the only one within Fifty Miles, is not only at Amity, but desirous to be Subjects to his Majesty King George, to have Lands given them among us, and to breed their Children at our Schools. Their Chief and his beloved Man, who is the Second Man in the Nation, desire to be instructed in the Christian Religion.*

This was an agreeable beginning, but much labor would be required to make the homes and lives that the Trustees and the settlers envisioned.

Oglethorpe set everybody to work and directed everything himself. Colonists unloaded the boats and transported the goods up the sandy bluff to the town site. Some cut down trees where the town was to be located and began to shape them into timbers. Others began building a fort and a palisade around the town. And finally there was a group which cleared land for planting. The sandy bluff was covered with pine trees which were excellent for the building needs of the new colony. At the Trustees' request, Governor Johnson sent Negro sawyers from South Carolina to assist in clearing the ground.

On February 9 Oglethorpe and Colonel William Bull laid out the town in the pattern which still gives Savannah real

---

* Oglethorpe to Trustees, Feb. 10, 1732/3, in *Collections, Georgia Historical Society*, I (Savannah, 1840), 233–34; reprinted in Charles C. Jones, Jr., *The History of Georgia* (2 vols., Boston, 1883), I, 122–23.

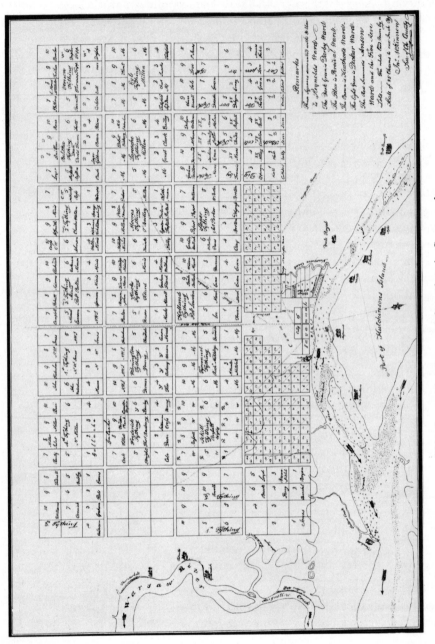

Plan for garden lots and farm lots in Savannah.

distinction. At regular intervals there were public squares which have always been important in Savannah's life. These were used for markets or open spaces in the city and may have been intended for a place where outlying settlers could camp if they had to come into Savannah because of danger of Indian or Spanish invasion. They were never used for this last purpose because the necessity never arose.

Physically and politically the town was laid out into lots, tithings, and wards. House lots sixty by ninety feet fronted on a street and backed upon an alley. Each block consisted of ten lots: five facing one street, five facing the next street, and an alley through the center. Four blocks, called tithings, made up a ward, at the center of which was a public square 315 by 270 feet. Fronting each square, and taking up the rest of the center of the ward were four Trustee lots, two on each side, intended for churches, markets, stores, etc. There were originally six wards in Savannah, and the same plan was used as the city expanded until about 1850. Beyond the town proper were garden and farm lots. This basic plan, with some modifications, was followed in all towns created in Georgia in the Trustee period and is clearly a descendant of Sir Robert Montgomery's plan for Azilia and of Governor Robert Johnson's 1730 township plan for the Carolina frontier.

The people had been divided into tithings on board the *Ann*, and this division determined neighbors when the original house lots were granted. At the head of each was a tithingman who was in charge of the ten men when they stood guard in the early days. Constables were the chief officials of the wards in much the same position as tithingmen for their units.

Work on the town progressed satisfactorily during the spring. When Samuel Eveleigh, a Charles Town merchant much interested in early Georgia, visited Savannah in late March he was impressed by Oglethorpe's abilities and how he kept things under control. "Mr. Oglethorpe is indefatigable, takes a vast deal of Pains. . . . He is extremely well beloved by all his People; the general Title they give him is Father. If any of them is sick, he immediately visits them, and takes a great deal of Care of them.

If any Difference arises, he is the Person that decides it. . . . He keeps a strict Discipline; I never saw one of his People drunk, or heard one swear, all the Time I was there. He does not allow them Rum, but in lieu gives them English Beer. It is surprising to see how chearfully the Men go to work, considering they have not been bred to it. There are no Idlers there; even the Boys and Girls do their Parts."* Land had been cleared and planted with wheat, herbs, vegetables, and fruit. The town site was cleared, four houses completed, and the palisade around the town almost finished. Said Eveleigh of Oglethorpe, "In short, he has done a vast deal of Work for the Time, and I think his Name justly deserves to be immortalized." And so it has been because of the founding of Georgia.

The first Savannah houses were all built upon the same plan. They were twenty-four feet long and sixteen feet wide, eight feet high exclusive of the garret or loft used for sleeping, built of feather-edged boards, and roofed with tarred shingles. The floors were made of one-and-a-half-inch planks and stood on log foundations two and a half feet above the ground. Oglethorpe was one of the last at Savannah to move out of his tent into a house, and his house was the same as the others.

By summer the defenses of the town had been completed—a palisade, a guardhouse, and two blockhouses proofed against musket shot. Cannon were installed in the blockhouses and a battery of six on the riverside. Oglethorpe estimated that 70 of the 160 inhabitants were able to bear arms, a rather high estimate under ordinary circumstances. Target practice was held from time to time with prizes for the winners to encourage the people to learn the use of firearms.

Food for the first year came from the South Carolina gifts, the gardens of the colonists, the Indians (especially venison and other game), the river, and from England or the other colonies. Several visitors commented that provisions were mainly salted, and at least one colonist was reprimanded by the Trustees for wasting

---

* *South Carolina Gazette*, March 24, 1732/3, reprinted in Allen D. Candler, ed., *Colonial Records of the State of Georgia* (26 vols., Atlanta, 1904–16), III, 406.

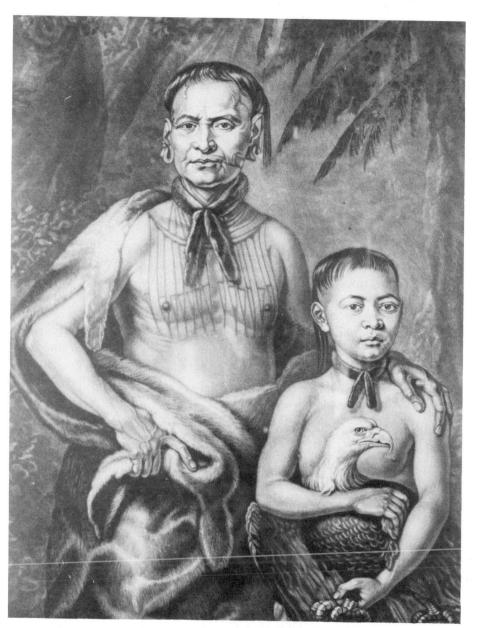

Tomo-Chi-Chi and Tooanahowi.

his time in hunting rather than tilling his land. Land in the immediate vicinity of Savannah was not very fertile, but good soil was reported several miles away. The basic diet of meat and flour was supplied by the Trustees under their plan to feed the settlers for their first year. The settlers had been townspeople—only three of the original settlers knew anything about agriculture—and the Trustees' plans concerned silk, wine, and spices. Food production was often inadequate in early Georgia, and the Trustees frequently had to feed the colonists for longer than a year.

Oglethorpe and the Trustees realized that the friendship of the Indians was of great importance. In truth, the colonists needed the Indians more than the Indians needed the colonists. Indian relations proved one of Oglethorpe's strong points, and he made a good beginning on this delicate subject. The small tribe of the Yamacraws who lived on the bluff named for them were headed by an old chieftain, Tomo-Chi-Chi, who was Oglethorpe's entry into Indian relations. The Indians came to welcome the whites with strange ceremonies which elicited some comments from the settlers. Speeches were made and translated, gifts were exchanged, and profusions of great friendship expressed. Tomo-Chi-Chi and the Yamacraws were glad to have Oglethorpe and the settlers, and the same proved true of the Lower Creeks in May when a treaty was agreed to.

Saturday, July 7, was a high point in the first summer in Savannah. Early in the morning the settlers met on the strand near the river and heard prayers of praise and thanksgiving read. Then they went to Johnson Square where the ceremony of naming the streets, wards, and tithings was held. Each freeholder was put into possession of his lot; now he felt himself a part of Georgia in a way he had never been before. There was a hearty dinner, and in the afternoon the Trustees' appointees for civil office were sworn in. The Trustees' order for establishing a court was read, a jury was impaneled, and a case was tried. Peter Gordon, William Waterland, and Thomas Causton were named bailiffs or magistrates, the chief officials of the colony and judges of the court. Thomas Christie was the recorder of the court, and

Joseph Fitzwalter and Samuel Parker were the constables. There were also tithingmen and conservators of the peace, all appointed by the Trustees from among the charity colonists.

The first recorded birth in Georgia was Georgia Close, born to Henry and Hannah Close on March 17, 1733. She received the silver boat and spoon, promised by James Hume of South Carolina to the first white child born in the new colony. She came soon enough to receive the ministrations of Dr. William Cox, the physician who came on the *Ann*, and the Reverend Henry Herbert, the minister. She had a fleeting sort of fame as the first white child born in the colony; but she lived less than ten months, dying late in December in the year of her birth.

During the first summer, death was a more common occurrence in Savannah than birth. Dr. Cox was the first to die, on April 6, leaving the colony without a doctor. The minister, Dr. Herbert, was ill in the early spring, when some ten fellow colonists had the bloody flux, thought to be caused by the cold and living in tents. He first went to Charles Town to try and recover his health, then embarked for England in May, dying at sea on June 15. July through September was the trying time for the colony and the colonists. During the summer about twenty of the *Ann*'s passengers died and perhaps the same number of settlers who came later.

Oglethorpe was sure that he knew the cause of both the deaths and a spirit of independence which manifested itself in the colony—the consumption of rum punch. To him this was the villain that caused all of the colony's troubles, and he believed that he had sufficient deathbed confessions to prove his point. He did not explain the deaths of infants, who hardly frequented public houses, but by implication rum punch was the cause here also. Oglethorpe certainly would have agreed with Baron von Reck, who brought the first Salzburgers to Georgia, when he called rum "that flattering and deceiptful liquor." Oglethorpe would not agree with the colonists who believed that the climate, especially the lack of a pure water supply, was to blame. As one reported to London, the people drank river water "polluted with putrid Marshes, and the numberless Insects that deposit their *Ova* there, together with the putrified Carcases of Animals and corrupted Vegetables; and this no doubt occasioned much of the Sickness that Swept off many." Acclimatization had been a problem in all colonies, especially during summer in southern colonies, but Oglethorpe would not recognize it.

Sometimes whole families were wiped out, but usually only a part. If one of the parents died, the other tended of necessity to remarry fairly soon. Several times a man or woman remarried after the troubles, only to have the second partner taken off soon thereafter. Sometimes the surviving partner and children returned to England, or sometimes children were put into foster homes at Trustees' expense. Neither God nor man seemed to favor Georgia in the summer of 1733.

In mid-July the troubles were at their worst. Some sixty people were ill, and little hope was held out for their recovery. Dr. Cox was dead. Noble Jones, who had medical training, helped until he became ill himself. Women who had experience in nursing did what they could, frequently until they too became ill. Indian and folk remedies were used to little effect. Then on July 11 when things looked very bleak and there seemed little hope, an unexpected ship arrived with some Jews who had come from England, unknown to the Trustees. One of these was Dr. Samuel Nunis, who went immediately to work with the sick. Oglethorpe soon reported that none of Nunis' patients had died, and the colony sang his praises. Though Oglethorpe praised Nunis' cures, he still insisted that rum had been the cause of the sickness. But the worst was over, and things were improving.

Besides the sickness of the summer Oglethorpe's other great trouble was what he called "this Petulancy." It was in reality a feeling of independence, a conviction on the part of the colonists that they knew how to get along in Georgia now. Oglethorpe wrote confidently in May that he had persuaded all the people to accept the prohibition of Negroes and rum. Yet when he returned from Charles Town in mid-June, after an absence of six to eight weeks, he reported to the Trustees that "some of the People began to be intemperate and then Disobedient so that at my Return I hardly knew them." Later he was more emphatic and reported that "the People were grown very mutinous and impatient of Labour and Discipline." People wanted their rations issued in larger amounts from the Trustees' store, Oglethorpe said, so they could trade them for rum. "By degrees I brought the People to Discipline," Oglethorpe reported, "but could not revive the Spirit of Labour: Idleness and Drunkeness was Succeeded by Sickness." He sent back to South Carolina the Negro sawyers, sorely needed, thinking that they might encourage idleness. He allowed a moderate amount of wine to satisfy thirst but staved all rum found. Yet rum could not be eliminated. John Musgrove sold it at his trading house less than a mile from Savannah, and Oglethorpe could not afford to antagonize John and his wife Mary. In Purrysburg, the new Carolina settlement about twenty-five miles upriver from Savannah, some deaths had been attributed to rum but others to exposure to the air during great heats.

Jean Pierre Purry, the founder of Purrysburg, had another explanation for the dissatisfaction in Georgia. He told the Earl of Egmont in London that the people at Savannah were uneasy because of the system of land tenure by which wives and daughters did not inherit, because of the prohibition of slaves, and because many "idle people" would not work while others could not work. Those able to work thought it unfair that they should labor for all. What Oglethorpe could not or would not see was that the settlers, having been in Georgia about six months, knew much more about what made for success there than they had upon arrival and were no longer willing to follow his leadership blindly. Joys of life were few in Savannah, and rum was one of the few that the poor could afford. Also the settlers must have realized that they were vital to the Trustees' plans and would have to be supported regardless of what Oglethorpe thought. Although later reports of good work and better spirits were to be sent to London, Oglethorpe's absolute control would never be reinstituted. His tenure as "father" had ended.

3

SETTLING THE COLONY: UNFORTUNATES WITHOUT DEBTORS

The most important element in any society is the people, and so it was in early Georgia. The Trustees might make elaborate plans for the colony; but it was the settlers who had to bring these plans to fruition or failure, a point that the Trustees never seem to have comprehended fully. Had they done so, they might have had fewer disappointments about their colony. They went to great lengths to interview personally the charity colonists although they never really understood what kind of people would make good colonists. Nor did the Trustees ever get over their misguided belief that the colonists should uncomplainingly follow directions from London.

Much of what has been written about the colony's population is overly concerned with the settlers who came on the *Ann*, only slightly over one hundred people. The Trustees continued to send over settlers, usually in relatively small numbers but sometimes in larger groups than came on the *Ann*. As more settlers arrived, Oglethorpe began to carry out his plans for settlements near Savannah. These outsettlements formed a perimeter around Savannah and were intended for defense purposes, at least as a warning of impending Spanish or Indian attack. Initially ten families were to be settled at each designated point, enough in theory to provide themselves with safety, to do their defense job, and to have some social intercourse.

In June of 1733, in the midst of the summer sickness and before there were enough settlers to carry out his plans, Oglethorpe and Captain James MacPherson of the South Carolina Rangers explored the country around Savannah, to select the locations for the outsettlements. The first of these was Fort Argyle, named for Oglethorpe's friend the Duke of Argyle, where an old Indian path to Carolina crossed the Ogeechee River about forty miles west and a little north of Savannah. Captain MacPherson and his rangers began building a fort here in August. When the fort was about half finished, it was abandoned because the Ogeechee became blocked with trees washed down by a flood. The fort was relocated some ten miles farther down the river at a place which was still navigable. By mid-September the new fort, also called Fort Argyle, was completed with mounted guns and houses for the garrison, and six families settled there. The original location, now called First Fort, became a point visited by the ranger patrols which went from Fort Argyle to Palachocalas on the Carolina side of the Savannah River. Because of the rangers stationed at Fort Argyle, it lasted longer than several of the other outsettlements.

Another early settlement was at Thunderbolt, about five miles southeast of Savannah on the Wilmington River, one of the water passages to the town. Here the settlers began in August a hexagonal fort with earthen breastworks and a battery of four cannon. Houses were built for the settlers, and Thunderbolt, as a place name, has remained until the present day.

Tybee Island at the mouth of the Savannah River was important in any protection plan. In September of 1733 Oglethorpe ordered ten families settled there and a fort built. The families arrived and the fort was begun, but the deep sand was impossible to cultivate and the island was hated by any who frequented it for this and its "musketoes." Besides its fort, which seems soon to have been forgotten, Tybee was to have a lighthouse to mark the entrance to the Savannah River. This lighthouse was begun in Savannah in the autumn of 1733 and aroused much wonder among those who saw it. When construction actually began on Tybee Island under the direction of

William Blitheman, a carpenter and one of the first settlers on the island, most of his original neighbors were dead and workmen had to be brought down from Savannah. There was continual trouble with drunken workers who did little work. When Oglethorpe returned from England in February 1736 he reportedly made dire threats against the workmen who had not finished the lighthouse. Work now went forward much more rapidly, and it was finished in the spring of 1736. When John Wesley visited Tybee in 1737, while a clergyman in the colony, he reported that the inhabitants had drunk themselves to death or gone away and the island "is now as before a Settlement of Opossums, Racoons, and the like Inhabitants." The lighthouse remained always in need of repairs, being repaired, or just repaired. By 1741 it was reported in ruinous circumstances and a new one was being built. And so it went throughout the colonial period. There seem to have been two reasons for the early lighthouse troubles. There was undoubtedly no builder in Georgia who understood the proper building and repair of such a building. Neither could a satisfactory structure be built of wood, the only material available.

The last settlement to the southeast of Savannah was made upon Skidaway Island in January of 1734. A guardhouse had been built on the northern end of the island in 1733, and a fort was built on the southern end in 1734. The island is about seven miles long with considerable high ground. The original settlers consisted of six single men and five families. In England the men had been perukemakers, clogmakers, ropemakers, weavers, dyers, victuallers, and bookbinders—hardly adequate training for pioneering on the Georgia coast. It was only at Skidaway that there was a Spanish Indian scare in 1734, but this was undoubtedly a false alarm. The original settlement was around the guardhouse at the northern end of the island. William Johnson Dalmas, a former soldier, was made tithingman in charge of the guard, which was complimented for its vigilance in allowing no boat to pass undetected day or night.

The original family which remained longest was Thomas Mouse, his wife, Lucy, and five daughters. He wrote a very proud letter to Oglethorpe while the latter was in England in January of 1735, in which he told of the improvements he had made in his property, the amount of livestock he had, and other things which would appeal to the Trustees and show Mouse as an industrious man, as indeed he must have been. The Mouses and William Ewen, a young single man, were the Skidaway settlers who tried hardest. They had some success for a short while but eventually failed and left Skidaway for Savannah, seeing all their hopes and dreams for success in Georgia and on Skidaway vanish, knowing full well that their feeble efforts would soon be effaced by nature. Before Ewen and the Mouses left Skidaway in 1740 after six backbreaking and disappointing years there, Ewen wrote to the Trustees, "I had now: almost broak my Constitution; with hard working; and hard Liveing and could not see any prospect; of any return of my Labour; now I am Obliged to leave my Settlement (tho, much against my Inclination) and Skidaway; without Inhabitants." He must now go back to Savannah "after that I had spent, all my time; all that I was worth; and had brought my self in Debt." Thomas Mouse could have told the same story. And so, in truth, could most of the colonists who really strove to succeed in one of the outsettlements which Oglethorpe set up mainly for defense reasons without any thought of the human misery and economic failure they would bring to those assigned to them.

There were other settlements away from the sea islands and to the south of Savannah. Here were the villages of Hampstead, settled by Germans, and Highgate, settled by French, very near each other, and Acton not far off. While they undoubtedly fit into the defense picture, they were not obviously so. Abercorn was the farthest north of the original outsettlements, being some fifteen miles upriver from Savannah. It seemed an especially good place for a settlement and had a guardhouse and two cannon.

These outsettlements never succeeded as planned. Frequently, as on Skidaway and Tybee, the land would not support the settlers. The physical isolation was more than most families could bear. Hence, as people died or abandoned these settlements, they were seldom replaced. By 1737 when John Wesley wrote his account of forts and settlements, he listed Abercorn as completely deserted. At Highgate there were six of the original ten families, at Hampstead five, at Skidaway one, at Tybee none, and at Fort Argyle only two. The forts at Argyle and Thunderbolt were reported as rotting and falling. "And the land . . . will in a few years be as it was before." Nature quickly reasserts itself on the Georgia coast.

Other settlements of the first few years, farther from Savannah, were created for certain non-English groups who wanted to live together in their new home. The first such group was the Salzburgers who arrived in March of 1734. Englishmen were interested in the plight of the Salzburgers even before the founding of Georgia. In 1729 the Archbishop of Salzburg, the ruler of an ecclesiastical state in the Holy Roman Empire, determined to convert his Lutheran subjects to Roman Catholicism. By 1732 he had succeeded in driving some thirty thousand of his subjects out of Salzburg. England, the leading Protestant state in Europe, was concerned about the plight of these and other Germans who were refugees from Catholic persecution, a number of whom were already settled in American colonies. Almost as soon as the Georgia charter was issued, the Society for Promoting Christian Knowledge queried the Trustees upon the possibility of sending the Salzburgers to Georgia. The Trustees were interested but did not feel that they had sufficient funds to send any Salzburgers immediately.

Having received a Parliamentary grant of £10,000 in 1733, the Trustees felt that they could accept the Salzburger request. The Reverend Samuel Urlsperger of Augsburg acted as the intermediary for the Salzburgers before and after their migration to Georgia. Seventy-eight people, consisting of forty-two families, left Augsburg in October 1733, to begin their journey to Georgia. In late November they were joined by the Reverend John Martin Bolzius and the Reverend Israel Christian Gronau, from the Latin Orphan School at Halle, who were to be the group's minister and assistant minister respectively.

The Salzburgers arrived in England in December, where they

The Reverend Samuel Urlsperger.

The Reverend John Martin Bolzius.

met the Trustees, took oaths as British citizens, impressed the English with their piety, and set sail for America. Upon arrival in Charles Town in March of 1734, they found Oglethorpe on his way to England. He returned to Georgia to see the Salzburgers settled. They arrived in Georgia on March 10, the second Sunday in Lent or Reminiscere Sunday in the Lutheran calendar. These people who had given up so much for their religion must have had fond hopes of a better day ahead. One of them wrote, "While we lay off the banks of our dear Georgia in the very lovely calm, and heard the birds singing sweetly, all was cheerful on board. It was really edifying to us that we came to the borders of the promised land, this day, when as we are taught in its lessons from the Gospel [Matthew 15:21–29], that Jesus came to the borders by the seacoast, after he had endured persecution and rejection by his countrymen." *

Because of their different language and customs, the Salzburgers wanted to settle separately from the English. Oglethorpe joined Baron Georg Phillipp von Reck, who had come with the group as its commissary or leader on the voyage, in searching out a location for the settlement. The site selected was on a creek which ran into the Savannah River about six miles away, some twenty-two miles above Savannah. Von Reck and the Salzburgers in the exploring party were enthusiastic about the site with its fine meadows, noble woods, and clear streams. The land seemed fertile and game was abundant. Here, they believed they would find their Ebenezer, their Rock of Help, for was it not to this spot that the Lord had helped them?

With their usual energy and faith, the Salzburgers began building their town, named Ebenezer, laid out for them by Oglethorpe. Characteristically, the first building completed was a clapboard chapel dedicated to the Lord with a special thanksgiving service on May 12. Von Reck soon returned to Germany, and the Reverend John Martin Bolzius assumed Salzburger leadership which he retained until his death in 1765 at the age of sixty-two.

---

* P. A. Strobel, *The Salzburgers and Their Descendants* (Baltimore, 1855; reprinted Athens, 1953), 60.

The building of the town went forward, land was cleared, and crops were planted. It was soon discovered that the soil was not nearly so fertile as was originally supposed, hence crop yields were disappointingly low. Also transportation of supplies from Savannah was difficult. While a road and seven bridges had been built from Abercorn to Ebenezer, the Salzburgers had only sledges for heavy freight. Ebenezer Creek proved a disappointment. Besides low water frequently, it became choked with logs, fallen trees, and other obstructions which were impossible to remove. Hence it was often necessary to bring goods overland on the backs of horses and of men.

Conditions at Ebenezer were bad by the end of 1734. There had been sickness and death despite all the ministrations of Apothecary Andreas Zwiffler, who acted as physician and frequently complained that he had inadequate and incorrect medicines. Neither Commissary von Reck nor Jean Vat, who came with the second transport of Salzburgers in late 1734, got along well with Pastor Bolzius. The authority of the minister and the commissaries, who were supposed to be in charge of secular affairs, was never made clear by Oglethorpe or the Trustees. Bolzius was a stronger man than either Von Reck or Vat, and neither of them remained very long at Ebenezer. Although Bolzius always phrased everything in spiritual language and gave the Lord all the credit, he always seemed sure that the Lord favored him over the commissaries.

When Oglethorpe returned to Georgia in early 1736, the Salzburger leaders insisted that they must move from Ebenezer because of its unproductiveness and inaccessibility. While Oglethorpe preferred that they remain at their original location, he seems to have been overpowered by the arguments of Bolzius and others and agreed to their removal to Red Bluff, where Ebenezer Creek flows into the Savannah River. He would not agree to the desired location north of Ebenezer Creek because this land had not been ceded by the Indians.

Immediately upon Oglethorpe's approval of the removal to Red Bluff, or New Ebenezer, the Salzburgers began making preparations to move. Clearing land, planting, and building public and private houses at New Ebenezer went forward rapidly so that most of the Salzburgers had moved the six miles to the new location by the end of May and Old Ebenezer became the site of a cowpen. Although the new location was better than the old one, it had much less good land than was originally anticipated, so that the Salzburgers continued to agitate for the use of Indian lands north of Ebenezer Creek.

After the initial Salzburger settlers, there was a second transport of sixty-five in December 1734, and a third of from sixty to eighty in February 1736. Oglethorpe wanted all the settlers he brought over in February 1736 in the "Great Embarkation" to settle at the new defense outpost of Frederica on St. Simons Island. But the Salzburgers wanted to settle at Ebenezer, and Oglethorpe gave in on this. However a small group under Captain Christian von Hermsdorf did go to Frederica and became the nucleus of a German settlement on St. Simons Island.

Besides the three transports of Salzburgers, a few came in small groups, and there was also some interchange of people between Ebenezer and Purrysburg, in South Carolina. A few non-Salzburger Germans and even non-Germans also settled at Ebenezer. But its population remained essentially Salzburger for several decades. The total number of Salzburgers who made up the three transports numbered between 200 and 250 people, but by 1738 there were only about 130 settlers at Ebenezer. The first and third transports were made up mainly of older people beyond the childbearing age, while the second transport, which had a number of young singles, had few women. Deaths of babies born at Ebenezer in the 1730s reached slightly over 50 percent, higher than usual for the colony. The women at Ebenezer came to believe that the soil there inhibited the growth of children as well as seeds. Adult deaths, augmented by acclimatization and the hard work of new settlements at two locations in such rapid order, were enough to make the early creation of an orphanage necessary.

Population began a gradual increase after 1738, reached about 250 by 1742, and increased further thereafter. Hence it took from

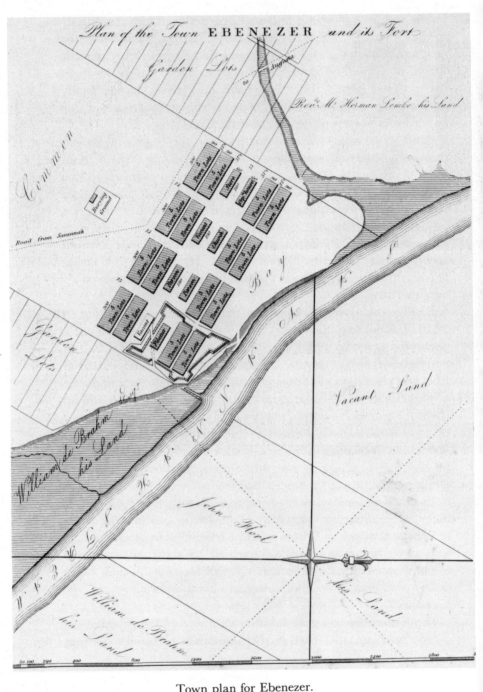

Town plan for Ebenezer.

A Salzburger house near Ebenezer. Few examples of the unusual construction features pictured here have survived until the present.

ten to fifteen years for the Salzburgers to become thoroughly acclimated and to begin slow growth and some prosperity. They could understand well and believe the old German proverb "Death for the first, hardship for the second, bread for the third."

But Ebenezer did last and eventually prosper because of hard work and excellent leadership. Much that happened at Ebenezer must be credited to John Martin Bolzius, who was the initiator and driving force there. Ebenezer was to a considerable degree during its first decades his elongated shadow.

Another group of German-speaking colonists was the Moravians, or members of the ancient religious order known as *Unitas Fratrum*. Count Nicholas Lewis von Zinzendorf allowed some of this persecuted sect to settle upon his Saxon estate. With the backing of Zinzendorf, August Gottlieb Spangenberg went to England in 1734 to negotiate with the Georgia Trustees about Moravian immigration to Georgia. Pleased with the Salzburgers, the Trustees agreed to allow the Moravians to come. A first transport of ten arrived in Savannah on April 6, 1735, under the leadership of Spangenberg, until recently a professor of theology at Halle and a friend of Bolzius and Gronau. A second transport of about twenty-five arrived in Savannah in February of 1736. A majority of the new colonists were men, and a number of them were about twenty years of age.

The Moravians came as indentured servants to Count Zinzendorf, but they never settled on the land granted to him on the Ogeechee. Instead they settled in Savannah and devoted themselves mainly to Indian education at nearby Irene. They steadfastly refused to engage in military duties, a right which the Trustees had accorded them before the initial settlement. With the increasing fear of the Spaniards from Florida by 1738 and the actual outbreak of war in 1739, this pacifist attitude made the Moravians most unpopular with other Georgians. Hence in 1738 and 1740 most of them left for Pennsylvania where they adapted much better than in Georgia.

Besides Germans, a second non-English group to come to Georgia were Scots. In 1734 about ninety Lowland Scots arrived. A group was granted lands at Joseph's Town on the Savannah

River about five miles below Abercorn. Others, including William Sterling and Andrew Grant and their relatives, were given lands on the Ogeechee at a point called Sterling's Bluff. These Scots were adventurers who brought servants with them and intended to make their living by farming. But they soon discovered that they could not live successfully upon the labor of their servants in a new area. Hence most of them had abandoned their farming operations by 1737 and moved to Savannah, where they rented out the servants who had not run away. In Savannah they organized the St. Andrew's Club, or the Scots Club as William Stephens called it, which was fraternal in its purpose but which became one of the centers of opposition to Oglethorpe and the Trustees' plans for Georgia.

Far better known are the Highland Scots who came in 1736. When Oglethorpe was in England in 1735 he commissioned Hugh Mackay and George Dunbar to recruit Highlanders in the Inverness region of Scotland. These men with their families and children were to be settled in the southern part of Georgia, to guard the boundary of the colony against the Spanish. On October 21, 1735, 166 Scotch Highlanders left Inverness for Georgia as a result of the efforts of Mackay and Dunbar. About 100 of these were soldiers, and the rest servants or families of the soldiers. Other transports of Highlanders came in 1737 and 1741, but the number never exceeded several hundred. Most of them were young, about twenty years of age, and many came as servants to the Trustees.

These Highlanders settled on the north bank of the Altamaha River, where Fort King George had been located, and initially called their town Darien, then New Inverness, and then Darien again which it has remained since. They built a battery of four cannons, a guardhouse, a chapel, and several huts. Hugh Mackay was in command and won early praise from Oglethorpe. The Scots as soldiers gave their greatest service during the Spanish War. Thirty-six were killed at the Battle of Fort Moosa in June of 1740, and forty were captured but later released and returned. In 1739 the population of Darien was reported as forty families, and in both 1740 and 1741 it was reported as about eighty people, but in 1741 forty-three new recruits were listed. With the ending of the active fighting against the Spanish, the Scots were left in relative peace and free to tend to their own affairs. From this relatively small group there came many who have been important in Georgia's history since.

Frederica was founded by no special national group but was most important in Oglethorpe's defense plan. Its site was on the inland passage side of St. Simons Island, some twenty miles below the Scottish settlement on the Altamaha, technically below Georgia's southern boundary. The site of the town had been tentatively selected by Oglethorpe in January of 1734 when he made his first exploration of the Georgia coast. With the arrival of the Great Embarkation in February 1736 there were settlers to found the town. Oglethorpe collected rangers and workmen in Savannah and proceeded to the site of Frederica on February 18 where he laid out the fort and town and began their construction. Supplies and colonists followed, mainly through the inland passage when the captains of the two ships from London refused to take their vessels into Jekyll Sound. The actual building of the town and fort went forward rapidly, so that by the end of March the general outlines of both were completed, cannon were mounted facing the inland passage, and other fortifications were begun. The life and death of Frederica was tied to the Spanish War, and it declined after 1748.

The most northern Georgia settlement, Augusta, was located at the falls of the Savannah River, at a site known to Charles Town Indian traders long before the founding of Georgia. Just below the new town on the Carolina side of the river was Savannah Town or Fort Moore where the Upper Creek Path crossed the Savannah River on its way to Charles Town. This place was a way station and a warehouse point for the pack horsemen who went into the Creek and Cherokee country, for below it goods could be transported on the Savannah River by boat.

Because of the obvious advantage of this spot, Oglethorpe in 1735 decided to locate a town there. A garrison was sent up in 1736, and in December of that year William Stephens reported that the fort there was nearly finished. Roger Lacy, one of the early settlers, seems to have been treated as a magistrate or representative of the government in Savannah before any official appointments for Augusta were made.

Storehouses and warehouses were built, and Augusta replaced Savannah Town as the main up-country town of the Carolina Indian trade. Carolinians who held lands on the Carolina side of the river began securing grants in Georgia as well and engaged in farming and Indian trade in both colonies, often with the same labor force. Carolina slaves were used in Georgia near Augusta regardless of the Trustee law against slavery. At the busy season of the Indian trading year, Augusta filled up with traders, warehousemen, packhorses, and Indians. The town seems to have developed fairly free from Trustee regulation or interference and probably without much Trustee knowledge. Thus its development was more "natural" than that of much of the rest of Georgia. Its settlers were mainly Carolinians who knew how to get along in the area, and its up-country location made it more healthful than the other Georgia settlements. The profits from the Indian trade went mainly to Charles Town merchants and contributed little to Georgia's prosperity in the Trustee period. The agriculture which developed around Augusta was modeled after that in up-country Carolina and was little affected by Trustee ideas or control.

Although non-English groups like the Salzburgers and Scottish Highlanders have received much emphasis in histories of early Georgia, it should be remembered that English settlers continued to arrive throughout the first decade both as charity colonists and as adventurers. They came usually in small groups and made no special impress on the colony upon their arrival. The "typical" charity colonists were perhaps best illustrated by the original settlers who came on the *Ann*—unfortunate poor who could not make a go of life in England and who were thought worthy of support in Georgia. The English settled in the Savannah area until the founding of Frederica and Augusta, when some located in these places as well. Closest to the English in background and beliefs were the Lowland Scots, who frequently cannot be separated from the English very clearly. Other British colonists consisted of the Highland Scots and a few Irish servants. A sizeable majority of the British in Georgia were always English, although lists and summary accounts of settlers never agree as to numbers. Charity colonists are given at between 1,700 and 1,850, with slightly over 1,000 of these as British. Of the more than 1,000 settlers who are known to have come to Georgia at their own expense, most were English. The 92 known Jews, over 100 Lowland Scots, and several hundred of Highland Scots made up the majority of the non-English in this group. About 1,400 of the charity colonists came in the first six years of the colony's life, and only about 100 English arrived during the next four years.

As a general rule, the Trustees did not send charity colonists after 1738. The plans for the original colonists had failed, and many of them were unsuccessful. Henceforth the Trustees sent mainly indentured servants (Scots, Germans, Swiss, Irish, and English) who might be sold to existing colonists or who might work out their indentures upon Trust projects in the colony. Such people were easier to control, could be used where most needed, and would be acclimated by the time they had served out their indentures and become independent economically. By the end of the Trustee period at least 1,100 indentured servants had been sent to Georgia by the Trustees. Proportionately there were fewer English among these indentured servants than among the colonists sent over in the first six years.

With the ending of the Spanish War in 1748 and the relaxation of the earlier Trustee regulations, especially the insistence upon small land grants and the prohibition against slavery, population began a new growth in Georgia. Many of these newer settlers were Carolinians who had not come earlier because of Trustee prohibitions against large land grants and slaves and the Spanish War. Now they came in increasing numbers and began to set up small rice plantations in the freshwater swamps along the Savannah and Ogeechee rivers.

With the disbanding of Oglethorpe's regiment in 1749, the soldiers, many of whom had families at Frederica, were offered a bounty of £5 sterling, 150 acres of land, and one year's subsistence if they would stay in Georgia. Of the approximately 650 soldiers and dependents available, about 150 remained in Georgia.

About 1750 there was a renewed interest in Germans coming to South Carolina and Georgia. In 1751 a group of 160 was conducted to Georgia by John Gerar William DeBrahm, an acquaintance of the Reverend Samuel Urlsperger at Augsburg who recommended him to the Trustees and to Bolzius in Georgia. These Germans established a settlement, Bethany, upon lands recently secured from the Indians north of Ebenezer Creek, lands which the Salzburgers had long desired and upon which some of them lived. About a year later a similar number of Germans came over and settled with the 1751 group.

The Trustees' greatest efforts toward settling Georgia came in its first decade, mainly before the Spanish War frightened off prospective colonists. The rate of population growth through 1738 reflected the availability of funds to the Trustees to send over charity colonists. The discontinuance of charity colonists, the closing of the Trustees' store in October of 1738, and fear of the Spanish all had an adverse effect upon Georgia's population growth by 1739. The closing of the store encouraged some Georgians to leave the colony as they had been supported by the store and knew not whence their support would come henceforth. The Spanish fear and war had a more drastic effect upon population. Frederica, Savannah, Darien, Bethesda, and other areas of the colony experienced an exodus to South Carolina and points north or lost population through military casualties. Frederica and Darien were most affected by combat deaths.

Some of those who fled during the Spanish fear returned by the mid and late 1740s. By 1747 Savannah's English population may have been less than it had been in 1735. Ebenezer's population grew slowly, if at all, during the Spanish War. Augusta was the one area in the colony which had a steady increase in population almost from its founding. Its settlement and economy were more spontaneous than the rest of the colony's during the first decade, and it was far enough north to escape the Spanish fear.

Low birth and high death rates retarded Georgia's early population growth. Many of the charity colonists were beyond the ordinary childbearing age. Disease and death rates, particularly among newborn infants and women during childbirth, were high in the first few years, as they were for all European immigrants to the southern colonies.

The renewed interest of settlers in Georgia at the very end of the Trustee period stemmed from the ending of the Spanish War in 1748 and the abandonment by the Trustees of their earlier and more visionary ideas and tight controls for Georgia. Plantations worked by slaves could now begin, and Georgia's population and economic growth would become more like that of South Carolina. People could choose their lands and the way they would use them, and no longer did the Trustees try to control the colony and its inhabitants. Had the Trustees allowed human selfishness freer reign from the beginning, the colony would have filled up more rapidly and would have experienced greater economic success. But as the Trustees said more than once, this was not their aim in settling Georgia. Aid to the unfortunate and security for the southern English frontier in North America were more noble aims, even though they interfered with the settling of the colony. A choice was necessary, and the Trustees held to their choice for almost two decades until they were convinced thoroughly that their scheme would not work. By 1750 many of the Trustees no longer cared about their dream for Georgia or even about what happened to the colony.

4

OGLETHORPE AND THE SPANISH WAR: DEFENSE WITHOUT CONQUEST

Oglethorpe's extraordinary energy and his concern for everything in Georgia were demonstrated well after his return from England in February of 1736. While founding Frederica he made a brief visit to the nearby Highland Scots on February 22 and 23 and complimented them by wearing Highland garb. Both town and people seemed to be progressing.

From March 18 through 25 Oglethorpe inspected the coast south of Frederica, accompanied by Tomo-Chi-Chi and forty Indians, Captain Hugh Mackay and thirty Highlanders, and several others. As Oglethorpe said, he wanted "to see where his Majesty's Dominions and the Spaniards joyn." The island below Jekyll, Oglethorpe named for the Duke of Cumberland at the request of Tooanahowi, Tomo-Chi-Chi's nephew. The duke had given Tooanahowi a watch in England, and the naming of an island for him did not seem too great an honor to the young Indian nor to Oglethorpe. On the northern end of the island, Oglethorpe directed a fort built by Captain Mackay and his Highlanders. Both the fort and the sound between Cumberland and Jekyll were to be called St. Andrews in honor of Scotland's patron saint. On the southern end of Cumberland, Oglethorpe planned Fort William to command Cumberland Sound.

Below Cumberland and the St. Marys River was a beautiful island which Oglethorpe named Amelia in honor of one of the royal princesses. After naming Talbot Island for England's lord high chancellor, Oglethorpe renamed the small island of San Juan, at the very mouth of the St. Johns River, George's Island. Here at last, Oglethorpe decided, the dominions of the king of England and the king of Spain joined. This decision was based in part on the claims of the Creek Indians to lands this far south and undoubtedly in part on what Oglethorpe felt he could claim realistically. By now the party was too close to St. Augustine to proceed farther. Here, to force the Spanish out into the ocean on any trip they might make to the north, was built Fort St. George. Thus Oglethorpe's tour ended, considerably south of Georgia's charter limits. Although he might not be able to control all the territory to the St. Johns, he could at least claim it for diplomatic purposes.

A diplomatic offensive against Spain was favored over a military one by the government in London. When Oglethorpe returned from England in early 1736, Captain Charles Dempsey came with him to investigate the Georgia-Florida situation and to negotiate with the Spanish. In the summer Antonio de Arrendondo came from Havana to Florida to secure the retreat of the English northward to at least Port Royal. The English responded by demanding that the Spanish give up all territory about the twenty-ninth parallel, south of St. Augustine. Initially, Oglethorpe professed to desire peace and wished the negotiators well, but his actions in founding forts below the Altamaha belied his professed desire for friendship. The opposing contentions of the English and Spanish about their boundaries made any peaceful settlement well nigh impossible.

Dempsey made several trips to St. Augustine. When Spaniards came to Frederica to negotiate, Oglethorpe moved men rapidly along the Spanish route, had many cannon fired from points near Frederica, and tried with some success to convince the Spaniards that he had more men and military supplies than he actually did. Real or intended attacks by Indians on Spanish emissaries were used by Oglethorpe to argue that he was trying to protect the Spaniards. In reality he probably knew of these attacks beforehand and may have helped to plan them with the Indians.

A treaty was agreed to at Frederica in October of 1736 between Dempsey and Arrendondo and accepted by Oglethorpe and Governor Francisco del Moral Sanchez in St. Augustine. Each side promised to control its Indian allies, to refrain from molesting the other, and to refer the troublesome question of a permanent boundary between the two colonies to the home governments. Oglethorpe agreed to evacuate Fort St. George at the mouth of the St. Johns River which, being closer to St. Augustine than to Frederica, was difficult to supply and protect in any case.

This Treaty of Frederica solved none of the problems between Georgia and Florida but perhaps did delay the outbreak of hostilities between the two colonies. Trouble may also have been delayed by Oglethorpe's presence in England from November 1736 to the end of 1738, his longest absence from Georgia since its founding.

Although the English were well satisfied with the Treaty of Frederica, the Spanish were not. Madrid immediately informed London that the treaty was made by the governor in St. Augustine without proper authority and was not acceptable. Governor Sanchez was recalled to Spain and removed from office. A story circulated in London in 1740, which the Earl of Egmont recorded in his diary, that the Spanish so disliked the treaty that Sanchez was hanged when he reached Madrid. Many historians repeated this story until 1954 when John Tate Lanning proved that it was not true and that in 1748 Governor Sanchez was cleared of all charges against him by the Council of the Indies.*

An interesting episode in the Spanish troubles of 1735–36 is the activity of John Savy, alias Don Miguel Wall. Wall, an Englishman who had lived in South Carolina and Georgia,

---

* See John Tate Lanning, "The Legend That Governor Moral Sanchez Was Hanged," *Georgia Historical Quarterly*, XXXVIII, 349–55.

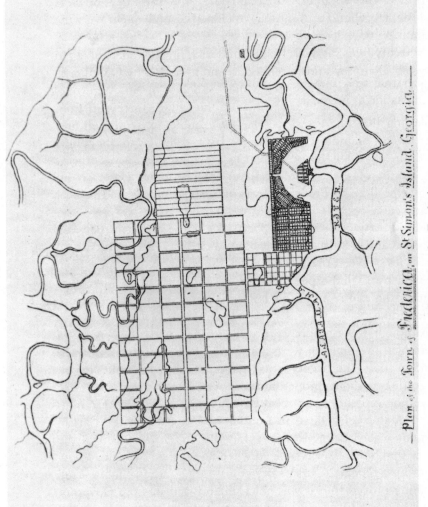

Town plan for Frederica.

presented himself to the Spanish minister in Paris in the summer of 1735 as one who wished to help the Spanish destroy the English settlements in these colonies. He went to Madrid, where he said that four to five hundred well-armed Spanish soldiers and six vessels would be enough to destroy Georgia. Naturally all this information was relayed to London by Benjamin Keene, British Ambassador to Madrid.

By the summer of 1736 the Spanish were preparing earnestly for an invasion of Georgia. Early in the summer Wall was in Cuba whose governor was made overall commander of the expedition. Supplies were dispatched to Florida and plans were made to send men and vessels. In Havana Wall talked a great deal to Englishmen and to Spaniards. What he said was relayed to Oglethorpe in Georgia and the governor in Charles Town. Authorities in Havana began to be doubtful of Wall and of his plan to capture Georgia. He was watched carefully and any authority he had possessed over the expedition was canceled. He remained an advisor because of his knowledge of the area.

In the fall of 1736, on orders from Madrid, the Spanish minister in London, Tomas Geraldion, began to insist that the English remove themselves from Florida, live up to the treaties between the two nations, and live in peace with Spain in America. The Duke of Newcastle and Sir Robert Walpole replied in soothing and evasive terms that the British government was not attempting to have Georgia extended beyond the borders specified in the original charter and that Oglethorpe might have made some mistakes by going too far south. The Georgia Trustees insisted that they had given no orders to Oglethorpe or their colonists to invade Spanish territory but had kept strictly within the limits of the charter. The attitude of the Spanish government, plus the blustering memorials of Geraldion prompted the belief that Spain would try to recapture all the territory she had once held.

Because of arguments with South Carolina and complaints from the Spanish minister in London as to Oglethorpe's activities in territory claimed by the Spanish, the Trustees urged Oglethorpe to return to England. His presence at the Parliamentary session of January 1737 was considered essential to quiet the objectors and to secure funds for the colony. So he left for London on November 23, 1736. In London he was thankfully received by his friends. Within a week he had convinced his fellow Trustees that his conduct in Georgia was free of all blame and they gave him a unanimous vote of thanks for his actions. But his interview with Geraldion did not quiet Spanish fears, and military reinforcements were soon sent to St. Augustine.

There were now increasingly insistent rumors in London and great fear in Georgia and South Carolina that the Spanish expedition had actually left Havana for Florida. Seven thousand troops and seven warships were reported ready for the invasion. In London, Oglethorpe used these rumors to back his January 25, 1737, request to Parliament for £30,000 for Georgia's defense. Oglethorpe insisted to Sir Robert Walpole that Georgia was important to the empire as a whole and must be supported by the British government. He was sure that if Britain abandoned Georgia, Spain would immediately grasp it. Further, Oglethorpe predicted that if this happened the French would then attack the Carolinas and Virginia. Having refused the proffered governorship of South Carolina, Oglethorpe agreed to take a military command in America. After Parliament granted £20,000 for Georgia, he asked for and received a regiment of seven hundred men with himself as colonel. He was made military commander of Georgia and South Carolina, a post which carried a courtesy title of general.

British Minister Keene in Madrid observed Spanish attitudes and actions to insure against a surprise Spanish attack on Georgia. By May he was certain that sooner or later an attack would come. Geraldion in London helped to influence Walpole to request Oglethorpe to disband his regiment. Oglethorpe insisted that Georgia should be protected, otherwise he would warn the colonists to leave. The Trustees petitioned for protection. Walpole gave way again, and Oglethorpe was commissioned colonel of his regiment on August 25, 1737.

Despite all this activity in London, possibly to a degree because of it, in March the governor of Cuba received orders from Madrid to suspend the campaign against Georgia which had been ordered earlier; and Geraldion was instructed to say that no attack had been made. Thus by late summer the greatest fears were ended in London and in Georgia. Having settled the major problems which brought him to London, Oglethorpe spent the next six months recruiting his regiment, trying to get an appropriation of £13,000 for it, attending the House of Commons, and enjoying London life.

In the fall of 1737, Wall returned to Europe where he offered his services to the English to aid in the destruction of Florida. He told the English a great deal about the Spanish preparations and maintained that he had spent all his time in Havana trying to collect information which would be of value to the British. Undoubtedly he was willing to back the winning side and the one which would do the most for him. Apparently he got nothing from either nation.

Throughout the negotiations in Madrid from 1736 to 1739 Ambassador Keene kept his eyes on the Georgia-Florida problem, although commercial depredations were of more importance. The Spanish never got satisfactory answers to their memorials presented in London, and Sir Robert Walpole was gradually being carried by public opinion closer to the war that he so earnestly sought to avoid.

One last try at negotiations came in January of 1739 when Britain and Spain signed a convention at El Pardo. This agreement specified that plenipotentiaries were to meet in Madrid to arrange for a settlement of commercial differences and of the Georgia-Florida boundaries. Until a settlement was reached, no changes were to take place in the disputed territory. This agreement amounted to nothing, and before the end of the year the two countries were at war with each other.

During this period of intense activity for Oglethorpe he found that he had a new and unexpected opponent—his fellow Trustees. The Trustees came to believe that Walpole did not want Oglethorpe to return to Georgia because of the fear that he would bring on unnecessary troubles with the Spanish in Florida. The Trustees continually gave Oglethorpe advice, struck many

items from the Georgia budget in their new policy of retrench-
ment, reminded Oglethorpe of their decreasing membership, and
chided him for his poor attendance at their meetings during his
stay in London. When, on March 29, 1738, Oglethorpe invited
his fellow Trustees to review his departing regiment and to
attend a "very elegant dinner" afterwards, only the Earl of
Egmont and three others came.

Despite this poor attendance, on May 1 Oglethorpe tendered a
farewell dinner to eleven Trustees at which James Vernon told
him frankly to look after military affairs and the Trustees would
look after civil ones. A week later, on May 8, George II
instructed Oglethorpe to avoid giving offense to the Spaniards
and to "maintain the strictest friendship." Finally on June 26
H.M.S. *Blandford*, with Oglethorpe on board, left Portsmouth;
and on July 5 in company with the man-of-war *Hector* and five
transports, Oglethorpe and his regiment set out for Georgia.
In many respects the most difficult and demanding part of
Oglethorpe's career lay before him, and he must have reflected
upon this as the vessels plowed across the Atlantic.

Back in Georgia in September of 1738, Oglethorpe found
administrative problems which demanded his attention, but he
was henceforth to devote most of his time to military affairs. His
regiment was headquartered at Frederica, thereafter Oglethorpe's main home, with the troops stationed there and at Fort
St. Simon on the south end of the island. The outlying forts and
posts throughout the colony were garrisoned by rangers and by
troops from the regiment rotated between these posts and St.
Simons Island. For the first time, Oglethorpe now had enough
troops to carry on his defense plans for the colony. He had about
a year to get Georgia's defenses in order before they were tested
in war against Spain.

The three naval vessels which accompanied Oglethorpe and
his regiment were ordered stationed on the coasts of Virginia,
South Carolina, and Georgia which received the *Blandford*. In
August 1738 the British West Indian Squadron was ordered to
act offensively against the Spanish and to cooperate with
Oglethorpe's troops.

In November, two months after his return to Georgia, Oglethorpe wrote to his fellow Trustee, Alderman George Heathcote: "I am here in one of the most delightful situations as any man could wish to be. A great number of Debts, empty Magazines, no money to supply them, Numbers of People to be fed, mutinous Soldiers to Command, a Spanish Claim & a large body of their Troops not far from us." *

The mutiny had just occurred among Oglethorpe's troops who had come from Gibraltar and who demanded full back pay for which Oglethorpe did not have funds at that time. One mutineer fired at Oglethorpe but only burned his cheek slightly. The mutineers were court-martialed and shot. Perhaps the incident aroused Oglethorpe's fighting spirit and it seems to have secured better treatment for him from the Trustees who had not been very happy with his military activities of late.

Georgia was ahead of London in declaring war against Spain. On September 8, 1739, a vessel arrived in Savannah from Rhode Island with the incorrect news that war had been declared. On October 3 Oglethorpe and the magistrates met in the courthouse in Savannah and the militia was formed outside. A formal declaration of war against the Spanish was made by Oglethorpe and the magistrates and duly celebrated by the Savannah militia. It was October 19 before the king's heralds proclaimed this war at Temple Bar in London amidst the ringing of bells and the rejoicing of the mob. This official declaration was read in Savannah on May 13, 1740, with proper ceremony.

The Georgia-Florida boundary dispute was only one of several causes of the War of Jenkins' Ear. The troubles of British illegal traders with Spanish *guarda-costas* resulted in Captain Thomas Jenkins' loss of his ear, but many other British seamen could have told similar stories of Spanish rough handling. Probably the main cause of the war was the desire of British merchants for more trade with Spanish colonies in America and the determination of the Spanish authorities to prevent it.

The Georgia-Florida boundary was the area where Ogle-

---

* *Collections, Georgia Historical Society,* III (Savannah, 1873), 62.

239

			£		
	Bro[t] from fol 1.	£	1470	7	
Feb 2[d]	By one Sett Bills Excha: pay[d] to A. Dedeon		20	„	„ v
18	By one Sett D[o] pay[d] to Tho[s] Jones to pay the heo[s] M[r] Whitefield to w[ch] build a Church		150	„	„ v
Mar 16	By one Sett D[o] pay[d] to D[o] to pay Mess[rs] Woodward & Fiewer		100	15	8 v
1740					
Ap[r] 2	By one Sett D[o] pay[d] to Tho[s] Jones		100	„	„ v
	By one Sett D[o] D[o]		99	„	„ v
10	By one Sett D[o] D[o] £150:0:0				
	one Sett D[o] D[o] 70:0:0		220	„	„ v
18	By one Sett D[o] pay[d] to D[o] 100:0:0				
	one Sett D[o] D[o] 60:0:0		160	„	„ v
June 7	By one Sett D[o] pay[d] to D[o] 100:0:0				
	one Sett D[o] D[o] 100:0:0		200	„	„ v
Sep 16	By one Sett D[o] pay[d] to D[o] 50:0:0				
	one Sett D[o] D[o] 30:0:0		80	„	„ v
Oct 6	By eight Setts D[o] pay[d] to D[o] G[o] Emery		391	7	6 v
28	By one Sett D[o] pay[d] to D[o] to pay Capt Wiggin		232	17	„ v
Jan 2	By one Sett D[o] pay[d] to D[o] for sundry Goo[ds] del into the Stores at Frederica		81	10	1 v
	By one Sett D[o] pay[d] to D[o] for a Cedar boat Sails &c		41	5	„ v
	By one Sett D[o] pay[d] to D[o] to pay Capt Brown's Men for Service on the Expedition		41	3	2 v
	Carr'd to fol 3	£	3371	6	.

Page of James Oglethorpe's account book for 1739–40.

thorpe and Georgians could hope for some practical gain from the war. Oglethorpe, immediately after the Savannah declaration of war, set out to strengthen Georgia's defenses against the Spanish. He worked to secure a thousand Indian warriors, raised a troop of horse, called for additional naval support, and began conferences with South Carolina authorities from whom help was also desired. He went to Frederica immediately after the funeral of Tomo-Chi-Chi to be nearer to the seat of any possible attack. The Spanish drew the first blood in mid-November by attacking and killing two men on Amelia Island, but did not attack the fort there. As soon as he had word of this action, Oglethorpe collected rangers, soldiers, and militia and set out for the St. Johns River, destroying all Spanish boats that he found en route. After a slight skirmish with some Spanish troops on the St. Johns, Oglethorpe and his party returned to Frederica.

The return to Frederica was only to prepare for a larger expedition against the Spanish. Oglethorpe and his troops started south on December 1, accompanied by several pieces of cannon and a considerable number of Indians. This expedition captured the Spanish Fort San Francisco de Pupa, which controlled navigation of the St. Johns River, and cut communications between St. Augustine and the Apalachee area to the west. Having captured the garrison of the fort, Oglethorpe left one there himself before his retirement to Frederica.

During Oglethorpe's expeditions in Florida there came to light a strange individual among the Cherokees. He was Christian Gottlieb Priber, a German Jesuit who envisioned a wilderness nation made up of Indians, runaway slaves, and fugitives from justice. He also envisioned a centralized Cherokee state with himself as secretary. He apparently received considerable backing from the Indians but was captured by Indian traders when he was near the French garrison. With his papers, he was sent to Frederica to await Oglethorpe's return and action. Priber was quite a linguist, knowing Latin, French, Spanish, English, and Cherokee well, and was considered dangerous or insane, perhaps both. His elaborate plans, revealed in his papers and conversation, show a man of imagination if not a very practical approach.

He died a natural death while imprisoned at Frederica, thus removing one of Oglethorpe's problems.

In March of 1740, after his two abortive expeditions into Florida, Oglethorpe went to Charles Town where the Assembly voted £120,000 South Carolina currency, a regiment of troops, and a troop of horse to aid in the attack on St. Augustine. Oglethorpe also secured promises of aid from British men-of-war to blockade St. Augustine. Upon his return from Charles Town, Oglethorpe sought Indian allies to join his and the Carolina forces, and trained and equipped his own men. He assembled at Frederica five hundred officers and men from his regiment, a troop of Scottish Highland rangers, a troop of English rangers, a company of Highland foot, a company of English foot, a Carolina regiment of six hundred men under Colonel Alexander Vanderdussen, some volunteers from Charles Town, and a sizeable number of Indians.

By May the army was ready to set out for St. Augustine. The Carolinians, the Highlanders, and the Indians went by land. Oglethorpe and the rest of the troops and the artillery went by water under convoy of men-of-war. Oglethorpe crossed the St. Johns on May 9 and the next day took Fort St. Diego, a small outlying post garrisoned by fifty-seven men and containing eleven cannon, small arms, and ammunition. The South Carolina forces soon arrived, and on May 15 the whole army continued toward St. Augustine. There were now about a thousand regular and provincial troops and some eleven hundred Indian allies. These were opposed by a Spanish force of about a thousand regulars, together with militia and Indian allies. The fort at St. Augustine had been considerably strengthened by Arrendondo and his engineers in the last five years.

With no opposition, Oglethorpe's force captured Fort Moosa, only two miles from St. Augustine, which the Spaniards had evacuated. Having failed to surprise and take the city by assault, it was decided to blockade the town and harbor with the seven British naval vessels present. Two hundred sailors were to be landed on Anastasia Island, opposite the city and fort, to bombard both. Oglethorpe was to attack from the land side. The

Spanish galleys inside the bar prevented the landing of troops and artillery on Anastasia Island, and the bar was too shallow for the English ships to enter and dislodge the Spanish galleys. Hence the projected attack could not be made.

After this failure on June 13, Oglethorpe decided to settle down to a siege. Flying parties were sent out to scout the countryside to confuse the Spanish as to the number and location of British troops and to prevent the Spanish from making contacts with Indians or any reinforcements which might seek to enter the city. On the night of June 25 the main scouting party was surprised by Spaniards at Fort Moosa. About twenty-five men were killed, a similar number were captured, but the rest escaped. The Spanish lost almost one hundred men but opened contact with the country which helped to provision the strained garrison. Psychologically and materially, Oglethorpe's forces were damaged considerably by this action.

Bombardment of the town and castle began in late June, but the distance was too great for cannon from either camp to do much damage. The Spanish refused Oglethorpe's demand to surrender, and he was not able to breach the walls of the fort or to coax the defenders out of the walls for a sortie. The greatest danger to the besieged was that they would exhaust their food supply. Just when it seemed that this was about to happen, three small vessels with food were able to slip into the harbor and relieve the Spaniards. The British naval commanders said that they would not risk the possibility of hurricanes by remaining on the unprotected coast after July 5. The Indians were restive and could be persuaded to remain longer only by high payments. The troops were increasingly sickly from hot weather; and desertions among the Carolinians, whose term of enlistment was running short, became frequent. Oglethorpe, deciding that he could do nothing else, ordered the siege raised on July 20, 1740, thirty-eight days after it began.

With little opposition from the Spaniards, the troops withdrew and arrived at Frederica by the end of the month. The British lost about fifty men killed, while the Spaniards reported four hundred men lost plus four forts with their munitions and supplies. Certainly the failure to capture St. Augustine was a major disappointment to Oglethorpe, to Georgians, and to South Carolinians. It is conceivable that the expedition prevented the proposed Spanish invasion of Georgia, but there was never any certainty that it would have come. The St. Augustine expedition must, therefore, be put down as a failure for Oglethorpe and all involved in it.

Almost before the South Carolina troops were back in Charles Town, arguments about the responsibility for the failure began. Both houses of the Carolina Assembly appointed committees to investigate the matter. These committees worked for a year and produced a lengthy report. Naturally the South Carolinians tried to blame Oglethorpe, while he and his partisans threw the blame on the South Carolinians. The truth is somewhere between.

If Oglethorpe is blamable, it is for not anticipating the difficulties the expedition might encounter. Although there was a two-month delay before all troops and supplies could be assembled at Frederica, making for much hotter campaigning weather, Oglethorpe should have known that all such logistical movements were beset with difficulties and that delay was the normal rule.

If the navy did not cooperate adequately, it was partially because of ignorance about the height of the bar and the depth of water at St. Augustine. On the other hand, there were people in Savannah and Charles Town who knew about these things, and to discover these facts at St. Augustine during the course of the expedition was disastrous.

The surprise assault at Fort Moosa by the Spanish seems to have resulted from carelessness of the local commander, something that Oglethorpe might have prevented by greater diligence. Certainly the shortages of long-range cannon made a great difference, for which South Carolina's failure to fulfill its promise to supply more artillery was partly responsible.

The Carolina troops under Vanderdussen, however, seem to have performed as well as Oglethorpe's and as well as could have been expected under the circumstances. The blame placed on them by Oglethorpe and his partisans does not seem justifiable, and these charges did not help to secure future cooperation when it was needed.

Oglethorpe's pride was hurt by his failure, and he sought a scapegoat. Besides his wounded pride, he was ill intermittently with a fever for two months during the campaign and for at least a month after his return to Frederica. In fact, according to William Stephens, Oglethorpe was ill much longer than most of the soldiers, whose bad health had been one of the reasons given for abandoning the siege.

While blame is being assessed, it is well to remember that the Spanish made no immediate attempt to follow up Oglethorpe's withdrawal. They were too weak or felt that the British were stronger than they actually were.

Oglethorpe realized that even though the Spanish did not immediately follow up his withdrawal from St. Augustine, an attack could be expected. Thus he kept parties of Indians and scout boats on the lookout for any invasion attempt. Occasionally, a Spanish prisoner was brought in, and there were incidents like the one in August of 1741 when Oglethorpe pursued some privateers to within sight of the castle at St. Augustine. The only indication of aid that Oglethorpe got from England was an order from the Admiralty to all officers in American waters to give Georgia and South Carolina all assistance possible against the Spanish at St. Augustine. From April to July of 1741 Oglethorpe was ill at Frederica, and the anxieties of the war and fear of trouble from the Spaniards continued.

When the war broadened into a general colonial and European war (the War of the Austrian Succession, or King George's War) in 1740, the Georgia-Florida frontier seemed to recede further into the background of the thinking of the officials at Whitehall and of the military and naval officers in America. The demands of England's allies in Europe received attention and seemed closer at hand and more important than Georgia. The British made an unsuccessful attempt to capture Cuba in 1741, which received all the reinforcements and supplies that were available, and Oglethorpe got nothing in response to his insistent entreaties. He wrote letters and sent over officers to plead for necessary supplies. Eventually Oglethorpe authorized Harman Verelst, the Trustees' accountant, to raise what money he could on Oglethorpe's estates and to spend his salary to pay the bills he drew for needed supplies.

In the fall of 1741 there was a royal order to the governor of Cuba for an attack on Georgia, and the governor began preparations for the expedition to be launched in April-June 1742. The actual expedition, which consisted of fifty-six vessels and about seven thousand men, left Cuba for St. Augustine in May. A storm dispersed the vessels but did not prevent most of them reaching St. Augustine. Oglethorpe, informed of this arrival by his Indian spies and the British navy, wrote the Duke of Newcastle "It is too late now to desire Your Grace to represent this to His Majesty and ask succours; before they can arrive the matter will be over. I hope I shall behave as well as one with so few men and so little Artillery can." South Carolina, now that the danger was so close, bestirred herself to send aid to Frederica.

After an unsuccessful attempt against Fort William on Cumberland Island, the Spanish fleet arrived at St. Simons Island on June 22, 1742. Oglethorpe's forces evacuated Fort St. Simon on the southern end of the island and concentrated all their strength at Frederica. Oglethorpe controlled the various aspects of the defense well and frequently anticipated Spanish activity. He brought in all available troops from the southern part of Georgia, requested aid from Charles Town, and did all else possible. The Spanish landed a force variously estimated at three thousand to five thousand men at Gascoigne's Bluff, below Frederica, and made their camp near the abandoned Fort St. Simon.

On July 7 Spanish troops marched against Frederica and were driven back by Oglethorpe's men. There were several other attacks and counterattacks. When the day's fighting ended the Spanish were back at their camp at Fort St. Simon under the protection of their cannon. Lieutenants Sutherland and Mackay had been promoted by Oglethorpe for their valor and success with the Scottish Highlanders. This Battle of Bloody Marsh was a victory for Oglethorpe, but it had not destroyed the Spanish army nor driven it off St. Simons Island. The Spanish still considerably outnumbered Oglethorpe's forces and might yet capture Frederica and the entire island.

Though Oglethorpe knew that he had won at Bloody Marsh, he did not have time to rest on his laurels. Nothing was safe as long as the Spanish remained on St. Simons. Frederica was strengthened as rapidly as possible, and Indians were kept on patrol to watch the Spanish. A second attempt by the Spanish to approach Frederica from the river side was unsuccessful. Oglethorpe's planned surprise night attack was foiled when a French marine deserted and warned the Spanish. Oglethorpe was afraid that the Frenchman would reveal the British weakness to the Spaniards who would then attack and destroy the defending force. Hence he resorted to a stratagem. He released a prisoner with a letter to the Frenchman instructing him to try to pilot the Spanish boats and galleys up under the woods where he knew the hidden batteries could destroy them. If he failed in this maneuver, he should endeavor to keep the Spanish on St. Simons for at least three more days until reinforcements of two thousand men and six men-of-war arrived. He was not to mention that Admiral Vernon was about to make a descent on St. Augustine.

The released prisoner was immediately taken before the Spanish commander when he arrived in the camp. Here his letter was discovered, and the Frenchman denied any knowledge of its contents or being a spy for Oglethorpe as the letter implied. While the Spanish thought this letter possibly a stratagem, many officers were afraid that it might be completely or partially true and favored immediate evacuation of St. Simons Island. Even before the letter was received, there was a division among the Spanish high command that was serious enough to impair its military efficiency. During the debate of the Spanish commanders, word was brought that three sails were seen off the bar. Supposing this was the first of the fleet suggested in the letter, the conference broke up immediately with a determination to evacuate the island. Having set fire to Fort St. Simon, the Spanish embarked in a great hurry by July 15, 1742, leaving behind several cannon and many military stores.

Oglethorpe gathered what boats he could to follow the

retreating Spaniards who apparently intended to attack Fort St. Andrew and Fort William on their voyage southward. However, Oglethorpe's vessels seem to have confused them further, so that they continued to St. Augustine without any serious damage to any of the fortifications between it and Frederica. A British fleet and troops from Jamaica, reported at Charles Town while the Spanish were on St. Simons, returned to Jamaica without even inquiring if Oglethorpe needed help. Only after the Spanish had left, did the forces sent by South Carolina arrive at Frederica.

Oglethorpe proclaimed a day of thanksgiving on July 25 to thank God "for his great deliverance, and the end that is put to this Spanish invasion." Seven colonial governors sent letters to congratulate him, and the rejoicing was great. The critical historian may well insist that Oglethorpe did not so much win on St. Simons as that the Spanish left without really trying to capture Frederica or Oglethorpe's troops. Oglethorpe certainly realized that with his small force, six hundred and fifty men, he must keep the Spanish on the defensive; and this he did. His letter to the deserting Frenchman could be called a stroke of genius, and Americans and Englishmen rightfully sang Oglethorpe's praises for having successfully defended Georgia from a Spanish force which by all the odds of warfare should have captured the colony and destroyed Oglethorpe's soldiers.

While the withdrawal of the Spanish from St. Simons Island ended the immediate threat to Georgia, there would be danger as long as the war lasted. Oglethorpe still was determined to capture Florida or at least to frighten the enemy from any further attack on Georgia. Rumors were soon rife that the Spanish and the French were about to join forces to invade Georgia. A message of the governor of Cuba was intercepted containing a plan to invade Georgia with forces already in Cuba. Oglethorpe made strong appeals to London. He was sure the Spaniards were an ever present danger in Florida, and that the British government needed to do something for the defense of its southern American frontier. All these appeals fell on deaf ears. Oglethorpe cruised off St. Augustine with several naval vessels in the late summer of 1742 but made no landing or attempts against the Spanish.

By February of 1743 Oglethorpe decided upon another attempt against St. Augustine before its garrison was reinforced from Cuba. Late in the month Highlanders, rangers, and Oglethorpe's regulars were ready to depart; they landed in Florida on March 9. Oglethorpe's Indians attacked what Spanish they could find, and the general himself tried to decoy troops out of the fortifications of the city into an ambush he had prepared with most of his troops. The Spanish refused to cooperate. Oglethorpe had no artillery or entrenching tools. He laid waste the surrounding country, cruised off the bar of St. Augustine, and then returned to Frederica by April without the loss of a man.

Oglethorpe was still concerned and tried especially to keep the Indians friendly. Although he was promoted to the rank of brigadier, he received no reinforcements. The War Office did approve recruiting for his regiment on June 23, 1743, but the order came too late to be of any value for activities in America. The Trustees, after the attempt against St. Augustine ended, wrote to Oglethorpe expressing sympathy and concern but furnished no tangible aid. On June 7 the Earl of Egmont, one of Oglethorpe's greatest backers among the Trustees, resigned as a member of the Georgia Common Council for reasons of health and because the ministry and Parliament did so little for Georgia.

Soon after Egmont's resignation, Lieutenant Colonel William Cooke, on leave in England from Oglethorpe's regiment, brought charges against Oglethorpe for his administration of the regiment. Because of a request from the War Office to answer these charges and for several reasons, Oglethorpe departed for England on July 23, 1743. This ended his career in Georgia.

Upon his return to London, Oglethorpe sought repayment of the funds he had advanced. He had pledged his estate, salary, and other resources to the amount of £91,705.13 .5, of which only £25,595.19 .7 had been repaid to date. He appealed to Parlia-

ment and on March 20, 1744, the House of Commons granted
the remaining £66,109.13 .10 due him. His court-martial met in
early June and cleared him on every count brought by Colonel
Cooke. Thus repaid and cleared of the charges against him,
Oglethorpe could concern himself with other things. He continued to attend meetings of the Georgia Trustees and Common
Council erratically until 1749 when his attendance ceased.

The second failure at St. Augustine and the exit of Oglethorpe
did not end the Spanish fear for Georgians. President William
Stephens and Captain William Horton, the senior officer present
in Oglethorpe's regiment, continued to believe that a calamity
might befall Georgia from a Spanish attack. Captain Noble
Jones continued to be concerned about local defense at Savannah. Stephens commented favorably about twenty men at
Savannah meeting for voluntary military activity in the late
afternoon and did all he could to encourage them. But Stephens
was not Oglethorpe, and could neither secure the loyalties of the
colonists nor lead troops in the field. Luckily for Georgians, the
expected attack never came.

The defenseless condition of the colony certainly had an
adverse effect upon its growth until peace. The Trustees continued to request more men and materials for defense, but the
authorities in Whitehall paid little heed to the needs of Georgia.
They said that they could see little result from what was spent in
Georgia after Oglethorpe's departure. The British government
had spent £100,000 for defense between 1738 and 1743, when the
real fighting took place.

With the entry of the French into the war of 1744 and its
expansion into a general European and colonial war, there was a
new danger in the American Southwest—the French. There was
fear for the Carolina backcountry and for the Indian trade.
Although the French took no action in this area, the possibility
made South Carolina even less concerned about the Spanish
threat to Georgia. Luckily nothing happened to require aid.

During the negotiations which preceded the peace of Aix-la-
Chapelle the Trustees brought their claims to the territory south
to the Altamaha to the attention of the government. However,

the treaty, signed late in 1748, ignored the Georgia-Florida boundary and returned all colonial conquests of the war. Georgia's boundaries were no better defined by the treaty and all the old fears and troubles continued.

With the ending of the war, Oglethorpe's regiment was disbanded in 1749, though some of the soldiers chose to remain in America. Any who remained in Georgia could secure lands from the Trustees. Already South Carolina had applied to the home government to station three independent companies in that colony for its defense. The first troops for these companies had arrived in Charles Town in 1746, and at the beginning of 1748 there were approximately one hundred soldiers in each of the three companies, stationed both in Charles Town and on the frontiers. With the disbanding of the regiment, the only protection Georgia could expect besides its militia was from these companies. But since they were stationed in South Carolina and under the control of the governor of that province, Georgians never felt that they were sufficiently protected by these independent companies even though detachments from them were also stationed in Georgia.

Georgia had survived her first and greatest threat from Spanish Florida. Georgians must have breathed a sigh of relief and must have realized that the Spanish threat was not as great as they had assumed. If the Spaniards could not capture St. Simons Island with several times as many troops as Oglethorpe had, they must not be too great a danger. Though many people had left Georgia because of fear of the Spanish, those who remained had fought well and had acquired a sense of unity and purpose under Oglethorpe's leadership. The Scots at Darien particularly had shown themselves superb fighting men. The worst days in colonial Georgia were now over.

For Oglethorpe the fighting years had been very important. Henceforth he would be known as General Oglethorpe the savior of Georgia as well as its founder. He had not shown himself the greatest of generals, but a part of his problem had been inadequate men and supplies. Surprise and speed were the only tactics which might have assured his capture of St. Augustine;

but with his several false starts, he had lost these advantages. He had not demonstrated sufficient leadership to weld together the divergent elements not under his direct control—the South Carolina troops and the British navy. Yet in his greatest challenge, the Spanish invasion of St. Simons Island, he had shown superb leadership and had succeeded completely. Although neither Oglethorpe nor the peace treaty settled the disputed Georgia-Florida boundary, Georgia lost no territory to Spain. Oglethorpe's finest hour and his greatest fame had come during his decade in Georgia, and henceforth he could rest on his accomplishments there.

5

INDIAN RELATIONS: FRIENDS AND ALLIES?

All early colonists in America found satisfactory relations with the native population near their settlements a considerable challenge. The importance of the Indians was especially obvious for Georgia, located as it was where the conflicting claims of the English, the Spanish, and the French overlapped. South Carolina's concern with frontier defense has already been treated as one of the causes for the founding of Georgia.

One of the more acceptable methods of dealing with Indians was through control of their trade. Threats to stop this trade were frequently used to get the Indians to agree to a white proposal. For the Indians, trade had become just as important as it was to the whites. Indians had lost their old wilderness self-sufficiency and were dependent upon the whites for guns, knives and hatchets, trinkets of many kinds, and some clothing and food. Southern Indians supported themselves to a considerable degree through the exchange of deerskins for manufactured goods.

By 1733 the deerskin trade was a major item in the economy of the southern colonies, and a part of the triangular conflict in the southeast was over which white nation would control and profit from this valuable trade. The British colonial traders possessed a decided advantage over their rivals in that they had more trade goods and sold them at a cheaper price than the French or the Spaniards. Besides being customers of the whites, the Indians were also allies, mercenary soldiers, interpreters, and spies.

Frequently they were enemies as well. Indians were vital to any white control of and expansion into any wilderness area.

The Creeks, the largest and strongest Indian tribe in the southeast and nearest to the Georgia settlements, were a confederacy which absorbed smaller groups and were thus growing in population, contrary to the condition of most Indian tribes by the 1730s. The nation consisted of two major divisions, the Upper Creeks who lived near the Coosa and Tallapoosa rivers in the Alabama country, and the Lower Creeks whose villages stood along the middle Chattahoochee River. There were in 1740 about seven hundred Lower Creek warriors, and about a thousand Upper Creek ones. Coweta, located on the Chattahoochee near the city of Columbus today, was the chief town and political center of the Lower Creeks. By the wilderness routes of the day, this placed the Lower Creeks squarely between the English and the French. The Creeks had been courted by the English, the Spanish, and the French long enough to understand how to play one white nation against the other for their benefit—in other words, to practice balance-of-power tactics. While they could never be taken entirely for granted, they tended to favor the English in this wilderness diplomacy.

The Cherokees lived in the mountainous area in what is today western South Carolina, northern Georgia, western North Carolina, eastern Tennessee, and northern Alabama. A trade path went from Augusta to the Cherokees, who had been friendly to the English since the visit of six Cherokees to England in 1730 under the leadership of Sir Alexander Cuming. The Cherokees were mainly important to Georgia for trade and for acting as a shield which protected the colony from the northern Indians but also probably kept out settlers coming down the mountain valleys from the north.

The Yamassees, who had lived in the Georgia area but had moved south of the Altamaha River after the Yamassee War of 1715-16, were entirely loyal to the Spanish during Georgia's early decades. The "Spanish Indians" frequently referred to by the English during the War of Jenkins' Ear were mainly Yamassees.

The very name of the place where the Georgia colonists landed and settled, Yamacraw Bluff, was derived from the only Indians within fifty miles of the new settlement. This small and outlawed group of Creeks had settled on this bluff in 1730. They numbered, by best estimates, about seventeen families or one hundred people. Their old and wise chieftain, Tomo-Chi-Chi, was hardly of great importance in the larger Creek Confederacy; but he was Oglethorpe's entrée into Indian relations, and Oglethorpe took the best advantage of Tomo-Chi-Chi's proffered friendship.

When Oglethorpe picked the Yamacraw Bluff site for the settlement, he conferred with the Yamacraws there and received their permission for the settlement. Once the settlers arrived at Yamacraw Bluff the Indians welcomed them with strange ceremonies and long and formal speeches. Gifts and profusions of great friendship were exchanged. Tomo-Chi-Chi and the Yamacraws welcomed Oglethorpe and the settlers, but what would be the feeling of the Lower Creeks with whom South Carolina had a long-standing agreement that there would be no settlements south of the Savannah River? Through Tomo-Chi-Chi, Oglethorpe invited the Lower Creeks to send representatives to meet him in Savannah. In mid-May about fifty-five Creeks came. After several days of the usual long and ornate speeches, ceremonials, and exchange of presents, a treaty was agreed to in which the Creeks ceded "all such Lands and Territories as we shall have no occasion to use." A schedule of prices for the Indian trade was also agreed to. Clearly Oglethorpe had established himself as a superb Indian negotiator and a friend of Tomo-Chi-Chi by the time the treaty was signed on May 21, 1733.

Indian traders John Musgrove and Thomas Wiggan acted as interpreters at this meeting, but it was Musgrove's wife, Mary, who soon became important to Georgia and Oglethorpe. Mary was a half-breed niece of the Old Emperor Brims, a Creek leader who had died a few years before the founding of Georgia. She was born at Coweta Town about 1700 and brought up both in the Indian country and among the whites. About 1730 John and Mary opened their trading post at Yamacraw Bluff, where John soon became one of the leading Carolina traders. Here they met Oglethorpe and the colonists when they arrived in 1733. Apparently Oglethorpe was immediately taken with Mary as a person who could be useful to him, and she undoubtedly saw that a connection with him could help her also. In many respects Mary became Oglethorpe's agent as well as interpreter in dealing with the Creeks; and, as long as Oglethorpe remained in the colony, she served him and Georgia well. John Musgrove died in 1735; and, the next year, Mary married Jacob Matthews, an Indian trader and captain of rangers who had once been a servant to the Musgroves. About this time, Mary, at Oglethorpe's request, opened a trading post at Mount Venture, where the Oconee and the Ocmulgee rivers unite to form the Altamaha. Here, as well as at Yamacraw, she carried on Indian trade and diplomacy for Oglethorpe.

Although the first Georgia regulation of the Indian trade was covered by the list of prices included in the Lower Creek treaty of 1733, this treaty was not primarily concerned with Indian trade but with general relations between Georgia and the Creeks. A more detailed treatment of the trade was reserved for the Trustees' "Act for Maintaining the Peace with the Indians in the Province of Georgia," which received royal approval in April 1735.

This act was based, with very little change, on the South Carolina Indian Act of 1733. The Georgia act provided for an Indian commissioner, who was to have control of all Indian affairs. He issued licenses to traders and could levy fines or withdraw licenses. Annual cost of licenses was not to be over £5 sterling, and a £100 sterling bond was required guaranteeing obedience to the commissioner. All traders were confined to the town or towns specified in their licenses.

Oglethorpe was appointed Indian commissioner by the Trustees in 1735 and retained the post until 1750. Secretary William Stephens was made co-commissioner in 1741 as Oglethorpe was now busy with military affairs. Oglethorpe appointed Captain Patrick Mackay in 1735 as agent to the Creeks and

Roger Lacy in 1736 as agent to the Cherokees. These agents lived among the Indians and reported on their doings. Mary Musgrove's duties as interpreter and de facto agent to the Creeks have already been mentioned.

As soon as this act of the Trustees about the Indian trade became known in Charles Town, there was great objection to it there. The Indian trade had become an important part of the economy of South Carolina, and most of the Charles Town trade was with Indians who either lived in Georgia or who could only be contacted by passing through Georgia. To object to the Trustees' act, a special session of the Assembly in late June 1736 denied Georgia's right to prohibit traders holding South Carolina licenses from trading in Georgia and promised to reimburse such traders for losses resulting from the Georgia law. In Augusta a committee of South Carolinians conferred with Oglethorpe and agreed to refer the matter to London for settlement. In the meantime the Georgia law would not be applied to Carolina traders.

Conflict soon developed in the Indian country between Georgia and Carolina agents and traders, and Oglethorpe said he feared an Indian war. At the same time, objections also resulted because agents under the Georgia prohibition act staved rum being transported up the Savannah River by Carolinians. South Carolina protested about both laws to London and asked that they not be enforced against Carolinians.

The Board of Trade heard arguments in 1737, and the Privy Council decided in July 1738 that Georgia could not charge a fee to Carolina licensed traders, that Carolinians had a right to the Georgia Indian trade, and that the navigation of the Savannah River should be open to residents of both colonies. It was recommended to the two colonies that they prepare acts to settle this controversy amicably.

The Trustees immediately approached the newly appointed governor of South Carolina, Samuel Horsey, who seemed sympathetic to their viewpoint. However, Horsey died within two weeks and was replaced by James Glen who was not so favorably inclined toward Georgia. Back in America, Oglethorpe and Lieutenant Governor William Bull tried unsuccessfully during the winter of 1738–39 to work out an agreement.

Finally in September 1741 the Trustees and Governor Glen worked out a compromise in London through which South Carolina would license half of the Indian traders in Georgia, and all Georgia traders might trade with Carolina Indians. It was agreed that the Trustees and the Carolina Assembly would pass parallel acts, worked out between representatives of the two colonies in America. While these acts were never passed, the essence of the agreement was observed by the two colonies for the remainder of the Trustee period in Georgia.

Besides the formal organization and problems of Georgia's Indian relations, actual happenings in Georgia must also be looked at. One policy which Oglethorpe adopted early was to build up the prestige of Tomo-Chi-Chi, his main contact with the Creeks. Thus in 1734 Oglethorpe took the old chieftain, his wife, Senauki, his nephew, Tooanahowi, and five other Indians to England. Oglethorpe's purpose was twofold: to dramatize Georgia to Englishmen through the Indians, and to impress the Indians with the strength and grandeur of England. The Indians visited, impressed, and were impressed by the king, the Trustees, the Archbishop of Canterbury, and many more Englishmen. Many presents were showered upon the Indians, and Oglethorpe's dual purpose was admirably achieved in the four months they were in England.

After Oglethorpe's return to Georgia, he continued to favor Tomo-Chi-Chi and to distribute some Indian presents through him. When Tomo-Chi-Chi died on October 5, 1739, Oglethorpe ordered an elaborate English military funeral. The burial took place in Percival Square in Savannah with Oglethorpe, William Stephens, and military officers as pallbearers. Truly Georgia and Oglethorpe had lost a friend, for Tomo-Chi-Chi's every act since the arrival of the *Ann* had been helpful to Georgia.

One of Oglethorpe's major triumphs as an Indian negotiator was his trip to Coweta in August of 1739 to a full meeting of the Creek Indian nation. Oglethorpe made this trip of about three hundred miles through the trackless wilderness with a few companions. At Coweta, he was royally received by the Creeks. The council lasted from August 11 to August 21, during which time Oglethorpe was laid low for several days by a severe fever. He reported to the Trustees that he answered satisfactorily all the complaints of the Creeks so that they agreed to be loyal to the English and confirmed the 1733 treaty made with Georgia. Here the Georgia-Creek boundary was somewhat clearer delineated than in the 1733 treaty. The lands ceded to the whites were described as "all the Lands upon the Savannah River as far as the Ogeechee and all Lands along the Sea-Coast as far as the River St. John's and as high as the tyde flows and all the Islands" except for a Creek reserve of lands from Pipemaker's Bluff to Savannah and the islands of St. Catherines, Ossabaw, and Sapelo. No lands were to be settled by whites outside these specified bounds. This was Oglethorpe's fullest meeting with the Creeks, and it showed well his abilities as an Indian negotiator. It was very important just at this time as Tomo-Chi-Chi was to die within a few weeks, and the Spanish War would soon break out.

From the time he met Mary Musgrove at the founding of Savannah, Oglethorpe was taken with her and what she could do for Georgia. They worked well together in maintaining Creek friendship for the English. Oglethorpe built up Mary's importance when she acted as his interpreter on most important occasions. When there was danger from the Spanish or the French, Oglethorpe always called on Mary to get the needed Indian aid, and she never failed him. When Creek friendship for Georgia was endangered, Mary helped to restore it. Mary seemed able to influence the Creeks more as Oglethorpe desired than anyone else who worked with them. There can be no doubt from Oglethorpe's letters and actions that he had a high regard for Mary and trusted and depended upon her fully.

In 1742 the Matthewses returned to Savannah from Mount Venture, because of Jacob's ill health. In the summer he died. During the Matthewses' absence from their trading post, Mount Venture was destroyed by Spanish Indians who looted the stock of trade goods there. Mary remained in Savannah and continued to entertain and help to control Indians who came there after Jacob's death.

When Oglethorpe left for England in July of 1743, Mary said that he promised her £100 a year for her services as interpreter. He gave her a diamond ring and £200 and promised her more. This ended Oglethorpe's active participation in Georgia's Indian affairs but not his interest in Mary, her efforts to get compensation for her past services and losses, and Oglethorpe's recommendations in her behalf to his successors in the military command in Georgia or officials in England who might be helpful to her.

A year after Oglethorpe's departure Mary married Thomas Bosomworth, who originally came to Georgia in late 1741 as a clerk to William Stephens. Back in England in late 1742, he took holy orders and returned to Savannah as an Anglican minister, a position that did not seem to interest him very much. In July 1744 Bosomworth and Mary Matthews were married, much to the surprise of Stephens and many other Georgians. Having given up his ministry in Savannah in 1746, he and Mary moved to her trading post at the forks of the Altamaha and engaged in the Indian trade for the next several years. Oglethorpe's successors continued to use Mary to secure Creek friendship and aid as long as the regiment remained in Georgia.

When Oglethorpe left the colony in 1743 no one could have known that Georgia's greatest danger in the remaining Trustee period was to come from Oglethorpe's old friend and interpreter, Mary Musgrove Matthews Bosomworth, her husband, and her Indian allies. Oglethorpe's departure and Mary's third marriage began her transformation from the friend and savior of Georgia. After the marriage, Bosomworth more and more promoted his wife's position among the Creeks and her claims against Georgia; and Mary was led to believe that she had been wronged by the Trustees and Georgia officials.

An early point of contention was the £100-a-year salary as interpreter which Mary said Oglethorpe had promised her when he left for England. In 1746 Mary petitioned the Trustees for £1,204 as her back salary as interpreter and bounties on crops of wheat, corn, peas, and potatoes raised in 1739 and 1742. Mary also asked for a grant to her husband of the land between Savannah and Pipemaker's Creek where Tomo-Chi-Chi's village of Yamacraw had been situated. The Trustees replied that they had never fixed any salary as interpreter and that Mary's services had been fully satisfied by now. The president and assistants were ordered to look into the bounties, but it was suggested that claims for bounties should have been made by Matthews in the years concerned.

The Bosomworths in January 1747 persuaded some Creek chieftains, especially Malatchee, a cousin of Mary's, to deed them the islands of St. Catherines, Sapelo, and Ossabaw, and the land between Savannah and Pipemaker's Creek—all reserved by the Indians for tribal use in the treaty of 1739. Such a deed was of doubtful legality under Indian custom. About a hundred Indians went down to Frederica and swore before Lieutenant Colonel Alexander Heron that Malatchee was king among the Creeks and that the reserved Creek lands had been correctly deeded to the Bosomworths. Documents to support these claims were carried to England by Abraham Bosomworth, the brother of Thomas, in an attempt to secure royal approval. Thomas Bosomworth purchased considerable cattle in South Carolina to stock his islands and needed money to pay for them. Major William Horton, Oglethorpe's military successor in Georgia, allowed Mary a salary for her services in preventing Indian troubles. When Colonel Heron replaced Horton in 1747 he refused to continue this salary. Mary also claimed payment for £650 worth of goods out of her store used in her Indian diplomacy.

On July 21, 1749, the Bosomworths and Malatchee came to Savannah with the rumor that Mary was to be sent to England in irons. They announced that they had come to meet Abraham Bosomworth upon his return from England to see the results of the petitions for the lands. If the petitions were not favorably acted upon, the Creeks warned that no more whites would be allowed to settle above the tidewater. On August 7 and 9 about two hundred Indians arrived, firing their guns as they came down the river. Savannah was thoroughly alarmed, and the militia was put into readiness. The next day the Indians were escorted into town by militia and volunteer horsemen under the command of Noble Jones. The Indians seemed confused and departed without taking any action.

The next afternoon a group of Indians marching down the street led by a drummer were almost fired on by excited townspeople. Just as a conference of whites and Indians began at William Stephens' house, Mary Bosomworth rushed in "like a Mad and Frantick Woman," threatening the lives of Georgia's leaders, the destruction of the colony, and declaring herself queen of the Creeks. She was arrested and removed to prevent further trouble. Thomas Bosomworth soon appeared and apologized for his wife's actions. The town was heavily patrolled that night, but there was no further trouble.

The Indians remained in town quietly until August 16, when presents were distributed in hopes that they would leave. At Malatchee's desire, a number of white and Indian leaders repaired to a tavern for the evening. Mary rushed into the tavern in high dudgeon and soon had Malatchee "foaming at the Mouth like a Mad Beast" and declaring he would support her fully. Mary was again arrested, Malatchee roused the Indians, and Thomas Bosomworth was full of threats. Again Savannah spent a sleepless night, but the next day Bosomworth apologized for his wife's actions. Malatchee, too, apologized and asked for another evening of mirth. Finally on August 19, the Indians departed, much to the relief of Savannahians.

There had been considerable fear in Savannah for the past month. Some feared that the town might be burned and a real war begun by the Indians. Yet only two Lower Creek towns were represented by the Indians in Savannah. No Upper Creeks were present, as the Bosomworths lacked popularity among them.

There were more apologies and appeals from the Bosomworths, but the president and assistants refused to make any payments for Mary's past services. Mary set out upon a tour of the Creek nation, mainly to Lower Creek towns, to secure signatures to her grant of the islands and Yamacraw area. At Coweta Town in August of 1750 she secured the signatures of seven chieftains to the deed for the desired lands to herself and her husband. William Stephens and other officials did what they could to persuade Indians not to back the Bosomworths.

In May of 1751 Patrick Graham was sent into the Creek country to secure a grant of the reserved lands from the Indians to the colony of Georgia. Graham bought for the colony the Yamacraw tract and the three islands. Twenty-six Upper Creek chieftains agreed to this sale and collected the goods given in exchange. At Coweta Town, Graham failed to secure Lower Creek agreement to this sale but was offered a lease on the desired territory. Malatchee and other chieftains denied that they had ever deeded the lands to the Bosomworths.

The Bosomworths again petitioned for royal approval for the desired lands and went to England in 1754 to press their claim in person. They appeared before the Board of Trade several times but with no success. Thus, when the Trustee period ended, the Bosomworth claims were still unsettled.

Georgia's first two royal governors, John Reynolds and Henry Ellis, and their councils were concerned with a settlement of the Bosomworth claims. In July 1759 word of royal disallowance of the claims arrived. At the same time Governor Ellis and his Council agreed that Mary should have £2,100 for her services as interpreter and her losses in the colony's service if that much could be realized from the sale of Ossabaw and Sapelo islands. St. Catherines Island, the third island claimed and where the Bosomworths then lived, was to be granted to them.

Ossabaw and Sapelo brought £2,050 upon sale, which was paid to the Bosomworths, and on June 13, 1760, Governor Ellis signed a grant to St. Catherines and the long matter was ended. The Bosomworths made great plans for planting operations and the building of a mansion. They did build a house, apparently not very grand, and there is a small shell mound on St. Catherines today which is pointed out as Mary's grave.

Despite the Bosomworth troubles at the end, Georgia's first two decades had been very fortunate so far as relations with the Creeks were concerned. Obviously much of the success through the Spanish War resulted from the work of Oglethorpe and Mary

Musgrove Matthews. They had a personal high regard for each other, and they cooperated fully to ensure Creek friendship.

One reason for the successful Indian relations was the mutual respect on both sides. Oglethorpe knew that Indian, especially Creek, friendship was essential to insure peace to the early settlement and to aid in the fighting against the Spaniards. He may have had humanitarian feelings about Indians, but they were not spelled out by him. Oglethorpe, who handled Indian relations personally, seemed to respect Indians as people, and he was much more interested in having their friendship than in allowing traders to make a profit from the Indian trade.

With the personalities and personal respect of Oglethorpe and Mary for each other and their personal domination of Indian relations, it is not surprising that there should have been trouble after Oglethorpe's departure from Georgia and Mary's third marriage. Perhaps no widespread Indian troubles resulted from the Bosomworth excitement because the Creeks generally believed, probably correctly, that trade with the English was essential to them and that there was little chance of any long-range or substantial help from the Spaniards or French if they broke with the English in Georgia and South Carolina. Georgians and Creeks needed each other and had to get along as best they could despite recurring immediate problems between them.

6

GOVERNMENT, 1733–1754: "THE TRUSTEES ARE THE GOVERNMENT"

Under the Trustees, Georgia was governed from both London and Savannah. The Trustees met personally as a full board and as the Common Council, a body of fifteen Trustees which was created to meet more often and carry on many of the detailed duties. The Common Council often could not secure its quorum of eight members, so that many meetings called as councils ended as full Trustees' meetings requiring no specific quorum. Both bodies were presided over by a rotating president (Trustees) or chairman (Common Council) who held office for one meeting and in the interim until the next meeting took place.

The Trustees maintained only two employees, Benjamin Martyn, the secretary, and Harman Verelst, the accountant, both of whom served for the entire life of the Trust. In practice their duties seem to have overlapped, and together they did the clerical work in the Georgia Office in Old Palace Yard, Westminster. Both knew much more about Georgia affairs than most Trustees and probably had considerable influence upon Trustee activities. Over its life the Trust had seventy-one Trustees, about forty-five of whom were active in Trust affairs and ten can be called leaders. The best known and most active were James Vernon, the Earl of Egmont, Henry L'Apostre, the Reverend Samuel Smith, Thomas Towers, and Oglethorpe.

Despite Oglethorpe's absence in Georgia much of the time, he had more to do with important decisions in the first ten years than any other Trustee.

The Trustees' original plan was to finance the colony from contributions. Georgia became a favorite charity of prominent Englishmen briefly in 1732, but only £2,000 was contributed in five months. After the initial enthusiasm, charity contributions fell off considerably, and the Trustees discovered that this was an impractical way to support the colony. Hence they began to agitate for Parliamentary grants, the first of which, £10,000, was voted in May of 1733. Of the over £260,000 ultimately accounted for by the Trustees, about 52 percent came from Parliament, almost 40 percent from adventurers, and the remaining 8 percent from charity contributions, mainly from London merchants. Georgia was the only colony whose settlement was financially aided by the British government. The reason for this Parliamentary expenditure was imperial defense, not philanthropy.

The Trustees, always short on funds, were rather parsimonious in spending, and refused to carry on deficit spending because of the uncertainty of their income. They tried to limit expenses in Georgia by the issuance of sola bills, Trustee promises to pay specific amounts to officials in Georgia to defray Trustee expenses. Sola bills circulated as currency in Georgia, were redeemed by the Trustees in London, but never controlled expenditures as it was hoped they would.

It has often been said, with partial truth, that the Georgia Trustees were so carried away with their economic and sociological ideas that they never got down to such pragmatic things as government. It is certain that the Trustees did not trust Georgia to the government of Sir Robert Walpole in England nor did they ever consider giving the colonists a substantial voice in their government. By the time Georgia was founded, there was a well worked out system of colonial government in which colonists participated. Yet the Trustees ignored this system and the English tradition of self-government. The charter gave the Trustees complete power to govern Georgia, except that any governor appointed or laws passed must be approved by the king.

Colonial experience had already proven that the day-to-day business of government could best be conducted within the colony rather than in London and that the colonists must be able to participate in their government, but the Trustees never seem to have learned either of these lessons.

The first and most obvious result of the Trustees' effort at making all important decisions was their failure to appoint a governor and their refusal to give any appointed chief executive adequate power to operate the colony successfully. From the arrival of the colonists in February until July 1733 Oglethorpe was the only government in Georgia. Though he had been given little specific authority by his fellow Trustees in London, they undoubtedly approved his actions and expected him to exercise authority in the new colony. Of course, he could occupy no office of profit or trust under the charter and at the same time remain a Trustee.

Before the first colonists sailed for Georgia, the Trustees created the "Town Court of Savannah and the Precincts thereof." This was the government which Oglethorpe instituted in Savannah on July 7, 1733. This court consisted of three justices, called bailiffs, and a recorder and was "to preserve the Peace and Administer Justice Without fear or affection, to the Terror of the Evil Doers and to the Comfort of those who do well." It was given complete criminal and civil jurisdiction "according to the Law & Custom of the Realm of England."

The Trustees appointed constables, tithingmen, and conservators of the peace. The constables and tithingmen were to summon juries and to execute warrants. The constables acted as prosecuting attorneys before the court, served the processes of the court, and became the officers of the militia. The tithingmen became the officers of the guard for the men in their tithing. Conservators of the peace dealt with petty offenses and suits for small sums, as did justices of the peace in England.

In 1735 when provisions were made for the settlement of Frederica, a town court identical to the one in Savannah was created for "Frederica and the precincts thereof." Both these courts were essentially local or municipal in character. The

villages near Savannah were always included in the jurisdiction
of the court there. As long as outlying settlements were physically
close to Savannah and Frederica, the extent of the jurisdiction of
the two courts caused no concern. But for settlements twenty or
more miles away like Darien, Ebenezer, and Augusta the
Trustees neglected for a long time to create adequate government. In Ebenezer the tight-knit Salzburgers got along well
without any further government because Bolzius exercised whatever leadership was needed. The Scots at Darien were also a
small homogeneous group where the absence of formal government did not cause immediate problems. It was Augusta, with its
more diverse population, which needed government. Yet the
Trustees appointed no conservators of the peace for Ebenezer
until 1745 when both clergymen, John Martin Bolzius and Israel
Christian Gronau, were appointed. It was 1750 before Augusta
received its first conservators, and 1751 before they were
appointed for Darien and for "Medway River and Great
Ogeechee."

Following the English tradition in local government, the
bailiffs were also the magistrates and possessed executive functions. But this pattern of government was clearly local in
character, and the colony outgrew it physically long before the
Trustees realized that the town-court system needed to be
changed to fit Georgia's growing needs.

All officials were appointed to serve during the pleasure of the
Trustees. The first officials were selected from the original charity
colonists. They knew no law and little English usage and
frequently argued with each other on the bench, with the juries,
and with those on trial. In an age when social status was
important, the fact that the officials were of the same lower social
class as the masses of the people did not help them to acquire
prestige. The fur-trimmed gowns and a mace sent by the
Trustees in 1737 did not provide the needed dignity and prestige.

While the Trustees recognized the importance of the executive
arm of government, instead of appointing a chief executive they
appointed a number of executive officers for different functions as
the need arose, each independent of the others and responsible

only to the Trustees in London. Among the officials thus appointed were a storekeeper, schoolmasters, clergymen, a collector for the port, a naval officer for the port, other port officials, a recorder, a botanist, a surveyor, a register of land grants, a secretary of Indian affairs, a receiver of fees for the Indian trade, an agent to the Cherokees, an agent to distribute Indian presents, a collector of benefactions for the orphans' house, overseers for Trust servants for the northern and southern districts, a prohibition agent, an overseer for the silk culture, a gardener, an overseer of the public garden, and many others.

With such a "Hydra of Magistracy" reporting directly to the Trustees, there was much confusion, especially when authority overlapped or when there were disputes between officials. If the matter were of sufficient importance, Oglethorpe would make a decision. Though he had no overall executive authority, he never hesitated to act when he thought it necessary. The Trustees never objected or tried to stop him. Since decisions had to be made, it was probably best for Georgia's beginnings that a man like Oglethorpe was present in the colony during its first years.

Despite the lack of authority, Oglethorpe was in reality the chief executive in Georgia during his first fifteen months in the colony. He made most important decisions, appointed subordinates where he felt necessary, and informed the Trustees of what he had done. As might be expected, Oglethorpe found that the original charity colonists did not make the best officials. Hence he was hard put to find adequate assistance to aid him in running the new colony.

The two men whom he appointed to most offices and who did most to assist him illustrate this problem very well. Noble Jones came on the *Ann* and in the first few years in Georgia acted as a doctor, a carpenter and builder, a conservator of the peace, a surveyor, and a militia officer. Jones was an able man who remained a leader in the colony until his death in 1775. If there were complaints because he did not survey the land rapidly enough to suit all the settlers or carry out certain of his other duties, it was because he had more duties than one man could perform.

Thomas Causton, who also came on the *Ann*, was the third bailiff in the Trustees' original appointments. Oglethorpe appointed him to take care of the stores of the colony, and he retained this office until October of 1738. He became first bailiff and the most important official in the colony. When Oglethorpe went to England in May of 1734 he designated Causton as the person in charge during his absence. Upon Oglethorpe's return to Georgia in February of 1736 he objected to some things which Causton had done, and Causton tried to resign as storekeeper. But Oglethorpe would not allow him to, probably because there was no other person in the colony whom Oglethorpe thought so well qualified for the job. Oglethorpe used what subordinates he could find, and he evidently considered Jones and Causton the two best available at first.

Oglethorpe's methods as an administrator are illustrated by the fact that most of his important instructions were oral and could not be definitely determined when he was out of the colony or too busy with the Spanish War. Neither did Oglethorpe support or condemn Causton when he was in trouble with the Trustees about the store accounts. Oglethorpe as an administrator disliked routine operations, was concerned with the immediate task at hand, used the best people available to him, and once the job was done showed little interest in the people he had used. McCain, the modern historian of the Trusteeship, thinks that Georgia would have been better off if Oglethorpe had never possessed any civil authority in the colony.* Had this happened, the Trustees would undoubtedly have been forced to appoint a governor and to centralize authority in the colony, something badly needed.

Like Oglethorpe, the bailiffs developed their power by an evolutionary process. Although the Trustees never spelled it out, there can be no doubt that they expected the bailiffs to act as the chief officials of the colony; yet the Trustees gave neither the bailiffs nor Oglethorpe any general instructions. Instead there were specific instructions for individual tasks. This procedure

---

* James R. McCain, *Georgia as a Proprietary Province* (Boston, 1917), 96.

considerably limited the power of the government and officials. An exception was the so-called "Rules for the Year 1735" issued by the Trustees when the settlers for Frederica were sent over in 1735. These rules brought together the regulations concerning settlement allowances, land granting, inheritance, and other topics of importance. While the Rules did not discuss political organization as such, it was the most important document issued by the Trustees for the guidance of officials and colonists for the next several years.

Both the Trustees in London and the officials and colonists in Georgia objected to this disjointed procedure, but the system continued for four years before the Trustees took the first steps to remedy it. As early as March of 1734, some of the Trustees complained that Oglethorpe did not write to them fully or often enough. The Trustees asked Oglethorpe to find a suitable person to correspond with them, a request with which he never complied. Had Oglethorpe corresponded with the Trustees as fully as they desired, he would have had time to do little else in Georgia. He was a man of action rather than a scribe. If the Trustees were to find out what was happening in Georgia, they must find someone else to inform them. In the spring of 1737 they sent William Stephens to Georgia to do this job.

Stephens was sixty-six years old, with an A.B. and an M.A. from King's College, Cambridge, and a representative of New-port, Isle of Wight, in the House of Commons for about thirty years before 1727. But he was now out of Parliament and in financial distress. In 1736 he came to South Carolina to supervise a survey of four baronies for Colonel Samuel Horsey. Here he became acquainted with Oglethorpe and Georgia. Upon his return to England he sent in a full report to Horsey, which the Earl of Egmont saw and by which he was immediately capti-vated. He wrote in his diary, "His journal is extremely well wrote, and it were to be wished it could be brought about to make him Governor of Georgia." Governor is not what the earl really meant, since the Trustees wanted no governor.

On April 27, 1737, Stephens was appointed by the Trustees as "Secretary for the Affairs of the Trust within the Province of

Georgia." He was directed to take a census, report on defense matters, check upon the attitudes of the people and the magistrates, report on trade and farming and all economic affairs, report on religion and education, and write to the Trustees on all possible occasions whether he had much or little information to impart. In Stephens the Trustees had found their source of information for happenings in Georgia.

Stephens kept a journal which he regularly sent to the Trustees. Nothing was ever too trivial for inclusion. While Stephens did not know everything that happened in Georgia, he undoubtedly knew as much as any other person and more than most. He early decided that it did not pay to go counter to the views of the Trustees in his reports. His desire to please probably resulted in the Trustees knowing less about unfavorable happenings in Georgia than they should have. But at his age and with a series of disappointing failures behind him, it is understandable why Stephens did not care to antagonize the Trustees and run the risk of losing his position. The journal from October 20, 1737, through October 28, 1741, was printed by the Trustees, but the 1741–1745 portion was not discovered until 1946 and was first published in 1958–59. No journal beyond 1745 is known to exist today, but it is certain that Stephens kept his journal until at least 1749.

From the very beginning, Stephens was more than a reporter to the Trustees. He soon began attending court and advising the bailiffs on English law and legal procedure, something that he knew much more about than they did. Being of a higher social and educational level than most Georgians, he was in a good position to influence the colonists. However both his age and his officious personality were against him, and he could never become a real leader. He was careful to consult Oglethorpe on most things and to defer to his judgment. Stephens was better at routine activities than at conceiving and carrying through large projects. Stephens' importance in the government grew gradually during his first four years in Georgia. After the Spanish War began in 1739 Oglethorpe had less time to devote to civilian affairs, and this increased Stephens' duties. He had a plantation, called Bewlie on the Vernon River, about thirteen miles from Savannah, to which he repaired at times when the hurry and bustle of Savannah and his governmental duties seemed too much for him.

But it would take more than an accurate report and advisor in Georgia to satisfy many of the colonists. Very soon after the colony's founding, people who did not find it as utopian as it had been advertised began to voice their objections—privately, to the Trustees, or publicly to the world. From the beginning such people were considered malcontents, unappreciative of what the Trustees did for them and unworthy of the aid they received.

Reports to London of Thomas Causton and William Stephens, a severe food crisis in 1737, and growing objections to limitations in land granting caused the Trustees to reexamine their Rules of 1735. Most objected to were the prohibition of rum and slaves and the limitation of land to five hundred acres per person granted in tail-male. The Trustees, in an unprecedented move, instructed Stephens to ask the colonists for their views on land tenure.

In December 1738, 119 freeholders of Savannah memorialized the Trustees for fee simple title to land and the use of Negro slaves. The memorialists insisted that they had tried hard to support themselves under the existing system but had found it impossible. Oglethorpe, who had first suggested slave and rum prohibition and who had worked to secure the laws which forbade them, opposed the memorialists. First, he said, to allow slavery would do injustice to innumerable blacks and would negate the entire original reason for the settling of Georgia. If the poor and unfortunate lost their lands, as he was sure they would do to slave traders if slaves were allowed, then they would be no better off than before they came to Georgia. Oglethorpe was saying that he still did not trust the charity colonists to be able to take care of themselves. Slaves would weaken the frontier that Georgia had been settled to strengthen and would discourage silk and wine production.

Reject the petition, said Oglethorpe, and the idle would leave and the industrious would go to work. He went to great lengths to represent the memorialists to the Trustees as people of doubtful motives. He collected petitions and depositions from Darien and Frederica and from Bolzius and the Salzburgers all opposing slavery and "proving" that Europeans could work in Georgia's hot weather with no real damage to themselves.

Oglethorpe's opponents in Georgia wrote directly to individual Trustees, charging that both rum and Negro slaves were freely used at Frederica among the officers and men of Oglethorpe's regiment, as apparently they were. Oglethorpe was also attacked as a tyrant who would allow no opposition and who was personally responsible for most of the ills of the colony.

The Trustees, who received the petition in April of 1739, were easily swayed by Oglethorpe's arguments. They blamed the colonists for any troubles and tended to minimize the conditions about which they complained. The Trustees denied both fee simple land titles and slavery and fired the magistrates who signed the petitions. As the worthy gentlemen in London lamented, "Many of the poor who had been useless in England were inclined to be useless also in Georgia."

It was almost a year before the colonists manifested any positive reaction to the Trustees' denial of the petition, but in this time additional resentment built up over the ending of credit at the Trustees' store and the lack of participation in the government. The outbreak of war with Spain in 1739 added to fear in the colony and increased hostility for the Trustees' viewpoints. In October 1739 Oglethorpe sent a long "State of Georgia" to the Trustees, defending their policies. On November 10 at the meeting of the court in Savannah, William Stephens offered a similar document entitled "A State of the Province of Georgia" for the signatures of all colonists. Stephens' document gave a rather rosy description of Georgia, especially its agricultural and other economic successes but asked for additional bounties on Georgia products. However only twenty-five men signed the statement.

Reaction to "The State of the Province of Georgia" was swift in Savannah. By November 22 a remonstrance to the Trustees had been drawn up and signed by sixty-four people. It went further than the petition of the previous year, asking that land might be granted where it was convenient to the settlers, that excessive quitrents be relaxed, that constables and tithingmen be under the order of the Trustees and the magistrates only, and that the people be allowed to choose their own bailiffs. Another petition, signed by seventy-eight men, was prepared for presentation to the king or to Parliament. This petition denied that the signers were "a set of clamorous people," but were instead people genuinely interested in improving conditions in Georgia.

The anti-Trustee faction, now dubbed the malcontents, summed up their opposition to Oglethorpe and the Trustees best in a book published in Charles Town in May of 1741. Entitled *A True and Historical Narrative of the Colony of Georgia in America* . . . , it bore the names of Patrick Tailfer, Hugh Anderson, and David Douglas as authors—the nucleus of the St. Andrews Club, or the leading malcontents according to William Stephens. Tailfer had practiced medicine in Savannah and had failed, if he had tried, as a planter in the Scots settlement on the Ogeechee River. Douglas was a Scot of the same settlement. Anderson was an English gentleman who had come to Georgia hoping to recoup his fortunes but had not succeeded.

The *True and Historical Narrative* . . . was satirical in the best eighteenth-century tradition and well written from a literary viewpoint. It contained a mock dedication to Oglethorpe and then recounted in great detail the old arguments and accusations against Oglethorpe and the Trustees. The Earl of Egmont prepared a long rebuttal and may have circulated it to other Trustees.

In 1741 the Trustees published two more booklets giving their side of the argument to be countered with another by Thomas Stephens, the malcontents' agent in London. Stephens, the son of William Stephens, was deputized by 141 landholders in Georgia to try to secure from any agency in England except the Trustees the following for Georgia: (1) the establishment of a regular government, (2) land grants as extensive and quitrents no higher than those in South Carolina, (3) the use of Negroes, and (4) encouragement for the making of potash, silk, wine, oil, indigo, hemp, flax, and other products desired in Britain. Finally, if no change in the government of Georgia could be obtained, any money granted for Georgia should be used to remove the settlers to some other colony where they could support themselves.

Thomas Stephens presented petitions to the Privy Council on March 30 and to the House of Commons on April 30. After hearings, the House of Commons resolved that Georgia ought to be supported and preserved. The petition of Stephens was condemned as containing false and malicious charges. On June 30 Thomas Stephens was compelled to fall on his knees and be reprimanded by the Speaker. While the Trustees had been upheld by the House of Commons, such unfavorable publicity was most undesirable to them, especially the call for more participation of the people in the government.

While some of the malcontents would have been satisfied with nothing that the Trustees did, others sincerely wanted to improve conditions in Georgia. This is especially true of the several magistrates who signed some of the petitions and the many signers who remained in Georgia to become substantial citizens and to occupy important offices. Such people saw that the Trustees' plans were not working to the benefit of the colony as a whole or for many individuals.

The Trustees reacted to these troubled years in several ways. Considerable changes in land tenure were made and will be treated in the next chapter. Slavery was eventually permitted. More and more after 1738 the Trustees mistrusted Oglethorpe and limited his authority. They had an excellent excuse for this—the Spanish War which took up most of the general's time. The creation of a new form of government for the colony, in theory at least, removed Oglethorpe from any political authority.

In December of 1740 Trustee James Vernon suggested the reorganization of Georgia's government in order to supplant Oglethorpe in civilian affairs and to achieve better what the Trustees desired. Vernon's suggestion was that the colony be divided into two districts, with an independent government for each. This would keep central authority in London in the hands of the Trustees and circumvent the charter provision that a governor must receive royal approval. The acceptance of this scheme by the Trustees made it clear that they thought Georgia's government needed reorganization but that they wanted to keep real power in their own hands.

The new plan approved by the Trustees on April 15, 1741, divided Georgia into two counties—Savannah and Frederica. The former was to include the settlements upon the Savannah and Ogeechee rivers, the rest of the colony would be in Frederica county. At the head of each county was to be a president and four assistants, to have such authority as the Trustees' Common Council gave them and to hold office at its pleasure. In reality the president and assistants were given little more authority than the old magistrates had possessed, their powers still being specific in nature rather than general.

The new system did not please everyone in the colony, since there were many who wanted some direct voice in the government themselves. The very day that the new government was instituted in Savannah, October 7, 1741, there were objections from the inhabitants. Said William Stephens, "and in the Evening they adjourned to *Penrose's* House to drink, and consider how to grow more troublesome than ever." Despite the attitude of these people, the new government was inaugurated in Savannah with William Stephens as president, with the bailiffs of the town court as assistants, and with the recorder of the old magistrates as clerk.

Oglethorpe was asked to recommend a suitable person for president of Frederica County, but he was too busy with the Spanish War and never made a choice. The population of the southern part of the colony had been diminished by the war, so that in April of 1743 the Common Council ordered the bailiffs at Frederica, who had been made assistants pending the appointment of a president, to be local magistrates only and subject to the authority of the president and assistants in Savannah. Now for the first time there was one unified government for the entire colony—ten years after it was founded. No further change in this administrative structure was made throughout the life of the Trust.

Stephens remained president for most of the Trustee period. The assistants appointed with him were Henry Parker, Thomas Jones, John Fallowfield, and Samuel Mercer. Parker had been appointed as a constable in 1733 and third bailiff in 1734. He was first bailiff in 1738 and the first assistant under the new government. In March of 1750 he was made vice-president, a new office created to give some relief to President Stephens; at the same time James Habersham replaced Stephens as secretary. Parker became president on May 24, 1751, when Stephens asked to be removed because of age and infirmities, and remained president until his death in 1752.

Certainly the government of the president and assistants, regardless of its lack of adequate authority, was the most complete and best organized government Georgia had under the Trustees. With the peace after the Spanish War and a gradually increasing population and prosperity, life in Georgia became more normal. The malcontents, who by their trouble helped in the creation of the new government, had left the colony or accepted the new government. Relations with South Carolina were generally good. Control of land granting by the president and assistants in Savannah solved one serious problem of the early years. The new government had a chief executive who was located in Georgia and who knew its problems firsthand. Although the people had no formal participation in the government, they could make their influence felt in Savannah much better than in London.

After the 1741 reorganization, the Trustees largely ignored Oglethorpe, who was busy with the Spanish War the rest of the time he remained in Georgia, and the officials in the colony were informed that Oglethorpe had no authority as a Trustee in Georgia. President Stephens and the assistants continued to consult with him and to ask his advice. However, they sometimes refused to accept his proposals when they thought them contrary to instructions from the Trustees. But Oglethorpe was still the strongest personality in the colony and could hardly be ignored.

The strangest feature of the Trustees' government was the absence of a legislature. The evidence on the drafting of the charter is insufficient to make it clear who was responsible for this omission. Probably the proposals made by the Associates of Dr. Bray contained no provisions for a legislature and none of the officials who worked on the charter inserted any. The charter gave the Trustees complete legislative power in the colony but, in fact, they enacted few formal laws or regulations for the colony. On August 10, 1732, a committee was appointed "to consider & propose Laws & proper Regulations for the Colony," but there is no evidence that it reported before January 9, 1735. On that date the committee proposed three laws: (1) prohibiting Negro slavery in Georgia; (2) prohibiting the use of rum, brandy, spirits or other strong drink; and (3) regulating the Indian trade. The Trustees passed all three laws the same day, and the Privy Council approved them on April 3. On April 1, 1737, a new committee was directed to bring in laws on several subjects, but it made no report.

On March 15, 1739, a Trustee committee was ordered to prepare a law allowing for female inheritance of land; but on July 25 the Trustees decided to change the land regulations upon their own authority. On the same day the Trustees approved a law for regulating pilotage and for laying port duties. When the Board of Trade raised some objections to this act, it was dropped. In 1742 the Trustees drew up acts to repeal the act of 1735 prohibiting the sale of rum and an act to regulate land tenures. The law officers of the crown raised technical objections to these acts, and they were dropped. Finally, the Trustees approved on August 8, 1750, an act to repeal the prohibition of slavery. The repeal act was sent to Georgia and presented to the people there in a mass meeting where it was approved. Neither the Board of Trade nor the Privy Council had considered this act before the Trustees surrendered their charter in 1752.

Obviously the colony could not be governed with only three laws, and the Trustees never intended that it should be. From their organization, they passed resolutions applying to Georgia which were as binding in Georgia from the Trustee viewpoint as were the more formal laws approved by the king and Council. The resolutions of the Trustees, called ordinances by some historians, might be a well worked out document like the "Rules of 1735" issued in conjunction with the settlement of Frederica. But more frequently they were simple statements or orders found among the Trustees' minutes and known in Georgia only from letters written by the Trustees' secretary to the proper official in the colony. Examples of such resolutions were appointment or removal of officials, enumeration of duties of officials, or directions on a specific subject. Most of these actions concerned a particular person or topic and were only a line or two in the Trustees' minutes. There was never any way for anyone in Georgia to know all the actions of the Trustees, and thus many decisions were ignored. Because of the informality of the early Georgia legislation, some historians have been misled into thinking that such legislation did not exist. Of course, the Trustees never carefully separated their legislation from their executive actions, and this has compounded the confusion.

While there was no Assembly in Trusteeship Georgia, there were times when the people came together in mass meetings to discuss matters of mutual concern. In the early days there were meetings to give out information from the Trustees and later to discuss problems of the colony. In a limited area with so small a population this was a natural phenomenon that influenced local officials and their actions. The meeting which went furthest was the one at which the inhabitants of Savannah were called together by the pindar, or cattle herder, to consider control of the cattle in the colony. This meeting held on August 6, 1739, agreed to regulations, apparently drawn up by the pindar. This incident may be, as McCain says, "the nearest approach made to self-government in Georgia during the first eighteen years of the colony."

Late in the period of their control, on March 19, 1750, the Trustees ordered the election of an Assembly in Georgia but were careful to specify that because the charter vested lawmaking power in the Trustees, this Assembly could "only propose, debate, and represent to the Trustees" what appeared to be for the welfare of the colony. The main reason given for calling the Assembly was to secure information about the colony, it now being so scattered that William Stephens could no longer collect all the desired information. The Common Council directed the president and assistants in Savannah to call the meeting at the most convenient time of the year, the deliberations to be completed within a month.

Every town, village, or district having ten families sent one deputy. Savannah was allowed four deputies, Augusta and Ebenezer two each, and Frederica two if it had thirty families. No deputy from Frederica attended, indicating its decline by this time. No qualifications were set for the deputies of the first Assembly, but in any Assembly called after June 24, 1751—annual assemblies were anticipated in the action of the Common Council—deputies were required to have one hundred mulberry trees planted and fenced upon every fifty acres of land which they owned. After June 24, 1753, every deputy must strictly conform to the limitations on the number of Negro slaves he owned in proportion to his white servants, must have one female in his family instructed in the art of reeling silk, and must every year produce fifteen pounds of silk for every fifty acres of land he owned—qualifications that probably nobody in Georgia could meet.

Each deputy was to hand in a written account of his district which should contain a census separating people by race, sex, and age; the amount of land cultivated by every inhabitant and how he cultivated it; the number of Negroes kept and the number of mulberry trees on each plantation; and the progress made by every family in the culture of wine, silk, indigo, cotton, etc. Probably none of these reports were made as specified, since none have been preserved among the records of the Trustees.

On January 14, 1751, sixteen deputies from eleven districts met in Savannah and elected Francis Harris, a leading merchant, as Speaker. Following usual legislative procedures, President Stephens addressed the Assembly upon its opening and it replied to his speech. An attempt of malcontents to create dissension failed. Most of the members owned five hundred acres of land, but a few were poorer men and not even freeholders.

Initially the Assembly concerned itself with problems which

the president and assistants could deal with, and they were asked to correct eleven grievances. Eight of these concerned trade and navigation at Savannah, two regulations for the guard and militia, and one the need of repairs on the courthouse. This list of needs was destined to be repeated regularly throughout the rest of the colonial period. The president and assistants generally agreed to the requests but insisted that the purchase of a pilot boat was too great an expense and must be referred to the Trustees.

During its last nine days, the Assembly prepared a report to the Trustees and made requests to them. There was a suggestion that the Georgia charter be renewed and a strong protest against the rumored annexation to South Carolina. Several suggestions about Indian relations were made including one that private persons be forbidden to purchase lands reserved to the Indians. There were petitions that the quitrent be reduced and that continued encouragement be given to silk production. It was asked that Negro slaves already in Georgia and those brought from other colonies be excused from the duty on slaves included in the proposed Negro act of the Trustees. There was a request for a pilot boat and for an engine to fight fires in Savannah. Conservators of the peace and constables were requested for districts where there were none. A small body of soldiers for defense was declared necessary. A court of equity ought to be established in Savannah to hear appeals from the town court. Finally, the Assembly earnestly petitioned that it might have the power to make bylaws for the colony to be in force from the time of passage until the Trustees might disapprove of them.

The Trustees approved or complied with all but three of these requests. The remission of the Negro duty was refused, probably because of the opposition of the Trustees to slavery and the refusal to do anything to aid its introduction into Georgia. The court of equity was denied with the reminder that all cases could be appealed to the Trustees without cost and that this should insure complete justice to all. Finally the request that the Assembly have the right to make bylaws for the colony was denied with the promise that the Trustees would consider promptly whatever was requested by future assemblies. The last two refusals indicated the Trustees' desire to keep governmental power in their own hands—something that had not changed since the founding of the colony.

Generally the Trustees and the colonists seemed pleased with the Assembly and its possibilities. However, before time for the next meeting, the Trustees had entered into negotiations with the crown to surrender their charter, so no further Assembly met. While this Assembly was not a legislative body, it might have developed into one had the Trustees continued to govern Georgia.

The original court, the town court of Savannah, continued to function with its composition unchanged throughout the Trustee period. There were always appeals from this court and the one established at Frederica to the Trustees. Under the governmental reorganization of 1741 the presidents and assistants were given appellate jurisdiction over the town courts. When in 1743 the government in Savannah was extended to the entire colony, it was given appellate jurisdiction over both town courts. Then in 1746 the Trustees suspended the town court at Frederica and the appellate jurisdiction of the president and assistants in Savannah. Thus there was only one court left for the entire colony.

In 1748 efforts were made to establish a court of vice-admiralty in Georgia. The commander of the regiment at Frederica recommended to the Admiralty Board in England the appointment of Mark Carr as judge of such a court. The Trustees approved the nominee but reserved the right to make all appointments in the province. It was then determined that no vice-admiralty powers had been granted to Georgia, and no judge could be appointed. The Trustees petitioned the king for the establishment of a court of vice-admiralty, especially to try condemned prizes captured in the war, but nothing was done.

Acting as a court of appeals, the Trustees generally gave prompt attention to appeals from the colony. While their tendency was to uphold the decisions of the colonial courts, they did not hesitate at times to overrule them. There is little record of objections to the Trustees' decisions in appeals cases.

The one known appeal from the Trustees' decision to the Privy Council concerns the case of Joseph Watson. Watson had engaged in the Indian trade in conjunction with John and Mary Musgrove and was brought to trial in 1734 for the death of an Indian whom Watson boasted he had killed through excessive drinking. The jury found Watson guilty of using unguarded expressions, probably not believing that he had actually been responsible for the death of the Indian, and recommended mercy on the grounds that Watson was not of a sound mind. Thomas Causton, the presiding bailiff at the trial, tried to get the finding changed to lunacy but was unsuccessful. Causton, nevertheless, ordered Watson confined as a lunatic. The Trustees ordered Watson kept in close confinement until they would send over a special commission for his trial, a commission which was never sent. Rumor circulated in Georgia that Watson was kept imprisoned because he did not agree with Oglethorpe and Causton and that they were trying to keep him quiet.

In England, Watson's wife appealed to the Trustees, but they refused to modify the confinement. She next petitioned the king and Privy Council for release of her husband. The Privy Council's request to the Trustees to answer Mrs. Watson's petition set the Trustees to work anew on the case. They sent to Georgia for information, wrote an answer to the petition, and became concerned lest this would set a precedent for further appeals to the Privy Council. Watson was now ordered released immediately, and the case ended. The Trustees undoubtedly approved the original action because they believed that severity was necessary to prevent whites taking advantage of Indians. The about-face when the Privy Council took up the case was the result of the well-known aversion of the Trustees to having Georgia's affairs taken up by the British government and the desire to prevent a decision being reached by the Privy Council.

Many historians have condemned the Trustees as impractical idealists, especially in regard to their governmental structure. The colonists also objected to the poorly organized and inadequate government and their lack of participation in it. A government with real authority in early Georgia would have made the Trustees' work easier and the lives of the colonists happier. Delay in securing decisions from the Trustees was vexing to the colonists, and petty problems which could have been better settled in Georgia took up too much of the Trustees' time. The colonists wanted to participate in the government, yet the Trustees never seem to have realized the importance of this to the colonists.

The malcontents showed that Georgians were maturing and had the desire to help control their own destiny more than the Trustees were willing to allow. More and more Georgians by 1740 were seeing themselves in the same light as the colonists in other British colonies in America and wanting the same rights. The governmental reorganization of 1741 did provide for a more fully organized government in Georgia and a centralization of authority in the president and assistants. Yet it was a halfhearted measure in that it still kept most real authority in the hands of the Trustees in London and did not provide for colonial participation through a legislature. Given the intelligence of the Trustees, this insistence upon retaining all authority in their own hands is strange because it went against English and colonial experience. The only explanation for this is that the Trustees put other priorities higher than government, that they did not understand the importance of the government and participation in it to the colonists, and that they believed they could ensure the success of their experiment only by retaining authority in their own hands.

Yet this insistence upon retaining power in London is one of the things that almost ruined Georgia. It is ironic that only the decline of the interest of the Trustees in Georgia after 1743 led to an increase in the powers and importance of the president and assistants. Located in Savannah these officials were more suscep-tible to influence by the colonists than were the Trustees in London. Yet there was never enough power in Georgia, even by default, to satisfy many Georgians. By the late 1740s, the colonists began to concentrate more and more upon making a living, at which they now had more success, and ignored many of the unpopular and impractical regulations of the Trustees.

For the colony to succeed, the colonists needed to face their own problems, and grow economically and politically. The Trustees never understood that human self-development is important and cannot be directed and molded from without. This inflexibility plus the failure to allow the colonists to participate in the government was the Trustees' greatest political failure.

7

AGRICULTURE, 1733–1752: DREAM AND REALITY

According to the mercantilistic beliefs of the day, the Trustees intended from the outset for Georgia to furnish products desired in the empire. Georgia's climate, Englishmen believed, was very favorable—on the thirty-third parallel, that of the Garden of Eden, according to some—and the colony should be able to produce the silk, wine, spices, and other semitropical products needed in England. The fact that these items had been tried unsuccessfully in other southern colonies never discouraged the Trustees.

Agricultural planning and land granting best illustrate how the Trustees tried to achieve their threefold purpose in Georgia—philanthropy, defense, and mercantilism. Poor unfortunates might lose their property if allowed economic freedom; hence land was not granted in fee simple so that it could be mortgaged or sold. As Georgians were to be citizen-soldiers to defend the empire's frontiers, land would only be granted and inherited in tail-male, which would insure a soldier for each fifty-acre grant, and grants must be contiguous to make defense easier. To feed the silkworms which loomed so large in the Trustees' thinking, all landowners must plant mulberry trees upon their cleared land.

The prohibition against slavery was also linked to the threefold objective. Poor unfortunates could not afford slaves and should not live in a slave society lest this discourage them from working. From a military viewpoint, slaves could not be soldiers and might desert to the enemy. Work with silk and wine was not considered arduous, so slaves were not needed to perform the labor of the colony. Every settler was envisioned as living contentedly under his own vine and mulberry tree, a view held only in London.

The predecessors of the Trustees—Thomas Nairne, Robert Montgomery, Jean Pierre Purry—were sure that the area could produce abundantly, and they helped to convince the Trustees of this. People like Sir Hans Sloane, president of the Royal Society and the founder of the Botanic Garden in London, and the Duke of Argyll urged the formation of a botanical garden in Georgia for the dissemination of useful plants collected from various parts of the world.

In August of 1732 the Trustees agreed to create a fund for "Encouraging and Improving Argiculture" in the colony, and a number of prominent people entered their subscriptions. The Trustees employed William Houstoun as a botanist to collect desirable plants to be sent to Georgia. Upon Houstoun's death in the summer of 1733, Robert Miller became his successor. Little that either of them collected ever found its way to Georgia. However, friends of the colony and the empire did contribute many plants including mulberry trees, olive trees, grape vines, Neapolitan chestnuts, Egyptian kale, cotton, madder roots, hop roots, coffee berries, date stones, tea plants, orange trees, hemp, flax, and many other plants.

A garden was begun in Charles Town in 1733 to receive these plants. Moved to Savannah in 1734, the garden was located on ten acres to the east of the settled area in a spot still known as Trustees Garden. The garden included sandy soil on top of the bluff, clay on the slope of the hill, and rich soil at the bottom of the bluff which was frequently "swamp overflowed." Here half-acre squares, separated by walks bordered with orange trees, contained different plants. Besides the mulberry trees which were so important in the early days, there were the varieties listed above, and more prosaic fruits, vegetables, and grains. Joseph Fitzwalter, the gardener, favored a practical garden with foodstuffs rather than exotic plants. Many species of plants sickened and died in the garden without ever having a chance to get into the hands of the colonists. The garden flourished for the first few years but fell into neglect by 1736 after Fitzwalter argued with the Amatis brothers and left its care to others. In 1736 Hugh Anderson was made "Inspector of the publick Gardens." He reemployed Fitzwalter, and with the help of indentured servants, the garden soon was returned "into decent Order again." In 1738 a bad frost and an unusually hot summer hurt the garden greatly, and Inspector Anderson lost interest. By 1740 the garden had lost its earlier importance, but it did continue as a mulberry nursery and was tried for grapes in 1740 and 1741. By 1741 the site contained only a few olive, orange, apple, plum, peach, cherry, mulberry, and locust trees. In 1755 the land was granted to the first royal governor, John Reynolds, and the garden ceased to exist.

In several respects the garden was symbolic of the Trustees' plans for Georgia and of their success and failure. Here were produced the mulberry trees, so essential to the silk industry; here were proven impractical many of the plants the Trustees hoped Georgia would produce. Fitzwalter planted practical foodstuffs in his first year, and this might well have been the best use for the garden. But, like so many of the Trustees' schemes, the garden failed in the end.

As mulberry trees were the most important plants propagated in the garden, so silk was the center of the mercantilistic hopes for Georgia. Silk was in great demand in England but could not be produced there. Virginia had long since given up silk for tobacco, but small amounts of silk had been produced in South Carolina for fifty years before the founding of Georgia, especially in recent years by the Swiss at Purrysburg. The Trustees believed that Georgia could save England the £500,000 paid out annually for silk imported from Italy and France and that twenty thousand persons could be employed in Georgia, with an additional twenty thousand in Britain in working up the silk and in producing manufactures to be exported to Georgia. Moreover, raising silkworms was considered an easy occupation in which women, children, and the elderly could be profitably engaged.

On the surface, the Trustees did better planning for silk production in Georgia than for most of their other ideas. They secured "silk experts" from Northern Italy, sent silkworm "seed" (eggs) with Oglethorpe on the *Ann*, and began to produce mulberry trees in the Charles Town garden in 1733. All colonists were required to plant five hundred white mulberry trees for each fifty acres of land, and women who learned to reel silk (unwind the thread from the cocoons) were to be given special rewards. But while hundreds and thousands of white mulberry seedlings were given out to colonists, they did not always do well. Frequently late frosts killed the early leaves, which was fatal to silk production as the hatching of the worms was timed for the first appearance of tender leaves. As late as the 1740s there were still complaints about this problem. In addition many of the mulberry seedlings given out were not properly cared for. Even in 1747 Pastor Bolzius at Ebenezer complained that there were not enough mulberry trees to feed the silkworms, although many had been planted in the last few years.

A recurring problem was the need for fresh supplies of silkworm eggs from Europe to replace the worms which died. Frequently the eggs hatched on the voyage over or were spoiled upon arrival so that they could not produce silkworms. Despite all these troubles, there were silkworms in the colony continuously from 1733. Equipment for silk production frequently was in short supply. The original reeling machines and copper basins sent over in 1733 were left in Charles Town and never reached Georgia. When Nicholas Amatis left Georgia in August of 1735 he broke or stole some of the reels and basins. A shortage of basins at Ebenezer was responsible for the loss of silk in the late 1740s.

A key to silk production was the knowledge of how to unwind the threads from the cocoons. This was carried on in a building called a filature. A filature existed in Savannah as early as 1734, but a permanent structure was not built for this purpose until 1750, a strange delay. Although special rooms were used at Ebenezer, no filature was built there until 1751.

The silk experts brought over from Piedmont in northern Italy proved a disappointment. Paul Amatis, "brought from Piedmont to introduce silk in Georgia," came on the *Ann* with the original settlers, and his brother Nicholas arrived the following July. Paul seems to have lived in Charles Town and taken care of the garden there until its removal to Georgia in September of 1734. He came to Savannah with the mulberry trees and assumed that he was still in charge of the garden. But he reckoned without Joseph Fitzwalter, who had been the gardener at Savannah and insisted that he should continue to be. A great argument arose between the two which was finally settled in the favor of Amatis by the Trustees. In August of 1735 Nicholas was discharged by Paul and left the colony, after having broken or destroyed reels and basins and silkworm eggs. Paul remained in charge of silk production until his death in December of 1736.

Nicholas Amatis brought with him as servants Jacob Camuse, his wife, Mary, and their three sons. With the departure of Nicholas and the death of Paul Amatis, the Camuses became the silk experts. The division of labor between the two is not clear, but Mary came in for more notoriety because of her terrible temper and her desire to dominate silk production. She was supposed to instruct girls in the art of winding silk, but she refused to give them a complete course of instruction for fear that her importance to the colony would be lessened. William Stephens tried unsuccessfully to convince Mrs. Camuse that the Trust would take care of her in her declining years when she was no longer able to work if she would train successors for her job, but to no avail. After having exhausted the patience of William Stephens and having refused to impart her secret to any of her charges, Mrs. Camuse was relieved of her duties by the Trustees in 1748. She was replaced three years later by Pickering Robinson, sent over by the Trustees. Robinson was probably the most popular of silk men in Georgia, but there is doubt as to his technical competence. Within two years he became ill and returned to England.

Silk raising never became the universal industry in Georgia that the Trustees envisioned. In Savannah it seemed to have been carried on centrally in the town, rather than by individual colonists. The worms were raised in a building under the supervision of whichever silk expert was currently in charge. At Ebenezer, under the watchful eyes of Pastor Bolzius and his wife, silkworms probably were raised by individual farmers. The same may have been true of some outlying areas nearer Savannah. Although the distance from Ebenezer to Savannah hurt the Salzburgers, their superior industry and patience together with the leadership of Bolzius resulted in more silk being raised per worker and for longer periods of time than by most other colonists.

Despite all the problems, silk production did increase throughout the Trustee period. Oglethorpe in 1734 carried to England eight pounds of raw silk, and some of the next year's production reputedly went into a dress for the queen to wear at the king's birthday celebration. In 1739 twenty pounds were sent to England. Finally in 1751, the peak year in silk production under the Trustees, 496 pounds of raw silk were exported. Silk processors in England consistently reported Georgia silk of quality superior to that from France and Italy. Although enough silk was never produced to be of great value to the colony or to England, hopes for a better day continued past the Trustee period.

Wine production would have been considered by many Englishmen as important for Georgia as silk. Although the Trustees encouraged wine production, they never gave it the emphasis that they did to silk. European wine grapes were early brought over and cultivated by a few colonists and in the Trustees' Garden, and new grape stock from Europe continued to be sent over into the 1740s. In 1738 Abraham DeLyon, one of the original Jews, received from the Trustees a £200 loan to perfect his vineyard. The results of his efforts are not known, but three years later he was reported to have left the colony.

Secretary William Stephens at his plantation Bewlie devoted himself especially to the propagation of a vineyard, which seemed to be his favorite agricultural pursuit. Stephens apparently began his planting of a vineyard in 1740 and had nine hundred vines by 1742 and two thousand the next year. In 1743 he made four gallons of wine which was too bitter for his taste, but he had great hopes for the future. By 1744 he was able to distribute over three thousand vine cuttings to Captain William Horton, Captain Mark Carr, and others. That year he reported his grapes very promising; but just as they were ripening and about to harvest, they fell off the vines and were lost. Stephens' vigneron said the problem was weather, and Stephens was hopeful for the next year, but in 1745 the grapes did not ripen properly, and again very little wine could be produced.

Stephens' problems were typical of others who attempted vineyards. He reported frequently receiving new vines from Europe, giving out cuttings from the Trustees' Garden or from his own vineyard, hopes for great wine production, and disappointments. A report in 1743 said that one colonist pressed thirty gallons of wine, and Patrick Houstoun reported that he made ten gallons of wine at Frederica in 1744, good enough to send a dozen bottles to Accountant Verelst in London. The years 1738 to 1745 seem to have been the period of greatest wine expectations. After that very little was heard of vineyards or wine pressing. Evidently there were climatic and/or soil difficulties to which European wine grapes did not adjust, and wine produced from native wild grapes was usually reported as inferior in quality. Thus wine became another unfulfilled dream of the Trustees and early Georgians.

Silk and wine were the only two agricultural products advocated by the Trustees that received any serious attempt at production by early Georgians. Tea, coffee, olives, spices, and other plants seldom got beyond the Trustees' Garden, and if they did, it was as curiosities rather than as practical crops with an economic potential.

Regardless of the Trustees' plans, the main thrust of Georgia's early agriculture needed to be food for the colonists. The Trustees did not object to food production, but they more or less took it for granted and did little about it. Seed and agricultural implements were furnished to all colonists upon arrival, and all were supposed to begin clearing their lands immediately.

Bounties were paid for food crops from 1734 to 1739 and irregularly thereafter. For at least three years the Salzburgers, in consideration of their "extraordinary industry on Joint Labour," and the settlers on the Ogeechee River were given a gratuity for their entire crop. The highest accolade which could be sent to London about a colonist was that he had cleared and cultivated his land.

The Trustees originally planned to feed the colonists for their first year, until they could support themselves. But self-sufficiency did not come this soon, and many settlers had to be supported out of the Trustees' store for several years. The emphasis on silk, wine, and spices had some adverse effect upon early food production. The fact that the colonists, other than the Salzburgers, were townspeople and did not understand agriculture was even more detrimental. Harvests for the first five years were scanty, blamed on drought, hot weather, and unproductive soil. There were food shortages, and hunger would have been very real for many colonists had it not been for the Trustees' store from which they were fed. Ample crops to feed the settlers were produced in 1738 and again in 1739. Although the colony was never in such a bad situation for food after 1740 and exported a little in a few good years, in years of scarcity it was necessary to import considerable foodstuffs as in 1744, 1747, and 1749.

In 1738, for the first time, the people at Ebenezer produced enough to have a small surplus to sell or to feed to their livestock. By 1738 a little over a thousand acres had been cleared in the entire colony according to the best records available. Almost half of this was in the Savannah area, a third at Frederica, and the rest mainly at Ebenezer and Darien. When it is remembered that the population of the colony was between two thousand and three thousand at this time, the inadequacy is immediately obvious and is only partially explained by the difficult work of clearing land for cultivation.

The main food crops were corn, Indian peas, potatoes, rice, and garden vegetables. Corn was the most important, and rice was just beginning at Ebenezer. Much disappointment was still expressed because of the infertile land which had been cleared and cultivated, at least in part the result of the policy of granting land in contiguous lots. There was less success at Frederica and at Darien than in the Savannah area. Ebenezer had the greatest success, probably because many of the settlers had been peasants in Salzburg. Lands above Ebenezer were reported better and, although they were reserved to the Indians, some Salzburgers and others began to encroach upon them by 1740. Lands around Augusta were probably the best in the colony.

An illustration of agricultural failure in early Georgia is that of Andrew Grant and William Sterling, each of whom had five hundred acres on the Ogeechee River thirty miles from its mouth. With twenty-five servants they had cleared only fifty to sixty acres by 1739 and claimed to have lost some £900 on their operation. Thus it is not surprising that they abandoned the plantation in the fall of 1739 and moved to Savannah before going to South Carolina the next year. Several other adventurers also complained that the results of their planting efforts with servants did not pay expenses. By the end of the first decade the Salzburgers grew about a thousand bushels of upland rice a year and a few other people were beginning to produce it. Indigo, cotton, tobacco, hemp, and flax were tried on a small scale but were of no economic value.

There were several reasons for this agricultural failure. Much of the soil was sandy and unfertile using the methods known to the settlers. Sandy, pine barren land was especially looked down on by the colonists, and generally was not considered good enough to produce crops. Swamp land was more fertile, but its flooding by heavy rains made it very difficult to use. Little fertilizer was used or available. Climate was another problem for people and crops. The long, hot, dry summers were new to the settlers and to some of the crops that they attempted to raise. Sudden temperature changes, especially late spring frosts, caused trouble. Only about one-eighth of the British settlers in the colony's first decade had any agricultural experience. Besides the lack of experience, there was the psychological barrier of townspeople doing the hard manual labor necessary for the successful farming—a very real problem. Agricultural techniques were primitive but no different from those used in other newly settled colonies, except that Georgians had no slaves. Trees were often girdled and left to rot in the fields. Such fields could not be plowed, but must be tilled with hoes, sticks, etc. Plows were seldom used in the early years.

The Salzburgers were the most successful farmers. They were experienced and did not look down upon hard labor. They were a strong-knit group and labored in common instead of on individual tracts. Thus, all shared alike and could learn from each other. And Ebenezer had Pastor Bolzius, who encouraged the Salzburgers on to greater endeavors. While there were grumblers who thought they had to work too hard and got too little from their labor, there were fewer at Ebenezer than elsewhere in the colony.

Clearly the agricultural ideas of the Trustees, never revised in London, did not produce the expected results in Georgia. Silk was never worth the effort put into it. Wine hardly counted at all. Other tropical or semitropical items sent over to the Trustees' Garden were of no economic value in Georgia. Success came from hard work, harder than most settlers wanted to perform, and more agricultural knowledge than most settlers possessed. Yet by the end of the Trustee period, some people had succeeded in agriculture. These were the tough, the smart, and those able to do their own work or to secure adequate labor in the colony. Perhaps twenty years was not too long to achieve success, given the type of settlers who came to Georgia in its first decade.

In the last five years under the Trusteeship agriculture gradually changed. After the Spanish war and with the legalization of slavery, people began to take up the freshwater swamps along the Savannah and the Ogeechee, land which made ideal rice plantations. With the model of South Carolina, with a slave labor force, and with increased capital this change would bring increased prosperity. Many of the people who took up rice lands were experienced South Carolinians, and rice exportation increased from 797 hundredweight in 1740 to 1,783 in 1750 and rapidly thereafter.

The Trustees had no special interest in cattle raising, but this was one of the easiest occupations in Georgia and one which had been carried on previously in the region by the Spanish and South Carolinians. Cattle required little effort from the few herdsmen who attended them except for branding and slaughtering. There was much natural pasture both on the islands and on the mainland: canebreaks, swampy areas, upland forests, and open savannahs. The Musgroves had a cowpen near Savannah, from which they supplied beef for the early colonists. The Trustees themselves kept cattle to feed the colonists and had cowpens on Hutchinson's Island, at Old Ebenezer, and scattered throughout the colony. Besides the public herds of the Trustees, private herds developed, usually pastured on ungranted lands. There were by 1750 enough cattle in the colony to begin the registration of brands of individuals by the government. Cattle came mainly from South Carolina and were a small and inferior breed. The average steer slaughtered when he was three to four years old weighed only three to four hundred pounds.

Early colonists commented on the shortage of butter and cheese. Pastor Bolzius was sure that this was because the English did not understand animal husbandry. Yet when he had milch cows driven home every night for milking, the yield was rarely as high as two quarts per cow per day. Better food, care, and breeding were necessary to improve milk and beef production. Once the orphanage at Bethesda was well established, it supplied dairy products to its neighbors in the Savannah area. Imports of beef and dairy products were common in Trustee Georgia. Almost all foodstuffs produced in the colony were consumed there. To the modern palate, the amount of salt beef eaten would be repulsive.

Fundamental to almost any agricultural development in all American colonies was land granting. Cattle raising might be carried on upon ungranted lands, but no one would clear and cultivate lands which had not been granted to him. The Trustees were aware of the great importance of land-granting policies, for they intended to use them to ensure the kind of agriculture they desired, to effect certain social and political controls, and to aid in defense. Land was vital to their intentions for Georgia.

Georgia's charter contained only one land regulation, that five hundred acres of land was the maximum amount that could be granted to any one person. The Trustees' ideas about land granting were worked out by 1735 when the first overall land regulations were issued. How much Oglethorpe helped in formulating these regulations is not clear, but he did approve restrictions on the amount of land granting to individual colonists. When there were early requests to Oglethorpe by South Carolinians for grants of several thousand acres each, coupled with offers of gifts for Oglethorpe's aid in securing the grants, he always opposed them.

The 1735 regulations followed generally the terms upon which land had been granted before that time. For charity colonists these regulations specified (1) fifty acres to each head of family, (2) inheritance by tail-male only, with no alienation of land except by special permission from the Trustees, (3) land to be cleared and cultivated within ten years, (4) one hundred white mulberry trees to be planted for each ten acres cleared, and (5) any grant for which the above conditions were not met might be forfeited to the Trustees. For adventurers who came at their own expense, (1) up to five hundred acres might be granted but there must be at least six indentured servants to secure the maximum grant, (2) one-fifth of the grant must be cultivated in ten years, (3) one thousand white mulberry trees must be planted for each hundred acres cleared, and (4) no Negroes could be brought to Georgia. Indentured servants who had served their time were eligible for a grant of twenty to twenty-five acres.

The tail-male provision applied to charity and adventurer grants and was designed to insure a soldier upon each fifty acres. This provision undoubtedly kept many prospective settlers from coming to Georgia, but it was never rigidly enforced. If there was no male heir, women were freely allowed to inherit land upon special application to the Trustees. Tail-male was intended to aid in defense, to control the settlers coming into Georgia, to prevent the unfortunate charity settlers from losing their land, and to prevent individuals from acquiring more than the prescribed five hundred acres. Georgia was intended for unfortunates who would labor upon small land grants, not for economic opportunists to achieve wealth.

The pattern of settlement in early Georgia was best exemplified in Savannah, but a similar pattern existed at Ebenezer, Augusta, Darien, and Frederica. Savannah's township consisted of 24 square miles of 15,360 acres. Twelve thousand acres were intended for actual grants, while the remainder was to be roadways, streets, Trust reserves, commons, and the like. This amount of land would supply 240 freeholds of 50 acres each.

The town proper was laid off into six wards of forty building lots each, with each ward divided into four tithings of ten lots. Immediately beyond the area of the town were the triangular-shaped garden lots, which with the building lots, made up five acres to each grantee. Here settlers were supposed to raise vegetables and other garden truck for their tables. Beyond the garden lots were the forty-five-acre farm lots where mulberry trees, corn, and other crops were to be planted. Beyond these farm lots, and outside the planned township area, were to be the larger grants of adventurers. The location of adventurer grants was never so rigidly controlled as were those of charity settlers. There were always settlements outside this basic plan, such as the outsettlements around Savannah.

As other towns were settled, the same basic pattern was employed. There were local variations, and the pattern was never as well developed nor as completely carried out elsewhere as in Savannah. This settlement plan was based upon the belief that contiguous settlements were the best defense against Spanish, French, or Indian attacks. Many visitors to early Georgia commented upon the plan of Savannah and the other towns, especially the public squares.

Another problem was that the contiguous settlement pattern made no allowance for the type of land granted to settlers in their farm lots. People complained that their land was sandy and barren or swampy and flooded, repaying no amount of work. In the southern colonies settlers requested land which they considered good and ignored the inferior lands, but the Trustees' plan of contiguous settlement did not allow this. A man was supposed to make do with the land he was allotted. People were allowed to exchange farm lots which were obviously impossible to cultivate, but sometimes only after a year or more of hard labor.

One of the first problems concerning land granting was that Noble Jones, the surveyor, could not run out land lines rapidly enough for the needs of colonists. By 1734 there were repeated complaints that farm lots had not been surveyed and that consequently people were unable to support themselves. Certainly one trouble was that Jones was given too many jobs by Oglethorpe to do them adequately.

Once lands were surveyed and the grantees put in possession, some of them objected to the form of tenure. Demands for fee simple titles in place of tail-male became common by 1735. There was real doubt that tail-male grants were legal under English law plus the desire to be able to lease, mortgage, or sell lands. The Trustees did allow some sales or leases, but special permission was necessary in each case.

Complaints were responsible for the first major reexamination of land policy in 1738. In an unprecedented move, the Trustees ordered Secretary William Stephens to ask the colonists for their views on land policy. This resulted in the petition from 119 Savannah freeholders in December 1738 asking for fee simple titles and slaves. The memorialists insisted that it was impossible under existing regulations to support themselves on their land, and that as a result many settlers had abandoned agriculture and moved to Savannah where they sought work. Initially the Trustees rejected the petition, and Oglethorpe suggested that land granting be stopped until that already granted was cleared and cultivated.

But the 1738–39 objections caused the Trustees to reexamine their entire land policy. Between March 1739 and March 1742 several important changes were made which were incorporated into a complete land regulation adopted by the Common Council on the latter date. Inheritance of land was now allowed to wives, daughters, other relatives, and any heirs at law when there was no member of the immediate family to inherit. Widows were guaranteed all the rights of inheritance they had in England. Colonists could now acquire through inheritance or marriage up to two thousand acres and could lease their lands for not over twenty-one years. White mulberry planting for cleared land was reduced to a hundred trees for every fifty acres, and land did not need to be cleared and cultivated on as rapid a schedule as originally specified. These changes did not affect the basic land policy of the Trustees, which required colonists to hold land in tail-male, except that adequate inheritance provisions were made where there was no male heir. Lands still could not be bought and sold freely. In the summer of 1742 the above changes were incorporated into a draft of a law which never received royal approval. Finally on March 19, 1750, all grants heretofore made were converted to fee simple and all restrictions on inheritance and alienation removed. Now, for the first time, Georgia land could be used or disposed of as the owner wished.

Another matter of less concern to Georgians than land tenure was quitrents. The one form of governmental payment which the Trustees sought to collect in Georgia was the quitrents of four shillings per hundred acres specified in the charter, which must be paid by the Trustees to the crown beginning ten years after land grants were made. By 1735 the Trustees set twenty shillings per hundred acres as the quitrent on grants to adventurers, to begin ten years after the grants were made. This was undoubtedly the highest quitrent in any colony in America at that time.

The malcontents objected to these exorbitant rates in their 1739 petition, and members of the House of Commons in 1742 thought Georgia rents too high. Agitation to reduce quitrents continued, and the Trustees in 1741 and 1742 suggested that the rents on pine barren land be abolished, that the crown rents be reduced from four to two shillings per hundred acres, and that all quitrents payable to the crown be allowed to the Trustees. However the Privy Council approved no changes. In 1745, when the original ten-year exemption period was ending, the Trustees directed that rent rolls be drawn up in the colony preparatory to collection. However no satisfactory rent rolls were ever completed, and no quitrents were ever collected in Trusteeship Georgia.

By 1752, according to extant records, some 245,984 acres of land had been granted in 2,840 individual grants. Only 329 of these grants exceeded fifty acres in size. Not until June of 1752 were grants of more than 500 acres made. In addition 1,300 acres had been granted to Bethesda Orphanage and some 35,700 acres in discretionary grants by Oglethorpe to soldiers completing their military service, to servants of the Trust completing their indentures, and to persons from neighboring colonies.

Following the original compact settlement ideas of the Trustees, most of the granted lands were in the districts of Savannah, Darien, Augusta, and Little Ogeechee. Ex-servants tended to receive their grants from among the common lands reserved in each district, while charity settlers got the usual town, garden, and farm lot. Adventurers were granted lands in larger amounts in outlying districts such as Joseph's Town or Sterling's Bluff. Ethnic groups like the Salzburgers, Highland Scots, and Jews were given tracts of 1,000 to 3,000 acres to be subdivided into the usual 50-acre grants.

An analysis of available land records shows that over 85 percent of the 2,122 grants to charity colonists were made before 1741, and that these grants made up 37 percent of the total acreage granted between 1732 and 1752. The decline of such grants after 1741 indicates a change in the type of settlers coming to Georgia and the degree to which the Trustees' original ideas for the purpose of settling Georgia had been modified. This change was only incidentally aided, if at all, by the fact that after 1741 the president and assistants in Savannah granted lands rather than the Trustees in London or Oglethorpe in Georgia.

After 1747 the changing approach to agriculture was reflected in land granting. Now with the influx of Carolina planters to take up rice swamps, for the first time the majority of grants exceeded 50 acres. In the last five years of the Trustee period there were some 80,000 acres, usually in 300- to 500-acre tracts, granted to adventurers. Except for DeBrahm's Germans in 1750, there were only occasional grants to charity colonists this late.

Throughout the Trustee period, not all land use was controlled by the Trustees. People abandoned lands as they left the colony, and others cultivated these abandoned lands without permission or legal right. Ungranted lands were also used on the same basis. People drifted in from Carolina; discharged soldiers remained; other people came from unknown sources. William Stephens and Thomas Causton had no idea how or when 36 of the 119 petitioning Savannah freeholders in 1738 came into the colony and where 32 of them lived. The Trustees' officials could have done little to control such a situation had they tried, and there is little evidence that they did.

Despite the theory of the Trustees, consolidation of lands into small plantations began quite early in Georgia's history, certainly by the end of the colony's first decade. The first consolidations probably came from the marriage of widows, who had secured by special application their deceased husband's grants, and widowers. From almost any viewpoint the marriage of widows and widowers during the first decade made a great deal of sense, and this was certainly true so far as landholdings went. By 1739 there had been at least fourteen, probably more, such consolidations. By the early 1740s, small plantations had begun to be created by men who were then or soon would be economic leaders in the colony: Dr. Patrick Graham, Noble Jones, James Habersham, Thomas Causton, William Stephens, Joseph Ottolenghe, and others. Edward Kimber, an English visitor in the colony in 1743, commented on "several very pretty Plantations" which he saw in the Savannah area, "several very commodious Plantations" on St. Simons Island near Frederica, and at the Orphan House of Bethesda "the Plantation will soon surpass almost any Thing in the Country."

Several results of the Trustees' original land policy are obvious. First and perhaps foremost is the fact that this policy kept many good settlers from coming to Georgia, especially Carolinians who would have been in many ways the best colonists. Secondly, this policy prevented most settlers, charity or adventurers, from realizing their full economic potential or from freely using the land resources of the colony as they wished. The small size of grants and the rigid controls made it impossible to pick the best lands and to ignore those of less value.

Because of the land policy and the shortage of capital and labor it was impossible to develop the lumber and naval stores industries. Many settlers, after several bad crop years, abandoned their lands and went to Savannah or left the colony entirely. Had they owned their land in fee simple, they could have sold or mortgaged it to secure the needed capital to tide them over the bad years or to improve their land enough to make it pay. Much land simply remained unused. By 1738 some 58,995 acres had been granted but only about one thousand acres were reported as being under cultivation.

The land policy further made for a different settlement pattern than that of the other southern colonies. Georgia settlement was in compact villages or townships with much vacant land between places like Augusta, Savannah, and Darien. Of course this design was deliberate in its inception and may well have made for better defense and a more healthy social pattern in Georgia than the usual southern settlement on isolated farms and plantations. The Trustees' land policy was clearly a major part of their overall plan for Georgia. In fact it might be called the most important control mechanism they possessed to promote their ideas about the unfortunates, mercantilism, and defense.

The relatively small amount of land granted, the much smaller amount cultivated, and the granting pattern reveal a great deal about the economic plan of the Trustees and about what actually happened in Georgia. Clearly land granting and agricultural development went together. They explain why the colony's economy developed so slowly until the end of the Spanish War and why a plantation system like that in South Carolina began after 1747. Both the general and the economic progress of the colony may be observed from the amount of land granted and cultivated. It could have been observed by the Trustees as well had they been as interested in the facts about Georgia as they were in their dreams for the colony.

8

BUSINESS AND LABOR, 1733–1752: FAILURE OF THE WELFARE STATE

Georgia was not founded in an economic vacuum; trade with the rest of the world was essential to her welfare. Some of the colony's most ardent supporters were important London merchants with commercial connections throughout the empire and the world who sought in Georgia personal and imperial profits from silk, wine, spices, and similar products. True, the Georgia Trustees were more interested in philanthropy and imperialism than in mercantilism, but after 1732 trade became of increasing importance.

Upon settlement, the most important trade of the colony was supplies for the settlers. The Trustee plan to supply charity colonists for their first year in the colony made the Trustees initially the largest supply merchant. Upon arrival in Georgia the stores on board the *Ann* were entrusted by Oglethorpe to Thomas Causton as storekeeper. This began the Trustees' store, an institution which was to determine the economy of the colony for its first six years. The original store was in Savannah, but branches were opened later in Frederica and Ebenezer.

Upon arrival in the colony charity colonists were outfitted at the store with tools, seed, clothing, and food. Here they returned for their food and supplies as long as they were furnished necessities by the Trustees. Indentured servants assigned to the Trustees were outfitted, supplied, and given their work assignments from the store. The store became the financial office of the Trustees, and the largest business during Georgia's first decade. Here things produced by the colonists were marketed, goods sold to the colonists, bounties on silk and provisions paid, and the Trustees' sola bills dispensed. Trustee operations like the saw-mills, grist mills, cowpens, etc. were carried on under the supervision of Causton and the store. All Trustee employees— scouts, boatmen, rangers, workers at the lighthouse on Tybee Island, and ordinary civil servants from Secretary Stephens down—were paid from the store. The size of the store and the complexity of its operation increased as the colony grew. There were bookkeepers, clerks, and laborers. Most imports which came into the colony were destined for the store.

The store performed a necessary function in Georgia's first six years. Perhaps it served the colonists too well. When crops were inadequate, as they were in several of the early years, the store fed the settlers on credit or extended the time they were supplied at Trustees' expense. The poor did not starve in early Georgia; rather, they were supplied from the Trustees' store.

By 1738 some £5,000 was owed to the store by the settlers, too large an amount to hope to collect considering Georgia's economic condition. Storekeeper Causton was accused of buying too many goods for the store and increasing needlessly the Trustees' debts. By 1738 the store had grown considerably beyond what the Trustees originally envisioned for it, and they decided to close it. Oglethorpe brought word of this decision in October 1738 when he returned from England.

The closing of the store removed the security of the settlers and undoubtedly convinced some to try their fortunes elsewhere, especially as it came just as the Spanish War was beginning. Of course, the store had never been entirely an economic institution; it had helped to unify Georgia under Trustee control. Never again would such unity and control exist as had in those first few years. The ending of this tight control was a part of Georgia's inevitable and necessary growth, but it came as a traumatic shock to many Georgians. People owed money by the Trustees were paid in stock from the store. While some colonists took their pay and left the colony, others took the goods which they received and set up stores for themselves. This was especially true of Francis Harris and William Ewen, two employees of the store before it was closed. These men joined a small number of merchants who were already operating in the colony.

Georgia's first merchant was, of course, John Musgrove whose trading post and plantation were established on Pipemaker's Creek, a few miles west of Savannah's site, when Oglethorpe and the colonists arrived on the *Ann*. Here the Musgroves carried on an extensive Indian trade and supplied the early colonists with many things otherwise unobtainable closer than Charles Town.

After John Musgrove, the next merchant in Georgia was Robert Williams. Williams came in 1733 and substituted merchandising for farming within two years. His brother William joined him in 1736, and they tried to carry on a general exporting and importing business, primarily shipping lumber to the West Indies. Having failed in his efforts to secure slavery and rum for the colony to aid his business, Williams left in 1740. Another early merchant was Abraham Minis, one of the Jews who arrived in July of 1733. By 1736 he had a combination shop and tavern on Bull Street from which he acted primarily as a commission merchant for incoming goods, especially for Oglethorpe's regiment. Minis' mercantile business declined after 1743 with the end of the Spanish War in Georgia.

There were numerous problems for these early merchants. First and most obvious was the competition of the Trustees' store. Savannah had no wharves, and frequently there was not enough water in the river to allow a fully loaded vessel to come up to the town. The scarcity of exports and the general poverty of the colony discouraged imports and made trade unprofitable. Most of Georgia's trade went through Charles Town via the inland passage, thus adding to the cost of trade and reducing its profits. Another result was that it is impossible to arrive at any figures for Georgia exports and imports, as those of the two colonies are inextricably mixed. Generally speaking, Charles Town merchants were more important to Georgia mercantile life during its first decade than were Georgia merchants. Charles Town firms such as Jenys and Baker, Robert and Andrew Pringle, Samuel Montaigut, Charles Purry, and Peter Simond did considerable business with the Trustees' store.

Upon the closing of the Trustees' store, Francis Harris took the goods he received as pay for his work in the store and set up as a merchant in 1741. By 1747 he formed a partnership with James Habersham, and Harris and Habersham soon became the colony's leading merchant house. Until 1754 this house was the unofficial public store and fiscal office of the Trustees, paying bounties on silk, furnishing cash or credit to Trustee officials, and doing other things which had originally been done by the Trustees' store. Although the dissolution of Oglethorpe's regiment in 1749 removed the largest single market for Georgia merchants, Harris and Habersham supplied the few soldiers left at Frederica. The firm handled Indian presents for the Trustees and began to get into the Indian trade itself. It undoubtedly carried on the business affairs of Bethesda Orphanage for which Habersham was business manager.

In 1739 Savannah's first dock was begun by Andrew Duche, the potter. This wharf was not well built and did not last very long. In the late 1740s Harris and Habersham were granted a wharf lot and built the first municipal dock at Savannah, a badly needed improvement. When opened in 1750 or 1751, this helped trade and business generally. Thus the ending of the war in 1748, the changed attitude of the Trustees, the improved physical facilities, and the gradual growth of the colony began to help trade and the whole economy of the colony by 1750.

Customs laws and their enforcement in Trustee Georgia were a matter of speculation and doubt. The Trustees appointed customs officials in the summer of 1735, and in 1739 Oglethorpe named John Fallowfield collector at Savannah and James Grant searcher at St. Simons. Two years later there was still trouble in getting them approved by the commissioners of customs in England. There was a great deal of uncertainty whether duties should be charged in Georgia. Apparently they were charged sometimes and not at other times.

To sum up trade conditions, there was little production of

staple crops which could be exported to form the basis for extensive trade. Trustee regulations, the Spanish War, and the poverty of the population all militated against economic development and trade. Georgia hardly produced enough for its own use by 1750, certainly not enough to export.

Once the new colony was founded, it was only natural that some Charles Town Indian traders should want to move their operations to Georgia. The Indian trade was one of the more valuable economic operations in South Carolina, and much of it was in the area of the new colony. The Musgrove trading post at Yamacraw has already been mentioned. Some Charles Town merchants were interested in trade with white Georgians as well. Samuel Eveleigh, a Charles Town Indian merchant, was one of the first to envision Georgia's trade potential. Early in 1733, as head of a group of Charles Town merchants, Eveleigh asked for 250 acres of land on Kunyan's Bluff near Musgrove's plantation to carry on the Indian trade and to set up an industrial community where manufacturing would be carried on by varied artisans. Although the land was not granted, Eveleigh retained his interest in Georgia and in 1735 did export the colony's first deerskins direct to London, something which seldom happened thereafter until the end of the Trustee period. Eveleigh also tried cutting live oak in Georgia and carrying on general trade. But he discovered that there was little profit to be made in the new colony yet, so soon gave up his endeavors.

The plans of Eveleigh and his Charles Town colleagues went against the basic ideas of the Trustees for Georgia's development. Whenever any South Carolina merchants applied for land grants or trade monopolies in the early years they were always denied by Oglethorpe and the Trustees. Eveleigh in 1734 sought permission to build a fort at the mouth of the Altamaha River in return for a five-year monopoly of the Indian trade along the river. Another group of Charles Town merchants sought a monopoly of Georgia's Indian trade in return for the payment of £1,000 annually to the Trustees. Oglethorpe insisted that the value was at least £2,000 annually, so no agreement was concluded.

One of the three Trustees' laws which received royal approval on April 3, 1735, was an act to maintain peace with the Indians. Under this act, storekeeper Thomas Causton was appointed to issue Indian trade licenses as Oglethorpe's deputy and to receive any deerskins which the Indians brought to Savannah. After June of 1735 it was illegal to sell rum, brandy, or other strong drink to Indians—a matter which would interfere with the Indian trade. Commissioners were appointed to both the Cherokees and Creeks, the two Indian tribes with whom most trade would be carried on. Almost at once trouble between the Georgia agents and traders licensed in South Carolina began. Carolina traders insisted that they did not need Georgia licenses. When a few Carolina traders had their goods confiscated and their rum staved in the summer of 1735 a first-class argument between the two colonies developed. It was six years before the argument was settled and the Indian trade could be conducted peacefully again.

The Indian trade prompted the founding of Fort Augusta in 1735 at the falls of the Savannah, seven miles upriver from Fort Moore in South Carolina. Roger Lacy was to lay out the town and several men who soon became prominent Indian traders initially received lots. Augusta became a center of the Indian trade, essentially a warehouse center and a point for entry into the Indian country, almost from its beginning. Most of the traders who operated from Augusta were South Carolinians. But Augusta did prosper and become Georgia's second most important town during the Trustee period. By contrast, Savannah profited little from the Indian trade, mainly because it had no merchants with adequate capital and knowledge of the trade. Only by the end of the Trustee period was the Indian trade beginning to become important economically in Georgia.

Oglethorpe always considered that the Indian trade was of more importance to Georgia for diplomatic and military reasons than for economic ones. He fully realized that trade and Indian friendship went together and that the English traders had an advantage over the French. Oglethorpe's Indian diplomacy paid off well as long as he was in Georgia, and it secured Indian friendship in his war against the Spanish. With a different attitude on Oglethorpe's part, Indian trade might have developed faster than it did in Georgia; but the Spanish War and the general poverty of the colony would have worked against this. In the Trustee period, the groundwork for a lucrative Indian trade was laid, but it would not flourish until the royal period.

A necessary adjunct to internal trade is transportation. Waterways were the only means of transportation which nature provided, so settlements were along navigable streams and the coast throughout the Trustee period. Small boats were used between Charles Town, Savannah, Ebenezer, Augusta, Frederica, and Darien. By 1737 there was a regular packet boat from Savannah to Charles Town, and the coming of Oglethorpe's regiment to Frederica caused considerably more traffic between that town and Savannah.

The first roads developed in Georgia joined Savannah with the nearby outsettlements. In March of 1736 Oglethorpe ordered a military road built from Darien to Savannah. Construction was begun by the Scottish Highlanders at Barnwell's Bluff at Darien. The road was marked out and some work done on it, but it could hardly be called an improved road before the 1750s. The road on St. Simons Island, made famous by the fighting along it, had been built as a part of Oglethorpe's defense plan for the island.

Other trails came into existence to take care of local needs. In early 1739, Oglethorpe ordered a path laid out from Augusta to Ebenezer on the Georgia side of the river, and the route was marked by that fall. This joined the road from Ebenezer to Savannah and eventually became the river road from Savannah to Augusta. Although there were a few roads upon which wheeled vehicles could be used, horseback travel was much more widespread.

Informal postal connections with Charles Town were established as soon as the colony was settled, and a regular courier service was initiated in October of 1734. The packet boats usually carried letters between the two towns, as did most travelers. Letters were distributed throughout Georgia without any formal postal organization.

Fundamental to the economy and life of any society is labor, and labor had a special relationship to each of the three reasons of the Trustees for the founding of Georgia. One of their purposes was to afford opportunity for unproductive people in England to contribute to the economic welfare of the empire. In theory, people considered useful in England were not to be sent to Georgia. The Trustees made "strict examination of those who desire to go over, and [agreed] . . . to send none, who are in any respect useful at home." Yet the unfortunates were to be industrious and good people, for none were to be sent "who have the character of lazy or immoral men." There was never any hint in the thinking of the Trustees that there might be a conflict between being useless in England and being a hard worker in Georgia. That discovery would come only after the founding of the colony.

Realizing that the town poor would not be happy at the prospect of farm labor—something to which they had not been accustomed and to which they probably considered themselves superior—the Trustees emphasized the necessity of work for all settlers and insisted that farm labor in Georgia would not be so fatiguing as in England because "the climate is so much kinder and the soil so much more fruitful." Besides, settlers would be working for themselves on their own land—always an inducement to laborers.

At first things began well in Georgia with everyone laboring hard under Oglethorpe's careful and paternalistic eye. Throughout the spring of 1733 there were repeated comments about good labor, but with summer things began to change. Hot weather brought sickness, death, and discontent to many settlers. By mid-June Oglethorpe discovered that "the People were grown very mutinous and impatient of Labour and Discipline." Oglethorpe set out to revive the earlier spirit of discipline and labor; but he did not succeed, for his earlier paternal control was gone and could never be revived.

To Oglethorpe and the Trustees, idleness was one of the worst sins which the settlers could commit. "He is an industrious man," was what the Trustees most wanted to hear, especially when applied to clearing and cultivating land. But not all settlers were industrious, certainly not as farmers. Georgians were beginning to work out their own destiny, and not all agreed with Oglethorpe's definition of "an industrious man."

Few of the charity colonists would be able to afford laborers outside their own families, but the adventurers could. The intent of the Trustees was that nonfree labor should be performed by indentured servants, and the original provisions for grants of five hundred acres of land specified that the grantee must bring over at his own expense at least six indentured servants.

Servants died in the seasoning during their first year in the colony or ran away; and they were always difficult to replace. William Stephens and other planters frequently complained of the inadequacies of their servants, but the greatest complaint was that servants ran away before their time was out. Few runaways seem to have been returned, probably because they left the colony. Of at least fifteen of the larger tracts in the Savannah district owned by adventurers and provided originally with servants, all but three had been abandoned by 1741, undoubtedly because of servant difficulties. There is small wonder that Dr. Patrick Tailfer and his friends became unhappy with labor conditions in Georgia and wanted to replace servants with Negro slaves.

The largest user of indentured servants was the Trust itself. Trust servants were used as laborers in the store, in the garden, at the cowpens, and on whatever public work the Trustees were engaged in at the moment. Trust servants were often assigned to widows or other unfortunates to help them survive in Georgia. In late 1734 or early 1735 Oglethorpe bought the indentures of some forty Irish convicts who were on a ship forced into Savannah by bad weather and lack of food. He assigned one of these to each widow and offered to sell one to each magistrate at cost. Before the colony was through with the Irish transports, most Georgians wished they had never arrived. They committed murder, stole, ran away, and caused untold trouble.

Increasingly after 1735 the Trustees sent over charity colonists as indentured servants instead of as free settlers. Once in Georgia, these servants were used by the Trust, sold to adventurers, leased to individuals, or assigned to unfortunate colonists as a relief measure. The general tendency was for the Trust to keep control of servants, even those working for private individuals, until their time was out.

Servants were secured by Trustee agents in London and by private individuals in England, Germany, and Switzerland. Trust servants in Georgia were processed through the Trustees' store and controlled by an overseer of Trust servants. Generally all freeholders had a right to purchase or lease servants from the Trust except Jews. William Stephens objected to non-Christians holding Christians as servants, but some Jews did.

The proportion of servants in the colony was small, no more than 20 percent of the population in 1741, and tended to decline as the permanent population built up after the Spanish War. Considering the small number of servants and their inadequacy in agriculture, they did little to increase farm production or any other economic activity.

Once servants had served out their time, freedom dues consisted of twenty to twenty-five acres of land, a cash allowance of a few pounds, some cattle, and a few basic farming tools. Newly freed servants often worked in the Trustees' garden or on some other public project until they secured other work, farmed for themselves, or left the colony. William Stephens complained that single men left the colony, either before or after their time was out.

By the eighteenth century, indentured servitude was declining in importance as a source of non-free labor in America, and Negro slavery was replacing it. Although the Trustees expressed no formal opposition to slavery before Georgia's founding, slavery went against the philanthropic and military reasons for the colony's founding. From the original settlement, Oglethorpe opposed slavery and prevented Carolinians from bringing slaves into Georgia. In early 1735 the Trustees agreed that there should be no slaves in Georgia as slavery negated the concern for the poor unfortunates and changed the intended nature of the colony. The Trustees passed an act "for rendering the Colony of

Georgia more Defencible by Prohibiting the Importation and use of Black Slaves or Negroes." The main argument of this law was that it was in the interest of defense for the frontier colony. It was specified that after June 24, 1735, Negro slaves found within Georgia would become the property of the Trust, and that offenders under the act should be fined £50. Runaway slaves from South Carolina could be returned to their proper owners. Indian slaves, of whom there were a few in Georgia, were not affected by this law or any Trustee regulation.

Such was the law, but the facts did not always conform. South Carolina Indian traders who operated in Georgia continued to use slaves, especially at Augusta. There were also Carolina planters who owned lands in Georgia, near Augusta, and who used slaves to work them, transferring them back and forth from Carolina to Georgia lands at will. Negro slaves seem to have been used by the officers of Oglethorpe's regiment at Frederica and there is no known opposition to this by Oglethorpe. Thus, the slavery prohibition denied slaves mainly to the adventurers who came to Georgia at their own expense and who owned enough land to make the use of slaves economically sound. The law evidently prevented more South Carolinians from coming to Georgia. Such people, already familiar with what it took to succeed in this area, would have been good settlers for Georgia, but they would have worked to change Georgia from the type of colony which the Trustees wanted.

The prohibition of Negro slavery was responsible for a long and intense argument within the colony. Simply stated, advocates of slavery argued that whites could not do hard work in a climate such as Georgia's and that the prohibition of slavery prevented the colony from achieving its full development. They insisted that rice could not be produced by whites and cited as proof that rice production in South Carolina was carried on entirely by slaves. They argued that Negroes were cheaper to acquire and to maintain than were white servants. Certainly Carolinians raised more with slave labor than was raised in Georgia with free or servant labor. Thomas Stephens, the son of Secretary William Stephens, declared that Negroes were "as essentially necessary to the cultivation of Georgia, as axes, hoes, or any other utensil of agriculture."

Opponents insisted that whites could and did labor in Georgia climate to no great disadvantage. The Salzburgers and the Highland Scots so argued from their own experience. The Salzburgers produced a bountiful crop of rice in 1739 and "laughed at such a Tale" that they could not produce rice without Negroes. Officers of Oglethorpe's regiment, especially Lieutenant George Dunbar, reported that the men of the regiment worked at hard manual labor throughout the summer of 1738 at Frederica without adverse effect to their health and added "nor did I hear, that any of the men ever made the heat a pretence for not working."

Opposition to the Trustees' antislavery policy began, however, with the founding of the colony, coming initially from Carolinians who wanted to move their planting operations to Georgia. Objections of Georgians, especially of the Lowland Scots on the Ogeechee, soon followed, with the December 9, 1738, petition to the Trustees which asked for land in fee simple and slaves.

But the Trustees' denial of the petition in 1739 did not end the matter. Throughout the 1740s there were continual requests that slaves be allowed and repeated protests that Georgia was not progressing satisfactorily. Opponents of slavery like the Salzburgers, the Darien Scots, and James Habersham came to favor the admission of slaves, and the Trustees weakened in their resistance. Georgia's decline during the Spanish War must have convinced many people, in England and in America, that almost anything which might help recovery ought to be done. Finally in the summer of 1750 the Trustees drew up a law which repealed the 1735 law prohibiting Negro slavery. The proposed law was sent to Georgia where it was approved by a mass meeting of the people in Savannah. This law was never acted upon by either the Board of Trade or the Privy Council, but the Trustees allowed slavery upon their own authority. In reality, they legalized what already existed in the colony, for the slave law had not been enforced in recent years and more and more slaves had been coming into the colony. One way by which the Trustee law of

1735 had been circumvented was the leasing of slaves from Carolina owners for ninety-nine years, with the full purchase price being paid as advance rent.

The absence of Negro slaves in Georgia had one effect unanticipated by the Trustees—the wages of artisans and laborers were higher than in other southern colonies where Negro slaves often worked as artisans. There were continual complaints throughout the Trustee period of high wages, as much as two shillings a day in 1744, according to William Stephens. Stephens and others linked high wages to the lack of agricultural progress. Settlers insisted that it was not worth their time to work at clearing their lots or engaging in agriculture, when they could live better in town with less fatiguing labor.

In the early years, artisans were employed mainly by the Trust on its varied public works. Once Oglethorpe's regiment arrived at Frederica, a number of artisans gravitated there to serve the regiment and its personnel. Another center of artisans was Bethesda, near enough to Savannah to be used as a source of skilled labor by the town. In 1740 Bethesda had twenty-five tradesmen working for the community and acting as instructors and overseers of the children. Bethesda might well be called the artisan nursery of the colony, because its children were all taught trades. The dependence of the artisans upon the public works of the Trustees and Oglethorpe's regiment hurt them severely when the Trustees' store was closed in 1739 and Oglethorpe's regiment disbanded in 1749. After both of these events, a number of artisans deserted the colony, going mainly to Charles Town but probably to other colonies as well.

The mid-eighteenth century was generally a period of rapid economic growth for the British colonies in America. If Georgia did not grow as rapidly as her sister colonies, it was because of her newness, her exposed position on the southern frontier, and the economic plan of the Trustees. Georgia's economic development under the Trustees can be divided into three chronological periods: 1733–1737, 1737–1747, and 1747–1752.

The first period was one of settlement and expansion. In this period one-third of the population which came under the

Trustees arrived, 40 percent of the land was granted, and agriculture began. All the different national groups arrived, and all the towns and villages were founded. Any apparent prosperity really came from imported capital of the Trustees or the settlers. The colony did not support itself, but it could not be expected to so soon.

From 1737 through 1747 there was decline in most economic endeavors in the colony. This period saw the closing of the Trustees' store, the objections of the malcontents, and the Spanish War. Immigration slowed, people left, and population actually declined. Charitable contributions to the Trustees declined to almost nothing, and the colony was kept going only by Parliamentary grants totaling some £88,000 during the decade. The year 1740 was undoubtedly the low point economically in the colony's history. It was during this decade that the inadequacy of many of the charity colonists for a frontier area became clear. Undoubtedly Georgia was better off to lose many of the settlers who left. It was a severe time of testing, but the colony came out of it better than most colonists realized in 1747.

The last period, 1747–1752, showed the greatest economic growth. The fear engendered by the Spanish War no longer existed. More settlers arrived, slaves were allowed, land granting and inheritance regulations were liberalized, and more land was granted than in the previous fifteen years. Agricultural and general prosperity increased, and both a merchant and a planter class developed as exports in appreciable amounts became available for the first time. All the original Trustee uniqueness was gone by 1752 when the colony was surrendered to the crown.

In economic planning the Trustees were mainly concerned with the unfortunate poor and with mercantilism. Neither of these really helped the economy of the colony in the first two decades. Only towards the end of the second decade when the Trustees lost much interest in Georgia and liberalized their policies did economic improvement come.

It has frequently been said that in mercantilism the Trustees made their greatest failure. True, Georgia never produced enough silk, wine, spices, tea, coffee, or other such items to make any great difference in the economy of the colony nor of the empire. In what the Trustees attempted in this regard they failed. Yet they spent little money or effort in developing mercantilism. By 1752 Georgia was beginning to fit into the same economic pattern as South Carolina, and South Carolina was considered in London to be a valuable and desirable colony. Thus the lumber, naval stores, rice, indigo, and deerskins to be produced in royal Georgia were a direct result of the founding of the colony and an aid to British mercantilism.

9

LIFE-STYLE: AN EIGHTEENTH-CENTURY UTOPIA

By the time Georgia was founded, life-styles had developed among the southern colonies which had much in common. In a colony where the great majority of the early settlers came directly from Europe and where the Trustee regulations made for difference from the other colonies, this life-style would not be immediately apparent. Instead Georgians followed the patterns common to their class and area in Europe with those modifications made necessary by the new environment. As Georgians became more American and less European, they would develop more the life-style common to small farmers and frontiersmen in other southern colonies.

For any undertaking in which philanthropy was as important as it was in Georgia, the churches and religious leaders must be concerned for the spiritual and, to a degree, the material welfare of the colonists. Five Anglican clergymen were among the original Trustees, and two others were named later. The original five were Stephen Hales, John Burton, Richard Bundy, Arthur Bedford, and Samuel Smith. All of these except Burton had worked with Dr. Thomas Bray, in so many ways the spiritual father of Georgia, and the D'Allone fund for converting Indians and Negroes to Christianity. Smith, the rector of All Hallows on the Wall, London, and Hales were among the hardest-working Trustees. Oglethorpe, James Vernon, and the Earl of Egmont, the lay members of the Board most actively interested in the religious aspects of the colony, were all Anglicans though there is no indication that they were ardent churchmen. Egmont probably was the most loyal Anglican layman among the Trustees, yet he never opposed the aid given to other Protestant groups. Trustee John White seems to have been the dissenter who most opposed official church support in Georgia.

Although there was no legally established church in Trusteeship Georgia and the Trustees never officially expressed themselves on the matter of an establishment, most of them undoubtedly took governmental aid to religion for granted. In February of 1736 Egmont said that of the members of the Common Council, thirteen favored a religious establishment in Georgia, six opposed one, and the sentiments of five were unknown. Though Egmont did not say an Anglican establishment, that is undoubtedly what he meant. Certainly the Anglican church was favored by the Trustees, but Georgia was always noted for its religious toleration. The Trustees proclaimed and maintained freedom of conscience to all people except Roman Catholics.

To support an Anglican minister, the Trustees in January of 1733 applied to the Society for the Propagation of the Gospel in Foreign Parts for its usual support to colonial ministers until the glebe which Oglethorpe had been instructed to have laid out should be productive. The Society for the Propagation of the Gospel promptly agreed. At least one, and perhaps all, ministers were paid £20 out of the British treasury, a sum given to Anglican clergymen who went to the colonies. The Trustees usually gave some additional financial help to ministers to aid in their initial expenses.

Glebe land for the minister in Savannah caused trouble for several years. The original glebe was pine barren which the Reverend Samuel Quincy in 1735 decided was not worth cultivating and requested better land. After lengthy consideration, the Trustees agreed that three hundred acres of land be set aside as a trust and that the income from it should be used for religious purposes. Oglethorpe was directed to have the land cultivated, using the money which had been given to the

Trustees for religious purposes. By May of 1737 the land was surveyed and John Wesley, then minister in Savannah, planned to cultivate a part of it as a garden for poor relief.

The Society for the Propagation of the Gospel inquired in December of 1736 as to what had been done about the promised glebe, and it suspended the £50 which it had granted the missionary in Georgia when it learned that no glebe had been granted as promised. Egmont insisted that the Trustees were trying to uphold religion, not church discipline and episcopal authority, and that income from land held in trust would be just as useful to a minister as income from a glebe granted to him. In the 1737 request to Parliament for funds, the Trustees asked for twenty servants to clear and cultivate land for religious purposes, obviously intended to support ministers in the colony.

To pay the minister in Savannah, Trustee James Vernon subscribed £20 a year as did several other Trustees. But this was no permanent solution to the £200 a year needed to support the proposed four ministers in Georgia. In 1739 the Trustees made an earnest appeal to the Archbishop of Canterbury and the Society for the Propagation of the Gospel for £50 yearly to pay the missionary in Georgia. The society agreed and paid ministers henceforth though the Trustees never changed their regulation about a glebe.

With the founding of the town of Frederica and the stationing of Oglethorpe's regiment there, the Trustees also granted three hundred acres in trust for the minister there on the same basis as at Savannah. Since the minister at Frederica was also the chaplain of Oglethorpe's regiment, his income was assured as long as the regiment existed. The Trustees arranged for the cultivation of both tracts by indentured servants, but it is hardly likely that enough was produced to add materially to the income of the ministers at either place.

A little over a week before the *Ann* sailed, Dr. Henry Herbert, an Anglican clergyman, offered to go to the colony and perform needed religious duties without a salary. The Trustees accepted his offer and he sailed with the first colonists. Herbert had planned to remain for one year but soon became ill and left to

John Wesley.

return to England. Herbert was succeeded by the Reverend Samuel Quincy, who did not keep the Trustees informed of his work, a cardinal sin in their eyes. Oglethorpe did not feel that he was very diligent in his duties, and Quincy did not get along with the authorities in Georgia. On October 10, 1735, the Trustees revoked his license and appointed John Wesley to succeed him.

John Wesley, the best-known Anglican priest to serve in Georgia, intended to serve as a missionary to the Indians. When he arrived in February 1736 Oglethorpe told him that it was not a good time to work with the Indians and requested him to take charge of the Savannah church where there was no priest. That was as close as Wesley ever came to being a missionary to the Indians. In the parish work at Savannah, Wesley ministered to some seven hundred people, most of whom were not regular communicants and did not approve Wesley's High Church beliefs and practices. He instituted three services on Sunday: prayers at 5:00 A.M., sermon and communion at 11:00 A.M., and afternoon services at 3:00 P.M. He visited with his parishioners during the siesta hour and exhorted them to virtue and religion. Besides these regular parish duties, Wesley organized small groups for the study of religion and for mutual spiritual growth in which his High Church ideas were very plain. He did show some evangelistic tendencies in his approach to the nonchurched.

Wesley was well received at first in Savannah. He was welcomed to the houses of the leading people and soon became acquainted with Sophy Hopkey, the eighteen-year-old niece of Mrs. Thomas Causton. Just how interested the thirty-year-old priest was in Sophy the records do not make clear. He liked her company, but he did not act swiftly enough for Sophy who was in love with Wesley. Sophy soon married William Williamson. Four months after the marriage, Wesley reproved Sophy for her behavior; and a month later, in August 1737, he repelled her from communion on a technicality. Williamson sued Wesley for £1,000 for defamation of his wife's character. William Stephens, who had recently arrived in the colony, said Savannah was divided into two parties over the matter, and he implied that

Wesley was unhappy with Sophy's marriage to Williamson, as may well have been the case.

First Bailiff Causton pressed the grand jury's investigation of the charges against Wesley, and the jury made ten presentments. Wesley insisted that only one of the charges was a civil matter competent to be tried in Georgia's court. The rest, he maintained, were ecclesiastical and could not be tried in Georgia. The minority of the grand jury sent the Trustees a protest against the injustice being done to Wesley but did not present it to the court.

Wesley demanded trial on the first presentment at once, but the court postponed it at the next several sessions. By October Wesley decided he could accomplish nothing more in Georgia and should return to England. He appeared at the next two courts but was refused trial. He then announced to the magistrates and by a public notice that he intended to leave on December 2. No attempt was made to prevent his departure. As he wrote in his journal, "As soon as evening prayers were over, about eight o'clock, the tide then serving, I shook off the dust of my feet, and left Georgia, after having preached the gospel there with much weakness indeed and many infirmities, not as I ought, but as I was able, one year and nearly nine months."

Wesley's most revealing comment about his activities in Georgia was made on his landing in England on February 1, 1738, the anniversary of the first colonists' landing in Georgia. "It is now two years and almost four months since I left my native country," he wrote, "in order to teach the Georgia Indians the nature of Christianity. But what have I learned myself in the meantime? Why, what I the least of all suspected, that I, who went to America to convert others, was never myself converted to God." Wesley certainly must have been closer to his heartwarming experiences in Aldersgate Street upon his return to England than when he left it for Georgia.

On February 22, 1738, Wesley appeared before the Trustees and gave his account of events in Georgia. They seemed inclined to sympathize with him but took no formal action. On April 26 he resigned his appointment, thus ending his connections with the colony.

Charles Wesley preaching to the Indians.

Charles Wesley's stay in Georgia was much briefer than John's. He came at the same time as secretary for Indian affairs. He reached Frederica, Oglethorpe's residence, on March 9, 1736, and within a week had incurred the wrath of some of the civilian inhabitants. Wesley had trouble especially with Dr. John Hawkins, a rather contentious surgeon, and once had Hawkins arrested for firing off a gun during preaching. In May Wesley went to Savannah on business and never returned to Frederica. He wished to resign his duties, but Oglethorpe requested that he continue. In July Wesley was sent to England to carry dispatches and thus ended his career in Georgia.

Before John Wesley left Georgia, he had interested George Whitefield in coming to the colony as a missionary. Whitefield was approved by the Trustees to serve as deacon at Frederica and left England just as John Wesley returned. The Trustees authorized him to officiate in either Savannah or Frederica. He arrived in Georgia May 7, 1738, and left for England on August 28 to be ordained to the Anglican priesthood. During this first brief stay he worked mainly in Savannah and was better received by the people than Wesley had been.

After ordination Whitefield bombarded the Trustees with his proposed plans for Georgia. He was now appointed missionary to Savannah where he agreed to serve without pay. It was a year before Whitefield returned to Georgia after his appointment; and when he arrived he spent little time in parochial duties, devoting himself increasingly to the orphan house which he founded. Whitefield was becoming more and more an advocate of justification by faith and other evangelistic views. He sometimes gave extemporary prayers, and did other things that shocked many of his congregation, so that church attendance declined.

Whitefield's most notorious action while he bore the Trustees' appointment as minister at Savannah was his argument with the Reverend Alexander Garden, the Bishop of London's commissary for South Carolina. Garden reproved Whitefield for ignoring the Anglican ritual and eventually forbade him to preach in Charles Town, where Whitefield was a frequent visitor. Whitefield ignored Garden's actions. When brought to trial before the commissarial court in Charles Town in July of 1740, Whitefield denied the authority of the court to try a resident of Georgia where, he argued, the Bishop of London had no authority. Garden pronounced a sentence of suspension from the ministry of the Church of England which Whitefield ignored. Thus the matter ended. In July 1740 the Trustees removed Whitefield as minister in Savannah, before Commissary Garden had pronounced his sentence of suspension. The Trustees' removal did not affect Whitefield, who continued his evangelical work from his orphans' house with little or no church authority exercised over him.

William Norris, appointed minister to Savannah, arrived in the colony in October 1738 but removed to Frederica when Whitefield returned to Georgia in January 1740. Whitefield invited Norris to assist him, but soon accused him of preaching false doctrine and declared that he could never officiate in Whitefield's church again. At Frederica Norris alienated many of the people and was accused of idleness and neglect of duty, and of fathering a child by his maid, an accusation which was never proven. About June 1, 1741, after approximately a year's service in Frederica, he returned to England where he spoke disparagingly of Georgia.

Thomas Bosomworth, a former clerk to William Stephens and member of Oglethorpe's regiment, was appointed rector at Savannah in 1743. Upon arrival in Georgia he spent several months in Frederica before coming to Savannah to take up his duties. In fact he spent more time in Frederica than in Savannah and officiated as chaplain of the regiment. In 1745 he left Georgia without permission and without making any provisions for divine services in his absence. The Trustees thereupon revoked his commission as minister. Bosomworth had married Mary Musgrove Matthews while minister at Frederica and they were to return to the colony later and cause much trouble.

On November 1, 1745, the Trustees appointed their last minister for Savannah. The Reverend Bartholomew Zouberbuhler was a native of Switzerland who had been reared in South

Carolina and ordained an Anglican priest. He could use the German, French, and English languages so seemed the ideal person to fill the religious needs of the Savannah area. As early as 1741 the Germans at Savannah had requested that he be allowed to preach to them, but the Trustees had no way of paying him at that time. Now with the removal of Bosomworth, Zouberbuhler was appointed to the vacancy.

Zouberbuhler entered actively into his duties, preaching in both German and English. Yet his activities did not satisfy everyone. The settlers at Vernonburgh and Acton petitioned the Trustees to allow another Swiss living in South Carolina, the Reverend John J. Zubly, to serve them. The Trustees recommended to Zouberbuhler that he accept Zubly as an assistant at £10 a year and promised Zouberbuhler an additional servant if he agreed to this recommendation. However, Zouberbuhler refused. He apparently did not like Zubly, certainly not as a minister in his parish, and insisted that his salary was not enough to live on as it was. He went to England to confer about the inadequate income. The Trustees agreed that if Zouberbuhler returned to Savannah his salary would be doubled, his parsonage repaired, two servants provided, the glebe laid out in a better location, and 500 acres of land granted Zouberbuhler and each of his two brothers. By the time of his death in 1766 Zouberbuhler owned 3,337 acres of land and 52 slaves, a clear indication of improved economic status after 1746. He was undoubtedly the best fitted of the Anglican clergymen to serve in Georgia under the Trustees.

By 1749 there were enough people in Augusta who desired religious services to lead to the building of a church. Six of the leading traders asked the Trustees to secure a minister for the town and to grant land for his support. At the request of the Trustees the Society for the Propagation of the Gospel secured the Reverend Jonathan Copp, who arrived in Augusta in August of 1751 only to discover that the three hundred acres for his support had not yet been laid out and the £20 a year promised locally not yet raised. Since the Trustees were then terminating their control of Georgia, the matter of Copp's support was not easily resolved. But arrangements must have been worked out since he remained in Augusta for several years.

Most clergymen read services once or twice on Sunday, preached, did some visitation, and may have instructed children in the catechism and religious duties. A few, like John Wesley, instructed interested adults. William Stephens noted regularly Sunday services but seldom commented upon the sermons. In the frequent intervals between priests in Savannah, a layman usually read prayers and sometimes a sermon as well. For the ordinary colonists the services were probably similar to those he would have attended in England. Anglican clergymen were not especially responsive to the needs of the ordinary layman in the eighteenth century. The priest at Frederica must have performed similar activities. His duties as chaplain of the regiment ensured a salary but probably made little change in his activities. There is slight evidence of Anglican services elsewhere in the colony where there was no regular minister. There were frequent exchanges between the priests at Savannah and at Frederica, apparently by their own arrangement.

The accounting of the Anglican clergymen in Georgia certainly does not speak well of their abilities or accomplishments. Most of them were young men coming to their first station after ordination who lacked worldly experience. Oxford had never been like Savannah and Frederica, as the young priests must have often thought. They tended to be too concerned with religion in the formal and ritualistic sense, while their parishioners were mainly concerned with practical matters. Most of them were inclined to censure small failings and frequently lacked tact or knowledge of how to deal with the frontier conditions and people they found in Georgia. It was truly a missionary field where practical saints were required.

So far as the records indicate, all the money contributed to the Trustees for religious purposes was used for the Anglican church in Georgia. These contributions in England came in the first nine years of the Trust: £702 was contributed for building churches, £679 for Indian missions, and £522 for general religious purposes, a total of £1,903 which went through the hands of the Trustees. Besides this there was the money spent by the Society for the Propagation of the Gospel, the Society for Promoting Christian Knowledge, and similar organizations estimated at between £3,500 and £4,000. A total of about £7,500 spent on religious purposes in its first twenty years is a conservative estimate. The land granted for religious purposes, aids to clergymen in supplies and parsonages, servants furnished, and other expenditures would increase this by several thousand pounds.

The religious expense about which the Trustees had the greatest discussion was the erection of a church building in Savannah. Plans and contributions began with the founding of the colony. A tabernacle of rough boards, twelve by thirty-six feet, was first erected, and a courthouse built in 1736 was used for the church as well. In 1740 construction of a church was begun under George Whitefield but when the Trustees limited expenditure to £300 for the entire work, it soon stopped. It was resumed in early 1744 under William Stephens, and the cornerstone was laid on March 28. Stone was used for the foundations and the first three feet of the walls, with frame construction above that. The stonework and the framing of the walls and roof were finished by October, when the money was exhausted and the work stopped until 1747. The church finally was dedicated on July 7, 1750, the seventeenth anniversary of the institution of civil government in the colony and the eighth anniversary of the defeat of the Spanish at Bloody Marsh. The Reverend Bartholomew Zouberbuhler commented: "The Church is large & when finished will be both beautiful and comodious, I wish I could say as lasting."

Two other Anglican churches were built in Georgia under the Trustees. At Frederica there was a sixty- by twenty-foot chapel built in 1739 from lumber sawed by the Trustees' servants, at little cost when compared with the Savannah church. At Augusta a church was built about 1750 at the expense of the inhabitants. The Trustees sent over communion silver, a Bible, and a prayer book.

When the Highland Scots were preparing to come to Georgia

the Scottish Society for Promoting Christian Knowledge agreed
to support a missionary to work among the Scots if the Trustees
would license him. The society thereupon appointed the Reverend John McLeod, who had just been ordained in the Church of
Scotland, and he sailed with the original Highlanders in October
of 1735. McLeod seems to have worked hard among his
parishioners and to have been beloved by them. He was
disappointed in getting a church built, despite Oglethorpe's
promises. A number of the Scots were killed during the Spanish
War, and Darien did not flourish. McLeod also objected to what
he called Oglethorpe's control of the Scots' economy. For all
these reasons he left Darien in May of 1741 and soon took charge
of a church in South Carolina. He wrote very critical letters to
the Scottish Society about conditions in Georgia resulting in the
society's determination not to support further work in the colony.
Hence there was no other Scottish minister at Darien during the
Trustee period.

The first Moravians, ten in number, came to Georgia in the
spring of 1735. Several more came in the next three years, and
there were a handful of converts in Georgia. The early Moravians set up in Savannah with a common economy among
themselves and did relief and nursing work among the town's
unfortunates. Their most important work in Georgia was educational work among the Indians which will be discussed later.
John Wesley and Benjamin Ingham admired the Moravians a
great deal and frequently sought spiritual conversation and
advice from them on shipboard and in Savannah.

The religious group which caused least trouble in colonial
Georgia was beyond a doubt the Lutheran Salzburgers. The
Reverend John Martin Bolzius from the Latin Orphan House at
Halle was their pastor and leader throughout the entire Trustee
period. Bolzius was thirty years old when he came to Georgia,
where he labored for his God and his fellow men for the rest of
his life. The Reverend Israel Gronau, also from Halle, the second
minister among the Salzburgers, worked among them until his
death in 1745. At Ebenezer the Salzburgers did indeed find their
Rock of Help and enjoyed the religious toleration and freedom

which they could no longer have in their native Salzburg. While Bolzius was not a Salzburger or known to his parishioners before their trip to Georgia, he immediately assumed spiritual and temporal leadership in the community. He was an able and determined person, authoritarian in the German fashion, in a community made up mainly of peasants. There was from time to time some opposition to Bolzius and his direction, but generally he seems to have been loved and respected by his people who never doubted that he was their leader and had their best interests at heart. Otherwise he could not have dominated the settlement and the settlers as completely as he did.

At the initial settlement of old Ebenezer, a small chapel was one of the first buildings completed, but the move to New Ebenezer caused a considerable delay in building a church. During this interval the orphanage was used for services. A church building for Jerusalem Church was built at Ebenezer in the early 1740s, as was a second church called Zion some four miles below Ebenezer. In 1751 or soon after two more churches were built, at Bethany some five miles northwest of Ebenezer and at Goshen about ten miles below Ebenezer. There were Lutherans in Savannah also served by the Ebenezer ministers, and some at or near Frederica. Thus with four or five churches, the clergy was kept busy conducting services, giving spiritual advice, and running the secular affairs of the Salzburgers.

Support of the Lutheran clergy was always supplied by the Society for Promoting Christian Knowledge in London, which had handled the negotiations with the Trustees about the Salzburger immigrations. Bibles, hymnals, and other religious books were usually sent from Lutheran sources in Germany. Bolzius and Gronau worked well together, and both had the respect and love of their parishioners. After Gronau's death in 1745 Bolzius asked that a new chief pastor be sent to Ebenezer and that he be allowed to become the assistant. Instead the Reverend Herman Henry Lembke was sent as assistant. He and Bolzius worked satisfactorily together. Within about a year Lembke married the widow of Gronau who was a sister of Bolzius' wife. After the foundation of the fourth Lutheran church in 1751 a third minister was sent to Georgia, the Reverend Christian Rabenhorst, who arrived in 1752. At first he was not welcomed by Bolzius and Lembke, who did not feel that a third pastor was needed; but he was soon accepted and fit into the existing church pattern well.

The Salzburgers at Frederica were ministered to by the Reverend John Ulrich Driesler, who was also teacher to both English and German children there and whom the Trustees requested Oglethorpe to appoint as chaplain of his regiment. However, he died in 1744, about a year after his arrival at Frederica and no other Lutheran ministered regularly at Frederica.

Germans in Savannah had received only occasional services in their own language from one of the Ebenezer clergy until 1745. In that year the Reverend John J. Zubly, a Swiss whose father lived at Purrysburg, South Carolina, preached several times to the Germans and French in their own languages. William Stephens, in reporting these services, never mentioned the religious persuasion of Zubly's congregations. Zubly tried to secure a regular appointment from the Trustees, but he was not successful. In 1745 Savannah's new Anglican priest, Bartholomew Zouberbuhler, did preach in German for those who desired it. A Reverend Henry Chiffelle from Purrysburg was reported by Oglethorpe in 1743 to have preached to the French in Savannah for some five years. In early 1745 William Stephens reported that Chiffelle had preached in both French and German, but Zubly seems to have replaced him that year. Both of these ministers seemingly preached on their own, though they undoubtedly hoped for financial aid.

The original Jews who settled in Georgia in 1733 brought with them a scroll of the Law, a Hanukkah candelabrum, and a circumcision kit. They founded a synagogue, named Mickva Israel, in a rented room, where they carried on worship without benefit of a rabbi. By 1740 because of the exodus of Jews caused by the Spanish War services were suspended, and it is not clear just when they were resumed.

Certainly all these religious groups except the Jews were

welcomed by the Trustees, and all but the Moravians by Georgians. The Trustees always insisted that they had full religious authority in Georgia and must license any clergymen in the colony. The Trustees also refused to admit that the Bishop of London had any authority in the colony, a point which the bishop did not press. While the Trustees never considered that they should give aid to any but Anglicans, in effect they did to all Christian groups. All churches which asked for it got land for a church and to help support their clergymen. Most clergymen in Georgia received at least token aid from the Trustees. The Salzburgers received more aid than any other dissenting group, but they were the largest such group and had important friends in London to watch after their welfare.

Religion and education were closely associated in colonial Georgia in the thinking of most people. The Trustees from the beginning considered education, like religion, their responsibility. Naturally they sought financial aid from private contributions and from missionary organizations like the Society for Promoting Christian Knowledge.

The earliest school in Georgia, established by the Moravians in 1735 at Irene, was on the river about five miles above Savannah. This school was intended primarily for Tomo-Chi-Chi's Yamacraws, and the old chieftain was a good friend to the school and its proprietors. Several Moravians lived with the Indians and adopted their way of life, thus gaining their confidence and learning the Indian language. They soon began work on a Creek grammar. Initially the school seems to have been successful and to have appealed to a number of Indians. In 1737 the Reverend Benjamin Ingham, an Anglican priest who came from England with the Wesleys, joined the Moravians at Irene and remained about a year until he returned to England.

With the coming of the Spanish War and the death of Tomo-Chi-Chi, both in 1739, Moravian educational work among the Indians declined. Most of the Indian men went with Oglethorpe to the south. In 1740, with the last of the Moravians removed to Pennsylvania, the school was closed. A little later the Trustees sent John Hagen to try and resume the work at Irene, but he found only women and children there so the project was dropped. Trustee interest in Irene was shown by their yearly contributions of about £150 and by their attempt to revive the school after the Moravians left.

In 1734 the Trustees received a donation to employ a catechist in Georgia, and in 1735 a colonist petitioned to begin a school in Savannah, but nothing happened in either case. The first school in Savannah was begun by Charles Delamotte in February of 1736. He had come to Georgia with the Wesleys to do missionary work among the Indians, but when he found this not practical he began a school to instruct the small children. He taught his pupils to read, write, and cast accounts, and acted as a catechist. Delamotte remained in Savannah about two years and was beloved and respected as a schoolmaster. He was paid no salary, but the Trustees did vote him £15 upon his return to England. It was unfortunate that so able and kind a person was not retained in his position by the Trustees, but they seemed little concerned about his financial condition.

When Delamotte returned to England, the school was taken up by James Habersham, a young man who had come over with George Whitefield. Habersham gave both a secular and religious education to his charges at the same time looking for orphans and dependent children who might come to the orphanage he and Whitefield hoped to found. From 1738 to 1740 Habersham conducted in Savannah a combination orphanage and Trustee school, where orphans and poor children were instructed free of charge, while children able to pay were charged tuition. This school was open to all children in the colony, but most of its pupils were from Savannah. In November of 1740 the orphanage moved to its permanent quarters at Bethesda, ten miles from Savannah. Because of this distance, another school was needed in Savannah.

John Dobell, who had assisted both Delamotte and Habersham, was appointed schoolmaster in 1741 at £10 a year and register of the province so that he might live on his combined salaries. All students who could afford it were supposed to pay, and the school was to be free to the poor. The president and assistants could not resolve the problem of who should pay, so in 1743 the Trustees decided to make the school free to all and to double the schoolmaster's salary. For several years Dobell taught about twenty-five students. He seems to have been competent and popular as a teacher, but the other officials did not like him as a register. Hence in 1746 he resigned both his jobs and went to Charles Town. While he was in Savannah he often acted as an Anglican lay reader when there was no priest present. After Dobell's resignation, there was never a satisfactory schoolmaster at the Trustees' school in Savannah. The low state of education among the colonists and the poor pay of the schoolmaster made it very difficult to find a suitable person. There were several teachers for a few years each, but the school did not prosper.

The earliest suggestion for a school in Georgia came from Christopher Ortman, who on October 17, 1733, proposed to go to Georgia as schoolmaster and parish clerk for the Salzburgers. He came with the first Salzburgers and took up his duties as a teacher at Ebenezer. Ortman was especially urged by the Trustees to teach the English language to the Germans, but he could not speak English well himself and he was a poor teacher. Pastor Bolzius and others objected to him in 1739, and he was discharged by the Trustees. Bolzius and Gronau both taught children at Ebenezer, especially in the early years. There were several additional teachers at Ebenezer, usually young men sent over from Germany as catechists and under the watchful care of Pastor Bolzius. By 1748 the Salzburgers required a second schoolhouse for the children outside Ebenezer, and a third was being discussed in 1752 when the Trustee period ended.

There is no evidence that any school was ever contemplated at either Darien or Augusta by the Trustees or by the settlers, though the clergymen there may have done something. There was no regularly instituted school at either, or elsewhere in the colony besides those mentioned above.

Support of orphans and their education often went together in the colonial period. Orphan care began in Georgia during that fateful first summer of 1733 when so many colonists died. The original plan was to appoint trustees for orphans who placed the orphans with some family. The Georgia Trustees supported the orphans until they were old enough to be put out to service or apprenticed so that they could earn their own keep and learn a trade.

The Reverends Bolzius and Gronau, both from the Latin Orphan House at Halle, set up the first orphanage in Georgia in 1737 at Ebenezer. It soon had a population of three boys and eight girls. The term orphan was used to include indigent children who had one parent still alive. Soon there were orphans at Ebenezer from Purrysburg, South Carolina, and elsewhere. A few widows and disabled people also lived at the orphanage. The children worked and were given formal educational instruction. Some women about twenty years old also served there for a year or so to learn domestic economy which would serve them well once they were married. From the beginning the Georgia Trustees gave some financial support to the Ebenezer orphanage, and the colonial officials considered it their right to visit and inspect it.

Georgia had been taking care of its orphans from the very beginning of the colony's life, and there was already an orphanage in the colony before the Reverend George Whitefield decided to found his well known "House of Mercy," Bethesda. Whitefield said that he got his first idea of an orphanage in Georgia from Charles Wesley, whom the Trustees asked to draw up a plan for an orphanage in November of 1737. Whitefield maintained that upon his first arrival in Georgia in 1738 he found many orphans who were poorly cared for and who received little educational and no religious training. To this situation he attributed his determination to found an orphan house, which he recorded in his journal on May 19, 1738. The next month Whitefield visited Ebenezer where he was struck by the prosperity and serenity of the Salzburgers, and especially with the orphanage. Bolzius catechized the children, exhorted them, prayed with them, and led them in the singing of a hymn. Then, Whitefield said, "the little Lambs came and shook me by the hand one by one, and so we parted, and I scarce was ever better pleased in my Life." Whitefield's mind was definitely made up now. He must have little lambs of his own. Georgia, even if she did not know it, needed an orphanage at Savannah; and Whitefield would see to it that she received it.

Whitefield remained in Georgia less than three months on this his first visit, but he returned to England with the idea of an orphanage firmly implanted in his mind. While in England he was ordained as a priest in the Church of England and secured Trustees' approval for his orphanage, preached and collected funds for it. Before Whitefield left England in late July 1739 he had resigned the Trustees' commission to collect funds for the orphan house, not caring to be accountable to them. He had collected about £1,000 and had secured a grant of five hundred acres from the Trustees.

Whitefield returned to Savannah on January 11, 1740. His friend and co-worker, James Habersham, had already secured the five hundred acres for the orphanage ten miles from Savannah and had begun clearing the land. In his refusal to account to the Trustees for funds collected, in his demands that all charity funds for Georgia be given to him to spend as he wished, and in his insistence that the land be granted to him personally to be passed on to whomever he chose, Whitefield showed that he intended to be independent of authority in both Georgia and England. Within five days of his arrival in Georgia, Whitefield had announced to the Trustees that he intended to resign the Savannah pastorate because of his frequent absences from Savannah, a pastorate that he had insisted must be his while he was still in England. Egmont and other Trustees were sure that what Whitefield wanted to do was to be free to breed up Methodists at the orphanage. This was true, but he wanted freedom for himself more than anything else.

Whitefield acted swiftly to establish his position. On January 18, he took in his first Georgia orphans, Richard and Elizabeth Warren, who had come to Georgia on the *Ann* and whose father had died during that first summer. Whitefield rented quarters in Savannah and began collecting orphans and indigent children. On January 30 he and a carpenter laid out the orphanage buildings and he soon had employed all the available workmen

Whitefield's Orphan House, or Bethesda College.

Plan of Bethesda Orphanage.

in the area, to the detriment of getting the crops planted and providing recruits for Oglethorpe against the Spanish. The main building was sixty by forty feet in size, of brick and frame construction, and consisted of twenty rooms. Besides, there were several outbuildings set in a quadrangle, costing in all £4,000. The buildings were considered in a sufficient state of advancement for the orphanage to move from its temporary quarters in Savannah on November 3. A few weeks before this move the orphanage "family" consisted of 146 people: 61 orphans and children, 60 adults including servants, and 25 miscellaneous workers—quite a sizeable establishment to have built up in one year.

Whitefield, an impatient and an impetuous person, spent much of 1740 outside of Georgia preaching and collecting money and orphans. Even so important an event as the November 3 move had to be made without Whitefield, since he was absent to the northward on one of his progresses. With Bethesda as a base and its organization safely outside the control of the Trustees or the Anglican authorities, Whitefield was free to range far and wide in England and in the colonies preaching to large and enthusiastic crowds, collecting funds for a worthy cause, and enjoying his freedom.

Whitefield gathered orphans wherever he found them—in Georgia, in other colonies, and in England. In Georgia he assumed that all orphans belonged at Bethesda. He paid no attention to the desires of the orphans, their relatives, guardians, or masters. The most famous case concerned the Milledge children, Richard and Frances, aged thirteen and twelve. These orphans were taken from their brother John, aged eighteen, about a week after Whitefield returned to Georgia in January 1740. John Milledge had received several encouragements from Oglethorpe and was doing quite well for a youth of his age. John objected to Whitefield's actions, but to no effect. Oglethorpe said that Whitefield had exceeded his authority and should return the children to John. This Whitefield refused to do, and advised John to tell Oglethorpe.

Soon after Whitefield left Georgia, John Milledge returned his brother and sister to his home, where an older sister completed the young family. Whitefield complained to the Trustees that his prestige had been hurt by this removal, but the children remained with John. The fact that as a family the Milledges might love each other and want to live together was apparently of no concern to Whitefield.

Another case in June of 1741 showed that to some, Bethesda was not a house of mercy. A boy who must have been Charles Tondee, eleven years old, ran away from Bethesda to Magistrate Henry Parker. He had written Parker a letter earlier to complain of harsh treatment, and it had been discovered. Thus he was severely beaten by the Reverend Jonathan Barber, the Presbyterian minister in charge during Whitefield's absence. When Parker brought the boy to town ten days later, Charles' wounds were still not healed. Barber denied the authority of the magistrates to question him and said that he alone should be the judge of the discipline to be meted out to the boys under his charge. The magistrates reiterated their power to visit and examine the orphanage and to interrogate the Georgia children there, which they did from time to time. Tondee was not returned to Bethesda but placed under Thomas Bailey, a Savannah blacksmith.

The daily schedule at Bethesda was intended to make the children industrious and to crowd out idle time when the devil could make his appearance. The children rose at five and had private devotions before they dressed. Then came an hour in church with hymns, psalms, and sermon. At seven there was breakfast with more hymn singing, praying, talk of the tasks of the day, questioning of the children, exhortations, and food. Work was the order of the day from eight to ten and lessons at school from ten to noon. After the noon meal the children worked at some useful task until two, attended school from two to four, and again worked from four to six. Supper was at six when hymns were sung and the children's conversation watched over. At seven was another hour in church similar to that of the morning. At eight began the questioning of the children on religious topics, which was considered a high point of the day by the zealots at Bethesda. Whitefield or his assistants sought to make the children aware of their sinful lives and their need to call upon God for help if they were to be saved. At nine the children went to their bedrooms. More singing and prayer followed with an adult to assist those who did not pray spontaneously. All retired at ten except a few older ones who might sit up for an hour or so in private devotion, meditation, or conference. Sunday brought exemption from the usual labor but substituted four church services and food cooked the day before so that all might devote full time to the worship of the Lord.

There were people who objected that this was too long and strenuous a day for children. "Not a moment of innocent recreation tho necessary to the health and strengthening of growing children is allow'd in the whole day," opined the Earl of Egmont. But Whitefield could cite from his own boyhood examples of sin: an impudent temper, lying, filthy talk, foolish jesting, stealing money to buy fruit and tarts, reading romances, playing cards, etc. None of this could be allowed to creep in at Bethesda. All the children must be disciplined in the love and service of the Lord from the start.

In March of 1741 there came a "spontaneous" revival at Bethesda in which the boys and girls for several days became much more aware of their sinful nature and prayed to God to save them. This was all reported to Whitefield who was in London. Many of the children wrote letters to tell him of God's mercy to them. The letters show a remarkable similarity in content as well as a great familiarity with the epistles of St. Paul and the Old Testament prophets, suggesting that Barber and Habersham had as much to do with the contents of the letters as the children. Obviously these letters were too good not to be used when Whitefield wanted to raise money for the orphanage, so he had them published in a small volume in Glasgow that very year, *Orphan-House Letters to the Reverend Mr. Whitefield.*

Did Georgia need Bethesda or any other orphan house in 1740? A look at the number of orphans in the colony, the way they were cared for, and the number in Bethesda once it was founded all suggest otherwise. There is no indication that the method in use before Bethesda did not work well for the colony or for the orphans. Habersham said in September of 1741 that only thirty-two, or about half of the children at Bethesda, were Georgians. The next February there were only fourteen Georgia children out of sixty. So far as the welfare of the children was concerned and the cost of their care, the old system of having them housed and boarded by individual families seemed adequate.

Thus it is possible to argue that Whitefield needed Bethesda more than Georgia or the orphans needed it. It gave Whitefield the ecclesiastical independence that he so badly wanted and which he could not have so easily in England or in some colony where the Anglican church was better organized than it was in Georgia. It gave him a base from which to make his preaching missions and a cause for which he could collect funds.

As an educational institution, Bethesda has often been slighted because education did not rank high in the controversy about it or Whitefield. James Habersham was the first teacher there and he was followed by others after he became superintendent of outward affairs (business manager) of the orphanage. He probably continued to teach some until he left the orphanage. Initially he and Jonathan Barber, superintendent of spiritual affairs, divided the management of the orphanage between themselves when Whitefield was away. Undoubtedly Barber also taught, especially the boys who showed a spiritual interest and who might develop into evangelical preachers.

Initially the emphasis was upon learning a useful trade and a simple English education. The various artisans who were a part of the family performed their trade for the welfare of the orphanage and for the community and instructed the boys. Thus was the work of the orphanage done and money brought in by supplying the Savannah market with needed items and services. Both boys and girls in their latter teens were placed out with artisans to learn trades. Bethesda was the only trade school in the colony.

Formal education was also important. All children got an

elementary education, and some who showed talent might get more advanced education. As the institution increased in size and established itself more in the colony, facilities for formal education increased. Bethesda was the best school in the colony. It had continuity and sometimes several schoolmasters and mistresses were available, something that no other school in the colony could boast. It was, almost from the beginning, a boarding school as well as an orphanage and institution for indigent children. Its institutional character and outside support allowed it to do things that no other school could do in Trustee Georgia.

Besides education which took place in schools and at the orphanages at Ebenezer and Bethesda, there was informal education as well. Children learned agriculture and homemaking from their parents as a part of a working family. Boys early were assigned agricultural tasks, which increased with the boys' strength and understanding. The same was true for girls in cooking, sewing, and many other duties performed in the home. For both boys and girls in their teens, there were formal apprenticeships and work as well as learning in households like the two orphanages and in the homes of the more affluent colonists.

While most of the early Georgia colonists could read, finding out what they read is difficult and often impossible. The records of early books sent to Georgia, mainly as gifts from Englishmen, were heavily religious. There were Bibles, New Testaments, prayer books, books of sermons, religious treatises, and such books as the two hundred copies of *Friendly Admonition to the Drinkers of Brandy* early sent over. There were also textbooks for the schools. There grew up at Savannah at the house of the Anglican rector a sort of public library where books could be borrowed by ordinary colonists. Here the titles varied considerably and were not nearly all religious. A similar library was begun in Augusta in 1751 when the Trustees sent over 166 volumes. Naturally Bolzius had a library of German books at Ebenezer, either his personal property or gifts sent from friends and well-wishers in Germany. There was also a library at Bethesda which would have much to appeal to the evangelical Whitefield.

Besides reading for pleasure or profit, celebration of anniversaries of important people or events was popular in early Georgia. St. George's Day, St. Andrew's Day after the arrival of the Scots, the king's birthday, the anniversary of the king's accession to the throne, Oglethorpe's birthday on December 21, and the anniversary of the landing of the *Ann* at Savannah on February 1 were the major rejoicing days in Georgia.

A standard celebration for these days was to raise the flag, fire artillery salutes, and drink appropriate toasts with wine furnished by the Trustees. On St. George's Day in 1742 William Stephens reported that most of the people in Savannah assembled at noon when he had five cannon fired and produced wine for the toasts, "tho the small Estimate for rejoicing days would hardly allow it. And I was glad to see them [the people] all go off well pleased." On St. George's Day and St. Andrew's Day there might be a special church service and dinner. On Oglethorpe's birthday in 1737 in the evening "a handsome cold Entertainment was provided at a Tavern, by the Subscription of upwards of thirty, who (as many as could find them) brought Partners to dance; which they did and were merry." Dancing was frequently reported, sometimes with disapproval by the more puritanical colonists especially during the Spanish War.

Wedding feasts were popular. When the Reverend John Martin Bolzius was married in 1735, Magistrate Thomas Causton ordered a Trustees' steer killed for the feast and a hogshead of English beer sent up to Ebenezer. The marriage feast longest remembered in Savannah must have been that when four couples from Purrysburg, which lacked a minister at the time, came to Savannah to be married before Georgia was a year old. A procession of several boats came down the river, Oglethorpe received them in Savannah, food and drink were furnished, and the people danced the whole night through. The next morning, departure of the newly married couples was announced by the firing of the great guns. Most people did not get such special wedding celebrations in early Georgia.

When the men and boys of Savannah were called out in the early years to perform certain public works, like cleaning the town of weeds in 1739, beer and bread at public expense was furnished, and there must have been contests to see who could complete his assigned task fastest or best.

The first Masonic lodge in Georgia was organized probably on February 10, 1734, and began fraternal celebrations. In June the members usually held their annual feast with a special church service from which they marched in procession to the public house where the dinner was given. The St. Andrew's, or Scots, Club was an organization of the Lowland Scots originally fraternal in purpose. Soon it was transformed into the center of opposition against the Trustees, Oglethorpe, and Stephens— plotting while its members ate and drank together. In 1750 at the end of the Trustees' period, the Union Society was formed in Savannah. Originally its membership seems to have consisted mainly of artisans, and from the very beginning it included both Jews and gentiles. At first the society was apparently mainly fraternal, but it would take on civic duties as well in the royal period.

William Stephens remarked at Christmas 1737, his first in Georgia, that "Feasting here was not yet in Fashion," but there is evidence to the contrary from other sources. Church services were always held, but otherwise the holiday seems to have been celebrated or not according to individual preference. Easter was a high religious day, and Easter Monday was observed by the closing of business and public games in Savannah. There were also games on Whitsun Monday and Tuesday.

William Stephens and George Whitefield objected to the horse races held by the St. Andrew's Club in Savannah in 1740, but horse racing was a popular sport once there were enough horses in the colony. Whitefield became greatly concerned "that several Persons in this Town lived most scandalous Lives with their Whores," a sign that the oldest profession came early to Georgia.

Hunting and fishing became more common as ex-town dwellers learned the pleasures of these sports and the fresh meat they afforded. At one particularly fine oyster roast, the Indians lighted a fire on one of the small islands in a salt creek at low tide. This fire roasted the oysters on the island, and then they were gathered and eaten with relish.

The favorite recreation of many Georgians must have come at the public houses which sold food and drink and other good cheer. Those in Savannah are best documented, but they existed in any settlement large enough to be called a town and a few were noted in the small villages or outsettlements around Savannah. People who secured a license to operate a public house continually complained about people who kept such houses with no license. Why unlicensed houses were allowed to operate is not clear, but they were. The best-known keepers of a public house in early Savannah were John and Elizabeth Penrose, who came on the *Ann*. Penrose was the only husband-man listed among the passengers, but he refused to try and cultivate his sandy soil, opening his public house in Savannah instead. The Penroses were continually complained about as being unlicensed until December of 1736 when they secured a license. Their house seemed the most popular in Savannah and lasted longer than any of the other early ones. Penrose built a few boats, sailed one of them to New York, carried freight to Charles Town and Frederica, and became pilot at Tybee as well. When he was doing all these things, his wife carried on the public house very successfully. The best public houses always seemed to have served rum, regardless of Trustees' law; and few fines were assessed against them.

While all frequented Savannah's public houses in a most democratic fashion, there were class distinctions in the small Georgia population. Oglethorpe, William Stephens, the magistrates, the officers of Oglethorpe's regiment, the clergy, and other leaders in the colony stood at the top of the social scale. Generally speaking the adventurers were of a better economic and social status than the charity colonists. By the end of the Trustee period with about five thousand people, there was beginning to develop a social scale among Georgians which bespoke their ability to succeed more than their ancestry or official position.

So far as the records disclose, only one titled Englishman came to Georgia as a settler. He was Sir Francis Bathurst, Bart., who was in such financial distress that his brother, Lord Bathurst, gave him £100 with which to come to Georgia. He was granted two hundred acres of land, but his servants soon died or ran away, and his hopes to recoup his fortunes in Georgia faded. He came in December of 1734 and six months later was visited by Samuel Eveleigh at his house outside of Savannah. The house measured twenty by twelve and was divided into two rooms, a bedroom and a dining room. Eveleigh joined Sir Francis at breakfast which consisted of fresh catfish and perch and a piece of cold pork. Eveleigh contributed two bottles of punch which they drank after breakfast. Sir Francis' wife died in August of 1736, and he married a widow. She was dead in October and Sir Francis in November. Georgia had little to recommend it even to the bankrupt nobles in England. One other baronet, Sir Patrick Houstoun, lived in Trustee Georgia. He had come to the colony in 1734 but did not succeed to his title until 1751. Georgia was primarily a colony of and for common people, as were most frontier areas in America.

10

ROYAL GOVERNMENT BEGINS, 1752–1765: THE PATTERN SET

By 1750 the Trustees became disenchanted with Georgia, long after Georgians had become disenchanted with them. Only James Vernon and the Earl of Shaftesbury from the original Trustees remained loyal participants in Trustee affairs, while three members elected in 1749 helped to keep the group alive: Samuel Lloyd, Anthony Ewer, and Edward Hooper. Egmont was dead, Oglethorpe had stopped attending Trustee meetings, and English interest in both Georgia and the Trustees had decreased greatly.

In 1751 Parliament refused the Trustee request for funds. As the Trustees now had no other source of income, this left Georgia in a precarious position and led to negotiations with the king with no better success. By the charter, the political powers of the Trustees were to expire on June 9, 1753. With little interest and no money, the Trustees did what seemed inevitable; they agreed to surrender their powers to the crown a year before they officially ended. Although the charter gave the Trustees perpetual control over the colony's land, they agreed to give up all their rights under the charter to the crown. On June 23, 1752, only four men met for the final meeting of the Georgia Trustees. That body issued its terminal orders, received its final reports, defaced its seal, and ceased to exist nineteen years and eleven months after its first meeting.

Both the Trustees and Georgians opposed the suggestion that the colony be annexed to South Carolina. Georgians were sure that they were too far from Charles Town to be governed adequately from there and also feared inferior treatment if they were engulfed into South Carolina. There were the old jealousies over the Indian trade and other conflicts. The idea of union was unpopular in South Carolina and was never considered seriously in London. Still Georgians could not breathe freely until their new status was spelled out at Whitehall.

By 1752 the British government had a well developed system of government for royal colonies. Despite this, it took two years to put the new royal government into operation. A specific plan for Georgia had to be drawn up, the necessary instructions issued, and a governor appointed and sent to Georgia. Trustee officials remained in control until they were replaced by royal appointees in 1754.

As in all royal colonies, the governor was the representative of the king and executive head of the government. His salary was set at £600 a year initially but was raised to £1,000 a year in 1756. The salary was supplemented by fees which increased in value as the colony grew in size and population. As executive head of the government, the governor was authorized to appoint all officials not otherwise provided for, to pardon all crimes except treason and murder, and to remit fines and forfeitures up to £10 in value. He was the commander of the colony's militia and could erect forts and exercise martial law in time of emergency. As vice-admiral he could try maritime cases and sailors for offenses committed in Georgia, appoint captains for ships which he commissioned, and commission privateers. He issued warrants for spending provincial funds, although in practice the Assembly was to determine how the money which it raised in taxes was spent. One of the most important and

Noble Jones.

time-consuming duties of the governor and his Council was land granting. All these duties and powers of the governor were similar to those of governors in other royal colonies.

By his instructions, the governor could take few actions without the advice and consent of his Council. The twelve royal appointees who made up this body were usually leading citizens of the colony, and no governor could hope to succeed unless he led his Council in most important matters. Besides the governor and his Council, there were other executive officials. The secretary, whose main duty was to keep the records, throughout most of the royal period was James Habersham, who also became the senior councilor in 1762. The longtime colonial treasurer was Noble Jones. The attorney general was the crown prosecutor and legal advisor to the governor. The surveyor general oversaw land surveying and records. Sir Patrick Houstoun, father and son, held the offices of register of grants and receiver of quitrents. The records make it unclear if quitrents were ever collected in colonial Georgia, but the weight of evidence seems to be on the side of little or no collection throughout the entire colonial period. There were also customs officials for Savannah and Sunbury after it was created a port of entry.

The legislature consisted of three branches—the governor, the Commons House of Assembly, and the Upper House. The Commons House of Assembly, elected by the voters, initially consisted of nineteen members elected from twelve districts. When the colony was divided into parishes in 1758, representation came to be by parishes, excepting Christ Church Parish which was divided into Savannah and four additional one-member districts. In 1760, perhaps as a result of parish establishment and the growth of the colony, the number of members was increased to twenty-five. Electors in Georgia were required to own fifty acres of land and representatives, five hundred. The Upper House of Assembly, as was typical in royal colonies, was the governor's Council sitting as a legislative body without the governor present. While there were differences between the two houses from time to time, there was nothing serious until the pre-Revolutionary troubles after the Stamp Act of 1765.

The Assembly ordinarily met in the fall or winter, then took a lengthy Christmas recess, and resumed from January to March. There was no pay for assemblymen or councilors, and attendance at sessions was often poor. Frequently a person elected refused to serve and a by-election was necessary. Governor James Wright once told the Assembly that it could get through its business sooner with stricter attention to business. The governor was undoubtedly correct, but there was no change in the usual schedule.

The governor and his Council were given authority to establish such courts as they considered necessary. Following the prevalent English practice, two courts were created—the General Court for civil cases and the Court of Session of Oyer and Terminer and General Gaol Delivery for criminal cases. These two courts had the same justices, met at the same time, and were referred to as the General Court. Initially the justices were leading citizens of the colony with no special legal or judicial training. Governors John Reynolds and Henry Ellis complained of the irregular action of the courts and asked that a chief justice who had legal training be sent from England. William Grover arrived as the first chief justice in 1759. The chief justice was paid £500 a year plus fees, while the assistant justices received neither salary nor fees.

Besides the General Court, the courts of conscience, or justice of the peace courts, were carried over from the Trustee period. These courts tried petty crimes and civil cases involving amounts of not more than £8, and they did most of the judicial business in the colony. As in other colonies, the governor and his Council acted as the highest appeals court. They could hear cases on appeal involving more than £300 or criminal cases carrying fines of £200 or more. Important criminal cases and civil cases involving amounts above £500 could be appealed to the Privy Council in England, but few were.

In addition to these common law courts, there were the usual prerogative courts. These consisted of the Court of Chancery where the governor as ordinary probated wills, administered intestate estates, appointed guardians, and handled other such matters. There was a court of vice-admiralty, of which apparently the governor was originally judge. Probably there was a separate judge for this court late in the colonial period, but the records are most inadequate. There were also special commercial courts for the use of transient merchants and ship captains who could not await the regular terms of court.

The attorney general, paid a salary of £150, was the prosecuting attorney of the province; and the provost marshal, paid £100, was the executive officer of the General Court. The provost marshal was usually an absentee, with the duties of the office carried out by a deputy. Constables performed the same duties for the courts of conscience. Juries were used in both courts of conscience and the General Court.

Financial support of the government came from two sources, a Parliamentary grant and taxes levied by the Assembly. In the middle of the eighteenth century Parliament granted funds to at least four new and poor colonial governments—Georgia, Nova Scotia, and East and West Florida. The Georgia grant provided salaries for the governor and other royally appointed officials, a £1,000 silk bounty, and a £500 contingency fund which the governor could spend as he saw fit. The grant usually totaled about £4,000 a year. Taxes were levied by the Assembly on land, free Negroes, stock in trade, and money at interest. Beginning at about £250 a year, the amount reached £1,500 by 1763. These funds were spent as the Assembly directed. Income of some officials came from the Parliamentary grant, of others from the legislative appropriation, and of some from both. Most officials derived additional income from the fees connected with their office.

Most of this outline of the royal government was contained in the instructions of the first royal governor, naval Captain John Reynolds, "Captain-General and Governor-in-Chief in and over His Majesty's Colony of Georgia in America and Vice-Admiral of the same." Reynolds arrived at the somewhat decrepit Savannah on October 29, 1754, to inaugurate royal government. Bells rang, salutes were fired, and bonfires were lighted. The guardhouse provided fuel for a bonfire by the "lower Class of

People." If ever a governor was welcomed to his colony, Reynolds was in Georgia. Many colonists shared James Habersham's hopes that the frustrations and unfulfilled desires of the Trustee period would now end.

The inauguration of royal government came on October 31, when Governor Reynolds and his Council took the required oaths and assumed authority for the government. The president and assistants of the old government—Patrick Graham, James Habersham, Noble Jones; Pickering Robinson, and Francis Harris—were all made members of the new Council. Graham, who had been president of the colony, now became the senior councilor. On November 4 the governor and Council were considering the ruinous condition of the building in which they were meeting when a stack of chimneys at one end of the building fell. Georgians so fervently wished the new government success that few, if any, of them took this as a premonition of the success or failure of the governor's administration.

As a naval officer, Reynolds immediately saw the necessity of improved defense. Fear of the French and of the Spanish had not abated over the two decades since Georgia was founded. The troubles of young George Washington that summer with the French to the north were a warning that another war between the British and the French was coming, and the Creek Indians were still subject to French and Spanish influence. Since there were too few troops present for safety in case of trouble, Reynolds immediately asked for troops and supplies from England.

Georgia had, said Reynolds, 756 men in a badly equipped militia. There were no fortifications within the colony capable of defense. The few cannon were old and useless. With the aid of William Gerar DeBrahm, an engineer officer and royal surveyor, Reynolds prepared by January of 1756 a report upon Georgia's defense needs. To guard the frontier, requests were made for over 1,000 troops and rangers, 122 pieces of artillery, and 150 slaves to build a string of forts. This would cost more than the colony could afford or than the British government was willing to spend. So defense matters were left largely as they were when Reynolds arrived.

One thing that Reynolds might have done to improve defense which would have cost little except patience and diplomacy was to win the friendship of the neighboring Indians. He went to Augusta late in November of 1755 to meet Creek chiefs but refused to wait more than ten days for them. He returned to Savannah leaving William Little to distribute the gifts when the Indians arrived. The Indians were disappointed at not meeting Reynolds personally, and his action did not help to promote Indian friendship.

With the meeting of the first Assembly under the royal government in January of 1755, a challenge was presented which could easily test the governor's abilities as a political leader. Edmund Gray, or Grey, who had arrived at Augusta in 1750 from Virginia, was a skillful combination of dreamer and unscrupulous adventurer who could appeal to people's personal greed and their love of liberty at the same time. Just what he intended is not clear, but he set out to get control of the new Assembly by securing the election of his friends to it. He was elected from Augusta and his principal lieutenant, Charles Watson, was elected from Savannah. Several other people favorable to Gray failed to be elected.

When the Assembly met, the Gray faction challenged the election of several members, tried to paralyze the Commons House by absenting themselves to prevent a quorum, and called for a mass meeting of the people. All these attempts failed, and four members of the faction were expelled from the House for technical irregularities in their elections. Gray now left Savannah rather than appear before the House to be questioned. He, Watson, and two other cohorts were expelled by the House; and the session ended in March with the governor and his supporters in control. Gray and his followers withdrew to the area south of the Altamaha where Georgia's authority did not extend, thus ending their threat against the new government. Although Reynolds had won the fight against Gray and had the backing of the majority of the Commons House, he did nothing to cement his position.

Reynolds brought with him to Georgia William Little, a navy

surgeon, who became his chief lieutenant. Little held seven offices by the governor's appointment: private secretary, clerk of the assembly, clerk of the crown and peace, clerk of the General Court, justice of the peace, secretary and commissary for Indian affairs, and aide-de-camp to the governor. In September 1755 Little was accused by the Council of consorting with the enemies of government, of interfering with various officials and trying to render them contemptible, slandering and threatening the Council in public, of inefficiency and dishonesty in office, including extortion as clerk of the General Court, of drawing papers in incorrect form, and of illegal actions as justice of the peace. As clerk of the Assembly he was reported to have falsified the minutes of the Commons House, tried to influence legislation as the governor's supposed spokesman, and failed to present to the governor for his signature two bills passed by the Assembly. The governor was asked to remove Little from all his offices. Instead Reynolds removed Clement Martin from the Council for his part in the opposition to Little.

Maintaining that he had only tried to influence those unfriendly to government to change their ways, Little denied most of the specific allegations of the Council. He did admit, however, that there might have been small errors due to press of work and his "not having been bred a lawyer." But he stoutly denied any sins of commission or of intent. He did admit withholding from the governor's signature a bill which concerned illegal settlement of lands. This matter was covered, Little said, by royal instructions so "the Bill was not presented merely on Account of its Insignificancy and Non-Importance."

After another memorial from the Council, Reynolds replied that he would neither serve as the president of the Council nor be bound by it, that he would not show his instructions or letters to the Council as some desired, and that he intended to govern the colony himself. The Council insisted that its members had a right to speak freely to the governor and to differ with him. Reynolds did remove Little from two of his seven jobs, but the governor's defense of Little had alienated the Council completely.

Almost before the argument with the Council had run its

course, Reynolds entered into another with the Commons House of Assembly, the only other body in the colony which still might cooperate with him in carrying out his duties. When the Assembly met for its second session in February 1756, the governor questioned the right of the Commons House to pass on the seating of two newly elected members. He dissolved the Assembly rather than acknowledge this right, possessed by all British legislative bodies. Members of the Commons House maintained that the governor acted to prevent any inquiry into Little's conduct in refusing to present the two bills of the last session for the governor's signature. This viewpoint seems to be correct.

Before he dissolved this Assembly, the governor had not recommended a new tax bill, despite the inadequacy of the previous year's collections. He had expressed doubt that the Assembly would vote sufficient taxes, but he had not asked for any and had not given the Assembly a chance to work on this or any other needs of the colony.

By now leading Georgians were doubtful of Reynolds' abilities as governor. In April of 1756 Councilor Jonathan Bryan, one of the largest landowners in the colony, wrote to the Earl of Halifax, president of the Board of Trade, about the declining state of the colony. Alexander Kellett, provost marshal and councilor, went to England in the spring and was suspended by Reynolds from his offices after he left Georgia. At the request of the councilors, representatives, and people of substance in Georgia, Kellett presented a memorial to the Board of Trade in July which criticized the actions of Reynolds and Little and asked that Reynolds be called to England and an investigation made of his governorship. This was agreed to in August of 1756.

The Assembly elected in the fall of 1756 was favorable to Reynolds, since the election was maneuvered by Reynolds and Little. Several of the old Gray faction, now friendly to Reynolds, were elected and William Little was chosen Speaker of the Commons House. Reynolds still did not recommend additional taxes nor support for the defense structure. In fact, he only requested the renewal of the original tax bill and a few other minor items. Little appointed a committee to report on the state of the province, hoping thus to aid Reynolds' reputation in England. This document, completed in early February 1757, blamed the troubles of the colony on the old government of the president and assistants and their continued influence in Reynolds' Council and on Benjamin Martyn, the ex-secretary of the Trustees, now Board of Trade agent for Georgia in London. Speaker Little was delegated to deliver this document to the Board of Trade in London.

Lieutenant Governor Henry Ellis arrived in Georgia and took over the government from Reynolds on February 16, 1757. Reynolds and Little remained in Georgia for several weeks collecting evidence which they hoped to use in their defense in London. However, these papers were all lost when Reynolds was captured by a French privateer on his return to Europe. After investigation the Board of Trade decided to allow Reynolds to resign as governor of Georgia. He returned to the navy to fight the French further and to be promoted to admiral.

John Reynolds never understood that political leadership required compromise and the ability to get along with people. He could tolerate no differences of opinion from his political colleagues. He made no effort to get along with the leaders of the old government nor with his councilors, who certainly knew more about conditions in Georgia than he did. Instead, during his short administration, he suspended three councilors and two judges of the General Court, including Noble Jones.

Reynolds' relationship with William Little contributed greatly to his downfall. Little was a very willing henchman who probably originated some of the governor's program. Reynolds was unwilling to do the hard work necessary to be a good governor and used the navy's command and staff concept with Little as his chief subordinate. Reynolds' refusal to brook opposition made him support Little, who, in turn, undoubtedly encouraged Reynolds' obstinacy.

In evaluating Reynolds as governor it should be borne in mind that he instituted the first government in which Georgians had been able to participate. They lacked experience but were anxious to be heard. Tact and diplomacy were required on the governor's part, traits which Reynolds conspicuously lacked. While there were not large numbers of able men from whom to choose officeholders, it is hardly true, as Reynolds intimated, that he could not find adequate officials in the colony.

Reynolds failed in not trying to give positive leadership to the Council or to the Assembly. His one effort at leadership was his attempt to improve defense. He was correct in his estimate of the great defense needs when he arrived. Yet in asking for too many troops and supplies under DeBrahm's too elaborate plan, Reynolds demonstrated his lack of practical leadership. Instead of devising a workable plan for the colony, he argued with his Council and Assembly and blamed them for what was not done. He allowed the colony to drift leaderless when it needed leadership. From Reynolds' failure the leaders in the colony learned how to oppose the governor successfully. But they also learned that cooperation among the governor, Council, and Assembly was necessary for successful government.

The small and compact society in Georgia and the lack of records other than those sent to England by the governor make it impossible to document adequately the opposition to Reynolds and Little. Outside the Council and Assembly, absolutely nothing has been discovered about Reynolds' enemies or friends. Wanting to get rid of both men is understandable enough, even for a people with little political experience. How Reynolds and Little went about getting a favorable Assembly elected in 1756 is an intriguing question, but one for which no answer has been found.

Henry Ellis, Reynolds' replacement, was thirty-six years of age and had made voyages to Africa, the West Indies, and to the Hudson Bay region to search for the northwest passage. A book on the latter voyage had secured admission to the Royal Society. Ellis was a gifted dilettante who had devoted himself to scientific endeavors and who was now making his first try at political office. That Ellis was to succeed under conditions similar to those which produced Reynolds' failure was clearly a matter of difference in personality rather than of knowledge or previous

On Governour Reynolds Departure for England.

1

'Tis done at Length the Tumults past,
The storm that Threatned us blown o'er;
R...... D's Power has wreath'd its last,
Little's vile Threats are heard no more.

2

The Planter now, his Hopes elate,
Pursues the rural Healthy plan;
Foretels our Georgia's prosp'rous State.
The great Idea charms the man,—

3

Our Judgement Seat no more shall sigh,
Polluted with a mur'drer there);
Under our present Guardian's Eye,
Virtue her due Reward shall share.

4

× Philanthropos with a patriot Zeal;
Pleasing receives the high Command;
Faction and Discord vanquish'd fail,
Party, that Hydra, quits her Stand.

5

Thus have I known a stormy Night,
Strike each Beholder with Dismay;
Joyful Relief from dire Affright,
Behold a calm unclouded Day.

Americanus.

θ Threatning the Inhabitants with Martial Law.

× Φιλανθρωπος

These poems, written to celebrate the departure of Governor
Reynolds and the arrival of Governor Henry Ellis, indicate the
political climate of the day. Both have been preserved in manuscript.

On Governour Ellis's Arrival in Georgia.

1.

Welcome! thrice welcome! to our Land,
Georgia break forth in rapt'rous strain;
Great George our Sovereign is our Friend,
Be thankful and forget thy Pain—

2.

How has this infant Province shook,
Under a lawless Tyrants Sway;
But lo! the iron Rod is broke,
Ellis is come to cheer our Day—

3.

Ne'er was the Sun more welcome known,
To bless a weary Land's Increase;
Too long in Triumph Vice has shone,
And Discord harrow'd up our Peace.

4.

Laughter no more shall Drop a Tear,
Ellis the Patriot bids rejoice;
A long adieu to ev'ry Fear,
Let Ïo Pæans tune your Voice—

5.

Thanks to our Sov'reign great and good,
His royal Hand is swift to save;
Destruction seem'd a coming Flood,
Ellis our Guardian stems the Wave—

experience. In sum, Reynolds knew how to command; Ellis knew how to listen and how to persuade. Therein lay the difference of their administrations in Georgia and the feelings of Georgians about them.

Ellis landed in Charles Town on January 27, 1757, and remained two weeks to secure "advice and information" from Governor William Henry Lyttelton. Ellis wanted information about the problems of Georgia from a source closer than London. He also wanted to know Lyttelton's plans for South Carolina, especially military plans in which Georgia and South Carolina would have to cooperate. Ellis and Lyttelton got along well and carried on a regular correspondence until both left America in 1760. Ellis generally deferred to Lyttelton, who had greater resources at his command, but he stood up for Georgia and his own ideas when he felt it necessary.

On February 16, Ellis arrived at Savannah where he was met on the bluff by "loud Huzzas" from the people. As *Americanus* broke into poetry, many Georgians must have agreed with his ode entitled "On Governour Reynolds Departure for England":

> T'is done at Length the Tumults past,
> The storm that Threat'ned us blown o'er;
> R . . . ds's Power has breath'd it's last,
> Little's vile Threats are heard no more.

and a similar ode "On Governour Ellis's Arrival in Georgia."

> Welcome! thrice welcome! to our Land,
> Georgia break forth in rapt'rous strain;
> Great George our Sovereign is our Friend,
> Be thankful and forget thy Pain.

> "How has this infant Province shook,
> Under a lawless Tyrants Sway;
> But lo! the iron Rod is broke,
> Ellis is come to cheer our Day.

Bonfires were lit in celebration, and an effigy of William Little was burned.

Ellis met with Reynolds and the Council the day of his arrival in Savannah, produced his commission, and took the state oaths. Reynolds turned over the Great Seal of the province to Ellis, promised to turn over his official papers, and withdrew. With the division of feeling in the colony, Ellis adopted a wait and see policy until he could determine his course of action and be sure of enough backing to carry it out. Many people came to discuss the colony's problems; he listened politely but made no promises. He hoped that time would heal some of the wounds, and it did. Ellis summed up his waiting game in a letter to the Board of Trade. "Sensible to my own inexperience & of the violence of such Councils fearful of being misled & aiming rather at healing the wounds and extinguishing the flame of Party than stirring it anew, I forebode making any material alteration until I should be qualified to Act from observation & experience. . . . This suspense will give time for mens passions to subside & for truth to appear through the cloud of party prejudice that at present obscures it."

Ellis was sure that he must first reconcile the various factions before he could accomplish anything. He realized, too, that his Council should be his most loyal political ally, and so he assiduously sought its advice and soon won over its members as his friends. Even when he removed James Read and Patrick Mackay, who had been given interim appointments to the Council by Reynolds, he said this was so just an act that they did not object to his action.

Since the Commons House of Assembly was dominated by Speaker William Little and Reynolds partisans, Ellis had to work gingerly with it. First he prorogued the Assembly until Reynolds and Little were out of the colony. Hoping that he could win most members of the Commons House to his side, he did not dissolve the Assembly as many colonists urged him to. Early in March, Little dared Ellis to do just that, warning that he "had taken measures to have the same men rechosen." In May Little left for England, and Ellis decided to call the old Assembly back into session. Little instructed his followers to elect Patrick Mackay Speaker and to continue their opposition to the new governor and Council, but Mackay was not elected to the

Assembly. David Montaigut, who was elected Speaker, was favorable to Ellis; and this ended the threat of organized opposition. Ellis had won without a confrontation and without making any new enemies.

By the time Ellis called this Assembly into session on June 16, he had arrived at what he considered to be the three most important needs of the colony: improved defense, increased population, and greater wealth. He realized that since the three were tied together intimately, any solutions for one of necessity involved the others. He would keep these objectives uppermost in his mind throughout his three years in Georgia.

In Ellis' thinking, defense came first. Unlike Reynolds, Ellis tried to devise a plan which could be carried out by the colony itself. The only fort in the colony was a very decrepit one in Augusta. Ellis suggested that the men of the colony devote the labor which they usually gave to public roads to building fortifications. Thus, in August and September of 1757, men labored for twelve days to build a palisade around Savannah, a log fort north of Augusta, and three log forts south of Savannah. Reynolds had raised a troop of forty rangers late in his administration but had made no provisions for its support. Ellis kept the troop at his own expense until he could receive authorization for its support from the British army. He also requested and received arms for the militiamen. By July Ellis secured a promise of a hundred regular troops if Georgia would pay for their transportation from South Carolina and feed them. The Commons House said that the colony could only afford the transportation costs, but Ellis had the troops sent anyway. This convinced the governor that Georgia could support no further defense expenditure unless its population and wealth increased. Hence he set to work on these matters.

Ellis was able to persuade the Assembly to double the tax rate. This would bring in an estimated £500 a year, still not enough to meet the needs of the government. But Ellis feared that a higher tax would discourage new settlers. He also approved a bill to issue £630 in paper bills to help refund the public debt, to provide credit, and to increase the circulating medium. Ellis agreed to accept the £7,000 paper currency issued in 1755 and still unapproved in England in payment for public dues to prevent its depreciation.

In an attempt to increase population, the Assembly agreed with Ellis' idea aimed at drawing the poor from other colonies. Debtors from all British colonies except South Carolina who reached Georgia were to be protected against suit for collections of past debts for seven years. Ellis sought approval by the Board of Trade for limiting the size of land grants because of his belief that Georgia should be settled by white settlers and not Negro slaves if the frontier was to be safe from Indian attack. While Ellis could not secure the desired approval in England, he could be of considerable influence in the granting of lands in the colony.

This legislation of Ellis' first Assembly set the pattern which he was to follow in Georgia. In all three areas he achieved limited success. His idea that these areas were interdependent and could only achieve success together was borne out by events in his and the next administration.

Ellis realized that he could accomplish nothing of lasting value for Georgia if he did not keep peace with the neighboring Indians. Hence he put Indian relations high in his priorities and worked hard to keep Creek friendship. Although there was no fighting in or near Georgia at this time, the French were working to secure Creek allies. Ellis realized the divisions among the Creeks and their old game of playing one white nation against the other. He sought to deprecate any French friendship for the Creeks and to convince the Indians that their needed trade goods could only be secured from the English and that it would be to their advantage to be friendly with the English colonies and traders. To improve trade, the key to most Indian relations, Ellis worked out a plan to control traders and centralize relations in each Creek town through one headman. He sought to convince the Indians that attacks on Georgia or South Carolina would inevitably bring retaliation from both colonies. At an early meeting with Creek chieftains, Ellis came into the room with his sleeves pulled up and pointed out to the Indians that his arms were not red with their blood as the French had said they were. When Ellis received his first large delegation of Creeks in Savannah in October of 1757 he put on a very elaborate show with militia, royal troops, mounted inhabitants, and much ceremony. With imaginative diplomacy, attempts to improve trade, and subtle hints at military retaliation in case of any real trouble, Ellis went a long way toward securing Creek friendship and relative peace during his administration.

When the Cherokees attacked South Carolina's frontier in January 1760, Ellis alerted the militia, convinced the assembly to fortify Savannah and to build forts along the frontier, and sought to encourage the Creeks against the Cherokees. In May, Creeks killed several Georgia traders near Augusta. Because he now feared a general Creek war, Ellis tried to conciliate them. While the general war did not come, many settlers fled and Ellis feared his plan to increase population would be frustrated.

Certainly Ellis was a better governor than Reynolds. He conceived an initial program, and he had some success in implementing it. Whereas Reynolds had let things flounder in the colony, Ellis exercised positive leadership. He made specific suggestions to both his Council and Assembly, sometimes sending draft bills to the Assembly. In personal popularity, he far surpassed Reynolds. The frontiers were more secure and escaped the devastating Cherokee War. Population and wealth increased more rapidly than at any time since the founding of the colony. Yet by late 1759 Ellis was discouraged and perhaps bored. He complained of the "intense heats" of the summers. He walked the sandy streets of Savannah in the summer of 1758 with a thermometer suspended under his umbrella. Ellis, who had visited equatorial Africa and the West Indies, decided that the people in Savannah breathed hotter air than any other human beings on the face of the earth. Even a weekend house "upon the salt water" twelve miles from Savannah brought him little relief from the summer heat.

Undoubtedly Henry Ellis missed the joys and excitement of London's sophisticated society and found little to interest him in Savannah. If he were unwell, as he complained, it must have been as much psychological as physical. Perhaps the hard work and lack of sympathetic companionship made the governorship harder than Ellis had expected. Probably he did not have the drive and determination to continue in what could be a difficult but rewarding position. After the first year he could still charm Georgians, but he lost interest in the colony and in doing a good job as its governor. Hence he asked to be relieved of his duties and was somewhat surprised at the quick approval in London. He did not want to spend another summer in Georgia, but it was October of 1760 before Lieutenant Governor James Wright arrived to replace him.

Back in London, Ellis was appointed governor of Nova Scotia, but he never went to this colony and soon resigned its governorship. He spent the rest of his life in scientific endeavors and enjoyed himself on the Continent, dying in Naples in 1806, a date which belied his contention that he was a worn out old man in 1760 at the age of thirty-nine.

By experience and inclination, James Wright was the best qualified of Georgia's three royal governors. Although he had undoubtedly been born in England, he had long lived in South Carolina, where his father, Thomas Wright, had been chief justice from 1731 to 1739. As early as 1734 young James began holding various jobs in the courts as well as practicing as an attorney. He studied at Gray's Inn in London and was called to the bar. In South Carolina he became acting attorney general in 1742 and held that office in his own right from 1747 to 1757. Then he went to London as South Carolina's provincial agent for three years. Thus his residence and official positions in South Carolina made him conversant with the government and life of the colony. His three years in London acquainted him with the British government and the officials with whom he would have to deal as governor.

Wright and his family arrived in Charles Town from London on September 7, 1760, and remained for about a month, before proceeding to Savannah. He took his oaths as lieutenant governor before the council on October 31, and assumed the administration from Ellis. Ellis resigned his governorship in 1761 and Wright succeeded him as governor, an office he would hold until 1782.

If Henry Ellis impressed people with his charming personality and cleverness, James Wright affected them by his businesslike manner, industry, and grasp of facts. He was an excellent administrator, an organization man who believed in and worked for Georgia and the British Empire—undoubtedly the two things which meant the most to him after 1760. Wright seems to have had few personal friends with whom he could relax fully, probably because of his personality and because he believed that he should not mix freely on a personal basis with those he must govern. While his letters to London were full of information and recommendations, they revealed little of his personality except that he was a hardworking official. In many ways Georgia became Wright's colony, which he watched as a fond father would his heir. Perhaps Wright became too involved personally or emotionally with Georgia and Georgians and could not see his own faults or how people could differ with him without being enemies of Georgia. Personally, as well as officially, Wright soon transferred his South Carolina interests and loyalties to Georgia. He sold his lands in South Carolina and purchased lands and began planting operations in Georgia.

Initially Wright made no radical departure from Ellis' program. Ellis remained in Savannah several weeks during which Wright learned what he could from his predecessor. With war against France still going on, Indian relations and defense continued to be important. Wright understood, as did Ellis, the need for more settlers to augment the colony's wealth and protection.

At first Wright was less an obvious leader for the Council and Assembly than Ellis had been. He did not make so many specific suggestions but sent general ones instead. The sense of urgency of the Ellis days departed with the dynamic governor and the return of peace in the next few years. As Georgia became larger and wealthier and its population more politically experienced there was less need for the individual leadership which Ellis had felt necessary. Certainly, Wright believed in the provincial system of government and society which was developing in Georgia. Generally he got along well with both his Council and the Commons House of Assembly.

Wright always realized the importance of good Indian relations and sought to give the natives justice according to the treaties in force. He also understood that Indians had different values than whites and were dependent upon the whites through the Indian trade. Though Wright insisted that Indians give satisfaction under their treaties when whites were murdered and property stolen, he was careful not to push the red men too far and to bring on open warfare. After 1763, Wright cooperated generally with Indian Superintendent John Stuart, who had oversight of Indian affairs for the Southern Department.

Wright soon decided that much of the Indian trouble came from Indian traders, the "worst & most abandoned Set of Men," who frequently cheated their customers. To try and bring better order into the Indian trade, in 1761 Wright adopted a scheme of licensing specific traders for each town. He cooperated with Stuart in his attempt to standardize Indian trade in the southern colonies, but this became impossible under the requirement of the Proclamation of 1763 that governors must issue licenses to all qualified persons who applied. Both Wright and Stuart realized that unrestricted Indian trade was bad for Indian relations, for one of the best ways to control the natives was to cut off or threaten to cut off their trade—something that the Indians could not do without.

Certainly Wright was more concerned with the growth of his colony than he was with the rights of Indians. In November of 1763 at a conference in Augusta Superintendent John Stuart and the four southern governors were to explain to the Indians the changes resulting from the recent peace, especially the departure of the French and Spanish from the area east of the Mississippi.

With the Spanish and French gone from the southeast, the Indians could no longer play one European nation against another. At Augusta, in the treaty signed on November 10, 1763, the whites and Indians reaffirmed their pledges of friendship and promised to keep peace. A sizeable cession of Creek land was

James Wright.

made to Georgia. This included lands between the Savannah and Ogeechee rivers from Ebenezer to Little River, just above Augusta, and an area about thirty miles wide along the coast from the Altamaha to the St. Marys, Georgia's new southern boundary. Although a part of this territory on the Savannah River, especially around Augusta, had long been settled, there was no record that it had ever been officially ceded by the Indians. Now the boundaries between the two races were to be clearly marked and this, hopefully, would make for fewer violations and improved Indian relations.

Both Wright and Stuart were pleased by the results of the Congress at Augusta. Wright was sure that the new Indian cession would add to Georgia's population and prosperity; Stuart believed that he had discovered how to handle the Creeks; both believed that Indian relations would now improve. They could hardly do otherwise, considering that the Indians were now completely dependent upon the British for their essential trade. Georgia was in better shape than she had ever been during her past thirty years. With the Treaty of Augusta, any real fear of Indian attack receded; and the government devoted itself more to economic development, as it had begun to do since 1760.

The Trustee dream of the self-sufficient peasantry raising silk and wine had long since disappeared. Now, for the first time, Georgians could safely and rapidly increase their rice and indigo production. The governor and Assembly had already turned their attention to agricultural production and foreign trade. The Assembly from 1761 to 1764 worked closely with the governor to facilitate and increase Georgia's trade. Steps were taken to clear streams, to repair the lighthouse on Tybee Island, and to hire pilots for Sunbury and Savannah. Georgia's first inspection law for exports, to ensure quality, was instituted. A tax was laid on deerskins sent from Augusta to Charles Town, aimed at diverting the skins for export through Savannah and thus increasing that port's business. Proceeds from this tax were to aid the building of Fort George on Cockspur Island, which would give added protection to Savannah and aid enforcement of the laws of trade. The approval in 1761 by London of the issue of £7,410 in paper money would aid business. In February of 1762, the appointment of William Knox, as Georgia's first agent to handle its affairs in London, was another indication of the colony's growth and desire to be heard in London.

Wright maintained good relations and leadership with his Council and assemblies. His argument with William Grover, Georgia's first chief justice, is an example of this. Grover became chief justice in April of 1759 and a member of the Council in November. He attended the next three meetings of the Council but never returned. His reasons for nonattendance seem to have been lack of interest in general governmental problems and inability to get along with governors Ellis or Wright. He refused to attend such ceremonial functions as the king's birthday celebrations or the proclamation of George III as king. Grover opposed before the Assembly Wright's requests for salary supplements to officials paid by Parliamentary grant, but eventually they were voted as requested.

Grover resigned from the Council, Wright persuaded him to withdraw his resignation, but he resigned two years later still having attended no more meetings. Wright finally suspended him as chief justice in November 1762, after twice being requested to do so by the Council. Grover did not meet Wright's standards for a high official as he gave the governor no backing in maintaining the dignity of government. He only attended court, hardly an arduous task in Georgia.

Just after Grover's suspension, a scandalous verse aimed at the governor was found inscribed on the wall of a building near the statehouse. It was thought to have been written by a Grover partisan or even by Grover himself, but no proof of authorship was ever determined. Both houses of the Assembly agreed that it was a "false Scandelous and Defamatory Libel" against governor and Assembly. This whole matter undoubtedly brought governor, Council, and Commons House closer together. Grover was removed from office by the king in 1763 and left the colony.

Something else that would help to bring Wright and Georgians closer together was the argument between South Carolina and Georgia over the land south of the Altamaha. Almost as soon as word of the treaty of peace of 1763 arrived in Charles Town, Governor Thomas Boone began accepting applications for grants in the area between the Altamaha and St. Marys rivers, the former debatable land. When Georgians heard of this, the Assembly instructed agent William Knox in London to oppose Boone's action. Wright sent Councilor Grey Elliott to Charles Town to protest, but to no avail. On April 5 Boone issued warrants for survey for some 343,000 acres of land in the disputed territory.

Boone had strict legality on his side. Georgia had been created out of lands between the Savannah and Altamaha rivers taken away from South Carolina. Hence the rest of South Carolina's old charter limits south of the Altamaha still belonged to her. But Boone realized that this land would undoubtedly be given to Georgia. Hence his rush to grant it while he still could. Most of the warrants for survey were issued to leading South Carolinians. Wright and Georgians were afraid that the grantees would hold the lands for speculation rather than settle and cultivate them. Thus Georgia's southern frontier would be left unsettled and exposed to Indian attack, something that most Georgians wanted to prevent at all costs.

Boone scarcely had time to act, for on May 30, 1763, the Board of Trade issued instructions forbidding him to make grants south of the Altamaha. By the time these instructions arrived in South Carolina, Boone had issued warrants of survey for over 500,000 acres south of the Altamaha to some 400 South Carolinians. Still, only 56 of these people completed their grants for a total of 90,000 acres before Boone's receipt of instructions from London to stop making such grants.

But the problem did not end when the royal proclamation in October gave the disputed lands to Georgia. The governors of Georgia and South Carolina were instructed to work out a method by which South Carolina grants should be legal in Georgia provided the grantees lived up to Georgia's regulations about settlement. To carry out these instructions, the Georgia Assembly passed an act specifying how the South Carolina grantees must proceed, but this act was disallowed in London on technicalities. At least eighteen of the South Carolina grants were perfected in Georgia, and the number was probably larger.

The results of the peace in 1763 had considerably more effect upon Georgia than this argument over which colony should grant lands in the area. With Florida ceded to Britain, it would now be necessary to establish a definite Georgia-Florida boundary, something that had been in dispute since Georgia's founding. The initial draft of the Proclamation of 1763 defined the Georgia-Florida boundary as a line drawn due west from the mouth of the St. Johns River (present-day Jacksonville) to the Chattahoochee or Flint rivers. The newly appointed governor of East Florida objected to a line so far south as he said it would take the better part of his province. Hence the line was moved north to the St. Marys River and a line drawn from its source to the junction of the Chattahoochee and Flint rivers. The Georgia-West Florida boundary by the proclamation was specified as the thirty-first parallel from the Mississippi to the Chattahoochee. The governor of West Florida also objected, and in 1764 the boundary was moved north to the juncture of the Yazoo and the Mississippi rivers ($32°30'$) east to the Chattahoochee. This boundary remained unchanged until the end of the War for Independence.

In this way, Georgia's southern boundary was fixed and certain for the first time since its founding. Though the Georgia charter had set the Altamaha as the southern boundary, Oglethorpe had never hesitated to violate it by locating Fort Frederica and other forts south of that river. Even more important than a definite boundary was the fact that two friendly British provinces were located south of this boundary. With the exit of the French and Spanish from the area east of the Mississippi the worry over them was ended and for the first time since its founding, Georgia now had only British territory nearby. This would make growth and expansion much easier than ever before.

Wright's relations with his assemblies during his first five years as governor may be summed up by a statement in the address of both houses of the Assembly in December of 1762 after the malicious verses at the end of the Grover affair. "Your Excellency whose Upright disinterested and Impartial Administration has on all Occasions been deservidly Approved of by Us and Justly requires our Utmost Efforts to support." As Wright became better acquainted with his job and with the leaders and problems of the colony, he gave more positive leadership to both the Council and Assembly. He had led the Council from the beginning, but he was at first somewhat hesitant in his dealings with the Commons House of Assembly. By the fall of 1762 he could recommend a comprehensive legislative program to the Assembly and have a substantial part of it accepted.

With the ending of the war in early 1763, Indian relations improved; and Wright was extremely optimistic about future development in Georgia. The Indian cession and the territory added to Georgia by the Proclamation of 1763 helped considerably. The dispute between Georgia and South Carolina over the territory south of the Altamaha served to bring the governor and his Assembly closer together. When the Assembly requested to be dissolved in February of 1764 it commented upon its close cooperation with the governor and declared its belief in the "Wisdom and Uprightness" of his administration. Though Wright could not know it then, he would never meet another Assembly with which he would get along as well.

When the new Assembly met in the fall of 1764, the governor made a number of general recommendations to it, including the extending of all provincial laws into the new parts of the province annexed by the Proclamation of 1763. By the end of March 1765, this Assembly had complied with all of Wright's recommendations. It created four new parishes south of the Altamaha—St. David, St. Patrick, St. Thomas, and St. Mary—and extended St. James to include Jekyll Island.

Certainly by 1765 James Wright had proven himself an able governor. After a somewhat hesitant beginning, which might have reflected only the caution inherent in a new position, Wright had asserted himself and exercised more positive political leadership than had ever been seen in Georgia before. He had proven himself a calm but efficient governor. He operated by the rules and got most of what he wanted. He had learned how to carry the colony's leaders along with him.

As governors both Ellis and Wright were the obvious leaders of Georgia's government. Ellis was such a great relief after Reynolds that most colonists were happy to follow his suggestions. There was no break in this executive leadership when Wright replaced Ellis in 1760. It is impossible to find any serious objections to either of these two governors by 1765. There is no assumption that there were no objectors in Georgia, but the records do not reveal any. This in itself makes their success seem greater than it may have been, but both were good leaders and very competent governors.

At the beginning of 1765 Wright and Georgians might well have looked forward to continued good relations, peace, and increasing prosperity. But before the end of the Assembly session in March, the seeds of trouble in all Britain's American colonies were being sown outside Georgia.

11

ECONOMICS, 1750–1775:
NORMALCY REPLACES UTOPIANISM

On March 15, 1756, James Habersham gave Benjamin Martyn a graphic description of Georgia's economic situation at the beginning of the royal period. "We are little better now in respect to trade than a province to South Carolina," he maintained, with all the money coming into Georgia being drained off to Charles Town to purchase necessities. What colonial Georgia's economic oracle said to the man in England most knowledgeable about Georgia is worthy of careful consideration. Actually Habersham might have broadened his statement to apply to most economic activities in Georgia, and many Georgians would have agreed with him that "our present situation is really melancholy." Part of this distressed condition was the result of the Trustees' interest declining during the last few years of their control, uncertainty as to what would happen once the Trusteeship ended, and the war between Britain and France (1756–1763) which could affect Georgia adversely. But Habersham wrote about more than immediate troubles.

Georgia had now existed for more than twenty years and had very little materially to show for it. It was spread out along the coast from Savannah to Darien and up the Savannah River to Augusta with centers of settlement at Savannah, the Midway-Sunbury area, Darien, Ebenezer, and Augusta. Most of the region between Ebenezer and Augusta was Indian territory with

James Habersham.

few white inhabitants. Savannah was the economic center and the colony's major port, even if it was an economic dependency of Charles Town. Augusta, the next largest town and the location of a lucrative Indian trade, was also a way station for the traders between the Indian country and Charles Town. Agriculture, whether on the coast or in the up-country, was increasingly a copy of South Carolina's. By now Georgia was in a position to begin a more normal economic development. In climate and soil the two colonies were so similar that nothing could be more natural than that they should pursue similar economic interests. This had become evident in the late Trustee period, and once royal government was instituted in 1754 the change became even easier. But the legacy of the past had to be overcome and the speed of change accelerated, not an easy task but one that many Georgians were willing to undertake.

Although there was no fighting in Georgia during the French and Indian War, there was always danger that war might come. This ever present threat delayed the colony's development for the first six or seven years of the royal period. But, by 1760, even though the war would last three more years, the greatest economic boom in Georgia's colonial period began and progressed steadily until rebellion broke out in 1775.

The economy of royal Georgia was based upon the exploitation of the colony's natural resources: land, timber, and deerskins. Though all of these were important, land was the most obvious and in many respects the most easily exploited in the eighteenth century. Just as the Trustees' dream had discouraged the adequate use of Georgia's lands and thus doomed the colony to poverty, now the royal government's desire to increase land use brought greater prosperity.

Aside from the Indian cession of 1773, all land was granted free in Georgia except for surveying and office fees. The basic headright allowance was one hundred acres for the head of the family and fifty acres for each additional member, including indentured servants and slaves. As families increased in size, additional land could be granted. This land allowance was a realistic basis for settling the colony and supporting the settlers.

It would, to a considerable degree, prevent the engrossing of large unsettled tracts held for speculative purposes which would have hampered frontier defense and the general development of the colony.

A problem in absentee ownership which worried all three of Georgia's royal governors was the farm lots granted by the Trustees to people who had abandoned them and left Georgia. Many of these lots were uncultivated and sometimes the owners were unknown. Yet the land was in a desirable location near Savannah and in demand by newer settlers. When the colony became royal, the Board of Trade ordered Governor Reynolds to record all Trustee grants, for which records were inadequate, and to issue new grants; but people who had left Georgia complicated this process by not applying for the royal grants. In March of 1758 the Assembly specified that people who had not yet received a grant for their Trustee land must apply within three years or forfeit the land. This problem should have been settled in 1761 except for minors and incompetents who were allowed three years to apply after they became competent.

Initially, instructions from England specified that 5 percent of all land granted must be cleared and cultivated annually, a specification which would result in all land being cleared within twenty years and no timber or firewood remaining. After complaints by Governors Reynolds and Ellis, the Privy Council in August of 1758 agreed that henceforth owners must "clear and work" three acres out of every fifty "accounted plantable" within three years. For barren lands, three cattle or six sheep or goats must be pastured per fifty acres. These new regulations were more realistic than the former ones, but enforcement of neither set of regulations was evident.

To receive a land grant, the applicant submitted to the governor and Council a request for the amount desired, its location, and the basis for making the application. Usually the petition was granted as requested, though sometimes the number of acres applied for was reduced or the application was rejected. All three governors were insistent that land not be granted unless it could be settled and used by the grantee. Land was sometimes granted beyond the headright entitlement, presumably because the governor and Council thought that the applicant could and would use it. Governor James Wright was the only governor who personally received large amounts of land, but the evidence is that his grants were based upon the increasing number of his slaves and therefore were legal.

Most of the 390,645 acres granted in the first decade of royal government, 1752-1763, were coastal—mainland or island. South Carolinians especially wanted freshwater swamps for rice land and usually brought slaves and rice planting experience with them. Land was granted in six districts during these years: Augusta, the only area out of reach of the coast and not yet formally ceded by the Indians; Ebenezer; Big and Little Ogeechee, spillovers from Savannah; Newport and Midway, both influenced by the movement of the South Carolina Puritans to Midway. Lots and land in the immediate vicinity of Savannah were still desirable. By 1760 Governor Wright reported to London that all good coastal land between the Savannah and the Altamaha had been granted as far inland as the edge of the tidewater, the Indian boundary. If Georgia were to receive more settlers she would have to obtain more cultivable land from the Creeks.

Thus the Treaty of Augusta of November 10, 1763, by which the Creeks ceded some 2,400,000 acres, was of great importance. Besides the coastal area between the Altamaha and the St. Marys, Georgia's new southern boundary, there was some additional land behind the original coastal Indian cession. But more important to the colony's development was the good land from north of Ebenezer Creek to the Little River just above Augusta. All this land between the Savannah and Ogeechee rivers was now open to white settlement. The fertile land north of Ebenezer had long been desired by the Salzburgers and others, and some of it was already occupied by whites.

The year 1763 in many ways pointed toward rapid growth for Georgia. The exit of the Spanish from Florida and of the French from the Alabama Country meant that the powerful Creeks would have only the English as a source of trade. Hence they would be much easier to manage and the frontier would be much safer. Georgia now had the best ungranted land in the southern piedmont, and many settlers in other colonies were anxious to secure it. In fact between 1763 and 1773 some 771,940 acres were granted, mainly in this northern district. Grants increased annually until 1769 when 129,971 acres were given out. Afterward, the amount declined until only 46,585 acres were granted in 1772, an indication that most of the desirable land of the 1763 cession was gone.

The size of the average grant tended to increase after 1763, sometimes ranging from five hundred to a thousand acres. One reason for this was because established planters frequently received larger grants than new settlers; another was that small planters were increasing in the up-country, something that Governor Wright and his Council greatly desired.

For the 1773 Indian cession, north and west of Augusta, there was a different plan of distribution. Since the traders to whom the Indians owed money were to be paid out of its proceeds, the land was sold at sixpence per acre. This land was available in lots of fifty acres per headright, with a thousand acres the top amount allowed to any one family. The price was high, but the land was considered of uncommon richness. Additionally, Wright recommended that the settlers be exempted from quitrents for ten years and from provincial taxes for up to seven years.

Wright made an extended personal survey of the cession in the fall and early winter of 1773 and was most favorably impressed with its potential. He believed that at least two-thirds of this cession was plantable. He picked a site for a town at the point where the Broad River flows into the Savannah and named it Dartmouth in honor of the Secretary of State for the Colonies. The governor was sure that there would be a rush of settlers into this desirable land, and he was correct. Wright and Surveyor General Henry Yonge reported in 1774 that there was not over 300,000 acres of good ungranted lands available for settlers in the colony. This did not include the 1773 cession which had not then been surveyed, although much had been granted there by the summer of 1774. Land was sold, and some of the Indian traders were paid, but revolutionary troubles arrived too soon to allow Wright's plan to be implemented fully.

Of course the main reason for land granting was to encourage and augment agriculture, a totally different agriculture from the peasant proprietorships envisioned by the Trustees in 1733. This type of agriculture had already disappeared before the first royal governor arrived in 1754. One of the most prosperous agricultural areas in Georgia at the beginning of the royal period was the Salzburger settlement at Ebenezer. Here was produced enough Indian corn, beans, rice (probably upland rice), potatoes, barley, and wheat to market in Charles Town, Purrysburg, and Savannah. There was a filature for silk, two sawmills, and one grist mill. The old German habit of hard work and cooperation and the excellent leadership of John Martin Bolzius made Ebenezer an outstanding area by now.

Silk, the legacy from the Trustees which may have seemed most unlikely, showed increased production in the royal period. This came about for several reasons. For those who persevered, like the Salzburgers at Ebenezer, silk methodology became regularized and comprehensible. Bolzius' leadership here eventually resulted in the creation of a filature at Ebenezer in 1759. Joseph Ottolenghe's work with silk accomplished more than that of the earlier and more erratic Amatises and Camuses. All the governors encouraged silk production.

In 1760, 1,205 pounds of raw silk, the first year of over 1,000 pounds, was exported. Thereafter until 1775, usually about 1,000 pounds of raw silk, valued at from £800 to £950, was exported annually, except for a few years when there is no record of silk export. The high year was 1767 with 1,961 pounds valued at £1,667.1.3. The traditional story is that silk production declined after the bounty was discontinued in 1768, but actually there was no dramatic change until the disruption of the war years after 1775. Some of the silk worked at the Ebenezer filature and exported through Savannah was undoubtedly produced at Purrysburg, South Carolina, but how much it is impossible to know.

A small beginning already had been made in rice plantations

along the Savannah River, but the real growth in plantation agriculture came in the royal period. The great changes which affected agriculture were the presence of slavery, almost unrestricted availability of land, the growth of staple crop economy, and the increased credit available to Georgians. Without all these, plantations could not have come into existence. It may not be too much to maintain that an "agricultural revolution" took place in Georgia between 1752 and 1775.

During this period there existed three main types of agricultural units: the coastal plantation, the family farm or small plantation mainly in the up-country, and the small subsistence farm on the frontier. The large plantations were located in the tidewater area and freshwater swamps along the streams for about twenty miles inland. In these freshwater swamps rice flourished. It was generally believed that rice could be cultivated only with Negro slaves who were not so adversely affected as whites by the fevers of the swampy areas. Rice became the greatest agricultural money crop in Georgia. Indigo and rice combined well on the same plantation, as indigo grew on upland and had a different work season than rice; but indigo never equaled rice in importance in Georgia. Corn and other foodstuffs were also produced on the upland of rice plantations, while livestock could be pastured on unused swamp or upland.

While medium-sized farms existed on the coast, they became much more common between Ebenezer and Augusta after 1763. Here by 1775 could be found many substantial farms worked by their owners and perhaps a few slaves as well. There were also an increasing number of smaller plantations worked mainly by slaves. Corn, some European small grain, and livestock were the main products of these farms and plantations. The most desirable land was along the Savannah and Ogeechee rivers and the navigable creeks emptying into them, where water transportation was available.

The smaller, more diverse plantations of the up-country had no staple crop like rice or indigo. One, about thirty miles west of Augusta, was described in 1772 as having 440 cattle grazed on ungranted nearby lands, a large peach orchard, 36 acres of

Indian corn, 26 acres of wheat, 12 acres of barley, and 16 acres of tobacco. Besides, it produced 40 barrels of pork, 26 of beef, 33 pounds of silk, 420 pounds of indigo, and some hides and fresh meat. Except for the silk, this was probably fairly typical of such up-country small plantations. Products were sold on the Augusta market, and some foodstuffs were shipped to coastal planters or exported to the West Indies. Many people hoped that the settlement of the up-country would result in the production of more wheat in Georgia so the colony would not have to depend upon Pennsylvania for its flour. Planters in the up-country were described as thriving though not yet rich.

West and north of the farms and small plantations were the small subsistence farms of the true frontiersmen, where corn and other foodstuffs were raised for home use and cattle and hogs were pastured upon nearby ungranted lands. There were also such farms south of the Altamaha but not very many. Frontier farmers were usually poor but hoped to improve their status. With good land and hard work they were usually able to do just that. Many areas which were fairly well settled with yeomen farmers by 1775 had been frontier in 1763. Small farmers hunted for pleasure and for food and sold some deerskins and lumber products if transportation was available.

Land in the up-country was more fertile than on the coast, and the area was much more healthful. In this area whites were believed able to live and do all the necessary work. Settlers always took up what they considered the best land first, usually oak and hickory land, except for the rice swamps. Pine barren was considered of little value except to grow pine trees and for pasturage of cattle. Thus the first rush of planters in the 1750s took up the rice swamps, but as most of this north of the Altamaha had been granted by 1763, the great concentration afterwards was on the land between Ebenezer and Augusta. This brought a different type of settler into Georgia than had come during the 1750s and resulted in a different kind of agriculture.

Plantations utilized slave labor, and the purchase of slaves required considerable credit, more than had been available in Trustee Georgia. Planters developing coastal rice swamps either

John Stuart's map of the Savannah area in 1780.

had to bring their slaves from Carolina or the West Indies or purchase newly imported slaves, an expensive procedure. Hence the development of credit facilities was most important to new rice planters. First this credit was extended by Charles Town merchants, and by 1763 by English merchants as well. Slaves working on good land could generally pay for themselves in a few years, and their children augmented the labor force of the planters. Much of the South Carolina capital sent to Georgia was actually used by Carolinians on their own land.

Because plantations had begun so late and perhaps because of the Trustee legacy, large plantations never displaced yeomen farmers and small planters in Georgia to the degree that they did in South Carolina. Lieutenant Governor John Graham owned 25,000 acres of land, and Governor Wright had some eleven plantations (10,000 to 15,000 acres) and 523 slaves. James Habersham, who combined planting with his mercantile interests, owned 198 slaves and over 10,000 acres. These are examples of the largest planters in colonial Georgia. More ordinary planters owned from 2,000 to 5,000 acres. In 1773 Wright reported that there were about 1,400 plantations or farms containing some 120,000 acres of improved land, which would average about 860 acres per unit.

Cattle were raised by farmers and planters on their own land or upon nearby public land, but they were also tended by herdsmen on public lands just as in the Trustee period. By 1755 many lowland South Carolina ranges were overstocked and were becoming unavailable as the land was granted to individuals, making Georgia ranges more desirable. Raising cattle on public lands was very cheap, as the only expense for a herd of several thousand was a few herdsmen and a little salt. By 1775 herds of 1,500 to 6,000 were reported in the area between the upper Ogeechee and Savannah rivers, which was becoming a favorite area for cattle drovers. Most of this range cattle was driven to the coast where they were slaughtered for local use or for export. From 1768 to 1772 nearly 1,000 barrels of beef were exported yearly, and the amount was increasing.

While most Georgians were directly concerned with agriculture for their income, merchants were of increasing importance in the colony's economic development after 1750. The slight growth in merchant houses and business in late Trustee and early royal Georgia reflected the equally meager growth in the economy. The complete transition from the old controlled economy of the Trustee period to a free one did not come until about 1760, concurrent with the colony's rapid growth.

The leading merchant house in Savannah as royal government began was undoubtedly that of Harris and Habersham, owned and operated by two of Georgia's leading citizens. Both Francis Harris and James Habersham had come to Georgia in the 1730s and their personal wealth and political and economic importance had increased as the years wore on. Its public wharf in Savannah was essential to the development of the colony's trade in the 1750s. The firm engaged in the general import and export business, in the Indian trade, and undoubtedly had many of the colony's largest planters as customers. This firm began practices that other merchants were to take up during the 1750s and 1760s.

Other merchant houses grew slowly through the 1750s, but much more rapidly after 1760. As though foreshadowing this increased prosperity, Thomas Lloyd moved from Charles Town to Savannah in the winter of 1758–59 and set up a counting house at the "public Stores and Market" in Savannah. Lloyd was essentially a factor or commission merchant who bought and sold cargoes but who did not engage in ordinary mercantile business. During the 1760s a few other commission merchants set up in Savannah, and ordinary importing merchants also engaged in commission business.

Basil Cowper and William and Edward Telfair came to Savannah from Antigua and began mercantile operations in 1767. This firm, alternately called Cowper and Telfairs, or Telfair and Telfair, became one of the leading merchant houses in Savannah and did increasing amounts of business throughout the colonial period. The firm acted as a factor for large planters in selling their rice and purchasing their supplies, served as wholesale merchant to smaller country houses, bought two vessels to engage in the coasting and West Indian trade, sent its sloop regularly to London once a year, and owned at least two brigs used in the Carolina-Georgia coasting trade. This firm exported rice, indigo, deerskins, lumber, silk, beef, pork, and other provision crops to the northern colonies, the West Indies, and to England. It imported Negroes, rum, and sugar from the West Indies, foodstuffs and manufactured goods from the northern colonies, and manufactured goods from Britain. By 1770 the company employed sailmakers and coopers, and entered increasingly into the ship supply business for vessels putting into Savannah and in need of repairs or supplies as well as cargoes. Other leading merchants did most of these things as well, but the Telfair house had as diversified a business as any Savannah merchant house. These houses are illustrative of the type of merchants who set up in Savannah in increasing numbers as the royal period progressed, but there were many others like Joseph Clay, Habersham's nephew, who came to Savannah about 1760 and entered into the mercantile business.

There were merchants outside Savannah, mainly at Sunbury, Darien, Ebenezer, and Augusta; but considerably less is known about them than those at Savannah. These outlying merchants tended to trade through Savannah houses rather than independently. Some Sunbury merchants engaged in direct trade with the West Indies and mainland colonies through coasting vessels.

The Indian trade was a business which had originally been conducted by Charles Town merchants, and they continued to control a part of it. Augusta early became the Georgia center for this trade and so continued throughout the colonial period. Originally, Augusta was essentially a warehousing center from which traders took off with their loaded packhorses for the Indian country and to which they returned with their deerskins. By the 1760s this business was in the hands of merchants from Charles Town, Savannah, and Augusta. Trade with the Creeks was carried on in what is today Georgia and Alabama, and that with the Chickasaws and Choctaws in present-day Mississippi. Cherokee trade in the Keowee country in Carolina was of less importance to Augusta. George Galphin became in the 1760s one of Augusta's leading Indian traders. He also traded with frontier whites and carried on farming operations in Georgia and South Carolina. The 1763 cession of the lands between Ebenezer and Augusta made for an increasing farm population near Augusta, and the merchants there began changing from Indian traders to farm suppliers or a combination of the two.

The general tendency throughout the royal period was for the number of merchant houses and the amount of business to increase. As partnerships were often of short duration, there were many changes of firm names, usually with continuity of the principal merchants. In 1764 twenty-four Savannah merchants advertised in the *Georgia Gazette*, and by 1769 the number had increased to thirty-two. In 1774 the number of houses was the same, but the volume of business was greater.

Business with planters, farmers, and country merchants was carried on a long-term credit basis by importing merchants, with a final accounting rare as long as the merchant and customer continued their usual business relationship. Thus it is difficult to know profits or financial worth. But profits were obvious from the expanding wealth of both merchants and planters. Frequently wealth was figured in land and slaves, and both were used in payment to merchants. Merchants, of necessity, acted as bankers and lending agencies, extending credit and cash for crops, bonds, and bills of exchange. Merchants were the only people who had intercolonial and British credit and were the only ones who regularly transmitted commercial paper or hard cash to other colonies or to the mother country.

Certainly the physical conditions for loading and unloading vessels at Savannah needed improvement. The wharf built by Harris and Habersham in 1751 has already been noted. In the 1760s a number of wharf lots were granted between the Trustees' Garden and Yamacraw Bluff, with the most desirable ones near Bull Street. The nine lots just west of Bull Street were important enough to be known as "commerce row." Wharves and warehouses were built on these lots to receive goods for incoming and outgoing vessels. These buildings were frequently four stories high so that the top story was level with the top of the bluff, while

Tybee lighthouse in 1764.

Fort on Cockspur Island.

the bottom story was level with vessels in the river. By 1764 there were sixteen such warehouses along the wharf used by merchants.

Docking and warehouse facilities could be built at Savannah, but the river itself could not be controlled and was one of the main hindrances to a thriving port business. Savannah is located some fifteen miles from the mouth of the river with sandbars and inadequate water depth between Savannah and Tybee. The river above Cockspur Island could not accommodate loaded vessels or those larger than 150 tons, despite legislation in the 1760s aimed at keeping it clear. Many vessels coming to Savannah had to load or unload at least a part of their cargo at Cockspur, using small boats which necessitated extra costs and delays. Some merchants kept lumber on Cockspur to give a vessel its full load once it had dropped down from Savannah. Few vessels larger than 150 tons stopped at Savannah. While this did not discourage the coasting trade, it did prevent more direct transatlantic trade, the very sort which was needed to increase Georgia's hoped-for prosperity and to escape from the control of Charles Town.

From relatively small beginnings in 1752, Savannah's direct trade with Britain increased fairly steadily. Rice and deerskins were the leading exports throughout the royal period. Smaller and less important amounts of lumber products, naval stores, indigo, silk, and beeswax were included. War with France in 1756 ended direct trade between Georgia and Britain in 1757 and 1758 because the British navy did not maintain convoy service for merchant vessels to Savannah. This trade began again in 1759 and increased yearly thereafter. By 1763 direct exports to Britain were £14,055, and a decade later had reached £40,974. Imports from Britain consisted mostly of manufactured goods and products from other European countries.

While lumber and naval stores exports to Britain remained small, lumber exports to the West Indies increased considerably. Indeed it seems that almost every vessel which sailed from Georgia to the West Indies from 1758 to 1775 carried at least some lumber products, sometimes cut to exact specifications of

the buyer. Georgia also exported small amounts of beef, pork,
corn, rice, other provisions, and a few horses to the West Indies.
The main imports from the islands were sugar and rum, with a
little molasses.

Trade with the northern colonies brought some flour and other
foodstuffs along with manufactured goods made in the colonies or
imported from Europe. Most trade with the Mediterranean area,
with rice exported and wine and a few other items imported, was
probably indirect through England or the northern colonies.

Any exact picture of Georgia's foreign trade is impossible for
several reasons. All the records of the Savannah customs office
were destroyed through military action in February of 1776.
Complete export and import figures have been found only for
trade with the British Isles. There is absolutely no way to know
how much of Georgia's foreign trade went via land or water to or
from Charles Town and is thus included in the records of that
port. Foreign trade figures in the *Georgia Gazette* after 1763 do not
give the original source of imports nor the ultimate destination of
exports. There are chance reports of customs officials and other
figures from which the general trend and value of Georgia's
foreign trade can be determined. The following tables, taken
from available figures, are believed to be reasonably accurate for
the amount and direction of trade throughout the entire royal
period. Certainly all sources indicate rapidly increasing trade
and agree with recent specialized studies of late colonial trade.*

Year	Tons exported	Value	No. of vessels used
1755		£15,744	52
1761	1,604	£15,870	45
1770	10,514	£99,383	186
1773	11,276	£121,677	225

While comparable import figures are not available, imports
probably increased similarly.

---

* See for instance, James F. Shepherd and Gary M. Walton, *Shipping,
Maritime Trade, and the Economic Development of Colonial North America* (Cambridge,
1972).

For the year October 1765 to October 1766 exports and imports by areas are as follows:

Imports from Britain	£ 83,000
Imports from West Indies	26,242
Imports from northern colonies	12,017
Imported Negroes from Africa	14,820
Total Imports	£136,079
Exports to Europe	£ 55,274
Exports to West Indies	24,481
Exports to northern colonies	5,074
Total Exports	£ 84,829

This proportional value of trade with the specified areas undoubtedly remained about the same for the remainder of the colonial period.

By 1772 Habersham's dire picture of 1756 had long ended, and he himself conceded that Georgia was more prosperous than at any time in her history, with more vessels in the harbor than ever before and such a great demand for the colony's products that it probably could not be fully met. The same year Governor Wright reported that since 1760, the year of his arrival in Georgia, the rice crop had increased from 4,000 barrels to 17,000 barrels and that Georgia was "making a very rapid progress towards being an opulent and considerable Province." Neither man was given to overstatement or enthusiasm not backed by substantial facts. Georgians now owned some thirty-six ocean-going vessels and more than fifty smaller vessels employed in river and inland passage local traffic, most of which traded between Charles Town, Savannah, and the rest of the colony.

By 1775 Georgia's economy was well on the way to fulfilling the greatest hopes of James Habersham and James Wright. It is interesting to speculate what Noble Jones, who came on the *Ann* with the original settlers, might have thought of the changes in Georgia in its forty-two years, but he left no record of his ideas. He had seen, undoubtedly as clearly as anyone, the change and progress. While he was not as wealthy as Habersham and

Wright, he had prospered. Peace and prosperity accompanied by sustained economic growth had been the most obvious characteristic of the colony during the years from 1760 to 1775. Nor did the political troubles pointing toward the revolt which would begin in 1775 slow the economic development. As that year opened there was little reason to suspect that Georgia's progress would not continue at an increased rate. Economically, it should have, but political considerations proved more determinative.

12

SOCIAL TONE AND FRONTIERSMEN:
A CONTRAST

In social as in economic affairs, royal Georgia underwent great change and became much more a typical southern colony. While part of this change had begun during the late years of the Trustee period, it came more rapidly and with more finality in the royal period. Frequently tied to economic change, social change became more pronounced after 1760, involving the type of people who moved to Georgia, their goals, the presence of an increasing number of Negro slaves, more schools and schoolmasters, and a sharper class structure. Of course all this came about in an evolutionary manner, but by 1775 someone who had known Georgia in 1752 might have considered it revolutionary.

Once the basic Trustee design of Georgia as a haven for unfortunate poor was abandoned, the type of settlers coming into the colony changed. Although most settlers continued to be poor, as in other colonies, they did not intend to remain peasant proprietors. Instead, like other frontiersmen, they hoped for increased wealth.

Greater population was the key to any improvement in Georgia. In 1751 just prior to the Trustee surrender, the Board of Trade reported 1,735 whites and 349 blacks. Like all population figures for the colonial period, this was a rough estimate. The next year the president and assistants in Savannah reported 3,000 whites and fewer than 500 blacks, probably closer to the truth than the previous year's estimate. In 1753 the Board of Trade estimated 2,261 whites and 1,600 slaves, probably too few whites and too many blacks. In 1755 Governor John Reynolds reported 4,500 whites and 1,855 blacks, probably too high a number of whites.

Clearly population had been increasing since 1750. The first group to arrive were 160 Germans brought to Georgia by William DeBrahm in 1751 who settled at Bethany, near Ebenezer. About the same number came the next year also. In 1752 DeBrahm estimated that 1,500 Germans were settled in and around Ebenezer, undoubtedly too high a figure.

Late in 1752 the first Puritans from Dorchester, on the Ashley River above Charles Town in South Carolina, arrived and settled on the coast midway between the Savannah and Altamaha rivers, thus giving the name Midway to that area. The removal was completed by the summer of 1754 when the church was constituted at Midway. The only real town of the Puritans was their port of Sunbury, a few miles from Midway church. These Puritans brought slaves from South Carolina and resumed the rice planting they had begun there. While perhaps not more than forty white families came from South Carolina, the Midway district became the largest nucleus of population south of the Ogeechee and one of the most prosperous in the colony. Other South Carolinians and West Indians with their slaves came in the late 1740s and early 1750s and settled along the Ogeechee or Altamaha rivers. By 1754 most of the good rice land north of the Altamaha had been taken up.

James Habersham reported that from 1750 to 1754 people came regularly to Georgia, but that immigration declined greatly after 1754 and did not really revive until about 1760. Of course one reason for this long interruption was the war which broke out between Britain and France in 1756. Georgia, an unprotected frontier colony with many Indian neighbors so close to the French in the Alabama country and to the Spaniards in Florida, was not the most desirable place to settle until the outcome of the war became evident. One group which did arrive at Savannah in December of 1755 was some four hundred Acadians, sent thither as a part of the deportation of the French from Nova Scotia. These Acadians, being Roman Catholic and French, were not welcomed; and little provision was made for their settlement. Most of them settled on the commons and other unused land near Savannah and eked out a subsistence. They died, left for South Carolina and other places, and did not prosper. Governor Henry Ellis noted in 1757 that only about one hundred remained. They made oars, handspikes, and other wooden implements which were easily sold to the West Indies. Ellis tried to help these people, but the last of them disappeared as a group when the land they had lived upon was sold in 1763.

There were always drifters, frequently economic failures, on the American frontier; and by the time of the arrival of Governor Ellis numbers of these drifters were beginning to settle on ungranted land of Georgia's frontier. This worried Ellis, but he was never able to prevent it. Such people, Ellis thought, were undesirable and could contribute little to the colony's prosperity.

The followers of Edmund Gray were a group which particularly bothered Ellis. In 1750 Gray, "a pretended Quaker," and a group of twenty families left Virginia to settle on the Little River above Augusta. The original settlement was abandoned in 1756 when the settlers moved to Cumberland Island in the debatable land between Georgia and Florida. The Spanish in St. Augustine moved to evict the English colonists, so Gray and many of his followers moved to the mainland and settled on the Satilla River, below the Altamaha, at a place which they called New Hanover. London in 1758 ordered Governors Henry Lyttelton of South Carolina and Henry Ellis of Georgia to get rid of New Hanover, and they sent representatives to New Hanover and Cumberland Island to order the settlers away. The next year New Hanover was reported abandoned and only a few persons were left on Cumberland Island.

There may have been three hundred people at New Hanover and a hundred on Cumberland, and the land and agriculture were reported unusually good. Despite the original order to move, Gray and some one hundred followers were on Cumberland Island in 1760. When this territory became British in 1763, further action against these settlers became unnecessary. But this area was too far south of Georgia's settlements to be safe or to be of any value to the colony.

Georgia's greatest population and economic growth began about 1760 and went on steadily until 1775. Soon after his arrival in Georgia in 1760, Wright reported fewer than 6,000 whites and 3,578 blacks. The governor, throughout the rest of the colonial period, continually objected to the frontier drifters in and around Augusta who were, he said, often worse than Indians and caused considerable trouble with the Creeks. James Habersham called such people "crackers" in 1772 and agreed that they were undesirable. Wright sought to secure what he called "the Middling Sort of People, such as have Families and a few negroes" to settle the 1763 and 1773 Indian cessions, people who would make the best economic and defense contribution to the colony. But both "crackers" and "middling" people continued to come to Georgia, and both made their contribution to her growth, the "middling sort" much more rapidly than the "crackers."

Settlement patterns from 1760 to 1775 show individuals coming from the West Indies, frequently friends or relatives of people already in Georgia, as well as increasing numbers from England, Scotland, and Ireland. Ordinarily these came as individuals or in small groups, though there were several large parties from Northern Ireland.

The major advocates of direct Scotch-Irish immigration to Georgia were George Galphin and John Rae, Indian traders and land speculators of Augusta. Both natives of Ulster, they backed an Irish settlement west of their holdings. In 1768 they secured a reserve of fifty thousand acres on the Ogeechee River near the present site of Louisville. Rae was especially interested in a settlement where Irish linen, a product in great demand in America, could be produced. He worked through his brother in Belfast to secure settlers, and with Galphin tried to get a law passed specifying that the colony should pay the ocean passage for poor settlers. Although this was dropped because of British opposition, some settlers did have their passage paid by the colony because they left for Georgia thinking that the law had been enacted. Rae and Galphin hoped to profit from supplying the new settlers once they arrived in Georgia.

The first 107 Rae- and Galphin-backed Irish settlers arrived in Savannah in late September 1768 and they were reinforced by several hundred Protestant Irish yearly until 1776. These settlers took land in or near Queensborough, also called the "Irish Settlement." By 1774 there were at least 900 Scotch-Irish immigrants, but some removed to South Carolina when they found conditions not to their liking at Queensborough. Indian troubles in 1771 and 1772 drove out some settlers, but a portion returned after the 1773 Indian cession.

Migration from the colonies to the north also took place between 1757 and 1775, largely from the Carolinas, Virginia, Maryland, and Pennsylvania in that order. Many were Scotch-Irish, with fewer Germans and English. These migrants were on the lookout for better land, and by 1765 the best land available in the southern piedmont was between Ebenezer and Augusta. Regulators from North Carolina, frequently considered undesirable by Wright and Habersham, came after their failure at the Battle of Alamance in 1771 and helped to fill the 1773 cession. Most of the settlers for this cession came from the Carolinas and Virginia and were small frontier farmers with no slaves. James Habersham reported in 1772 that 3,000 people had already settled in the area of the proposed cession and that 600 additional families were ready to purchase land in this area as soon as it could be done legally. During the first three months after sales began, 1,413 whites and 300 slaves moved in. In March 1774 Wright predicted that 10,000 more people would arrive by the next January, a figure which was undoubtedly too high.

Governor Wright had some interest in settling new arrivals in townships for protection and in encouraging better people, who would not add to political unrest, to come. Wright's most successful township settlements began in September of 1767, when representatives of 50 Quaker families from Hillsborough, North Carolina, applied for a reserve of land. Quakers were thrifty and industrious settlers who got along well with the Indians and who had few radical political ideas. So 12,000 acres of land were set aside near the Little River west of Augusta. This settlement was soon named Wrightsborough in honor of the governor. By 1775, 124 Quakers held title to over 30,000 acres in this area and the total population was over 600.

Generally Governor Wright's attempts to attract settlers were successful, but many would have come regardless of what was done by the government. By 1770 Wright estimated the population at 11,000 whites with 2,500 to 3,000 effective militiamen, which gave Georgia its first numerical superiority over its Creek warrior neighbors. In 1773 the governor reported 18,000 whites and 15,000 blacks, and there were probably 45–50,000 people in Georgia by the summer of 1776, a considerable increase from the 4,000–5,000 at the beginning of the royal period. Perhaps a third of the whites were Scotch-Irish, almost a sixth were Germans, mainly in the Ebenezer area; most of the rest were English, with only a few Highland Scots at Darien and about 100 Jews at Savannah.

Georgia's rapid population growth paralleled that of other mainland British colonies but was reinforced by her newness, the exit of the French and Spanish as neighbors in 1763, and the best land available in the southern piedmont after 1765. Wright realized that Georgia's immediate future lay in the rich piedmont lands, hence his great concern with the 1763 and 1773 Indian land cessions. Certainly the policies of Wright, implemented by the Assembly, helped population growth. By 1776 Georgia had enough settlers to think seriously of rebellion.

That portion of Georgia's population about which least is known, despite its importance to the colony's growing wealth, was the slaves who arrived in increasing numbers throughout the royal period. When slavery was first allowed legally by the Trustees in 1750, the proposed slave code which was never enacted into law showed unusual benevolence toward Negro slaves by eighteenth-century standards. By this code there was to be one white servant for each four Negro slaves, and no great differences were obvious in the punishment of slaves as opposed to whites. In royal Georgia the first slave code was passed in 1755 and was modeled after the 1740 South Carolina code. This act marks the abandonment of the Trustees' humanitarian ideals. Now only one white servant for every twenty slaves was required, and there were many more restrictions on slaves and more severe punishments prescribed for them than for whites. Sixteen hours of labor a day was allowed, and masters were required to furnish only minimal amounts of food and clothing. The same general pattern continued throughout the colonial period. The 1755 slave code expired in 1763, and the Assembly enacted a new law in 1765 which was disallowed. After slight alterations this act was approved in 1770 and governed for the remainder of the colonial period. Undoubtedly the 1765 act was the basis of the slave system between 1765 and 1770.

By the beginning of the royal period, most early opponents of slavery had changed their minds and no longer objected to its introduction. People like James Habersham and George White-field, many of the Salzburgers, and the Highland Scots at Darien were now willing to own slaves and to profit from their labor. At the beginning of plantation slavery in the late Trustee period, South Carolina and West Indian planters brought their slaves to the colony. Some Negroes continued to come from other colonies, but most brought into Georgia were new slaves direct from Africa, mainly from Angola, Gambia, and the Gold Coast. These slaves were sold by importing merchants in Savannah as a part of their general business.

With the introduction of slavery into the colony, the favored situation of white artisans was endangered. They banded to-gether to restrict the entry of slaves into the "mechanical skills." When an attempt was made to legislate these views in 1758, large planters and merchants fought this and prevented any meaning-ful enactment. However, Negro artisans never became as impor-tant in Georgia as they were in South Carolina.

Generally Negroes did the heavier jobs such as coopering, sawing, boatbuilding, and some blacksmithing. They served as boatmen on the colony's small boats and worked in the brickyards. Finer workmanship like cabinetmaking, bricklaying, and better blacksmithing was reserved usually to whites. There were, of course, overlapping jobs done by both races. Frequently slave artisans belonged to or worked for hire with white artisans as assistants or apprentices. The smaller proportion of slaves in Georgia and the greater importance of the middling sort of whites undoubtedly helped white artisans to maintain relatively favorable conditions.

Savannah's forty to fifty free Negroes and slaves who lived by themselves and hired out for day labor lived in the Negro district, below the Trustees Garden bluff by the 1760s. The total population of this district was ordinarily two hundred to three hundred by 1770.

To many people, the coming of Negro slavery to Georgia was associated with the growing prosperity of the royal period and thus contrasted favorably with the poverty of the Trustee period when slavery was not legal. Certainly Georgia now was more prosperous, and slavery did make its contribution to this prosperity. As the slave population increased, so did the white.

Population increase created a need for more clergy and churches. Neither grew sufficiently in the royal period to keep pace with population growth. The religious turbulence of the Trustee period declined, and the increased stability and prosperity of the royal period gave churches a firmer base than most had enjoyed earlier in the colony.

As in other southern colonies, there was a move to establish the Anglican church as Georgia's official church. This began in 1755 in the first session of the royal Assembly, but it was 1758 before an establishment act was passed. This act was largely the work of Joseph Ottolenghe, a former Italian Jew converted to Anglicanism in England. He came to Georgia in 1751 to oversee the silk industry and to act as catechist for Negroes. Ottolenghe was helped in the Commons House of Assembly by Edward Barnard of Augusta and Henry Yonge, brother to the Bishop of Norwich. Since the German Lutherans, Midway Congregationalists, and Presbyterians differed so much from each other, Ottolenghe managed to keep their representatives from uniting against his proposed measure; and he understood parliamentary procedure well enough to circumvent the opposition in the Upper House.

The establishment act divided Georgia into eight parishes. Christ Church in Savannah comprised the largest parish congregation, while St. Matthew's at Ebenezer took in most of the non-Anglican German Salzburgers. Between Augusta and Ebenezer lay sparsely settled St. George, then called Halifax District. St. Paul included Augusta and the surrounding countryside. Southwest of Savannah, Hardwick and the area twelve miles distant from Christ Church made up St. Philip. Adjacent was St. John, dominated by the Midway Congregationalists. St. Andrew included the district around Darien, while St. James was principally St. Simons Island. In 1765 the territory south of the Altamaha was made into four new parishes—St. David, St. Patrick, St. Thomas, and St. Mary.

In 1758 there were only two Anglican congregations in Georgia, Christ Church and St. Paul. The act did nothing to prevent dissenting churches from functioning as they had previously. Indeed, the Assembly guaranteed the right of dissenters to worship by specifically stating that no Anglican rector might "exercise any Eclesiastical Law or Jurisdiction whatsoever."

Each Monday after Easter, all freeholders and householders in each parish should assemble at the church or at some designated place where they should elect two church wardens and a vestry of five to ten persons. The vestry was empowered to levy taxes upon all parish citizens for poor relief and church expenses. The taxes could produce only £30 annually in Christ Church or St. Paul and £10 in the other parishes where there was no church. The vestry and church wardens were the only local government organization in Georgia and carried on political as well as religious duties. Dissenters voted in parish elections and were sometimes elected to parish offices. In St. Matthew's Parish the deacons and elders of Lutheran Jerusalem Church at one time were elected as vestry of the parish, and the vestry of St. John's undoubtedly was heavily Congregational.

On the whole the establishment of the Anglican Church did not affect discernibly the colony's religious life. There were too few churches and Anglicans in Georgia. St. George's Parish built a church in the 1770s, and there were rectors for St. George, St. Philip, and St. John at some time; but there were seldom more than three Anglicans doing parish duty in the colony at one time. Sometimes one of the rectors or one of the clergymen at Bethesda officiated in parishes that lacked a regular priest, but usually these parishes were without Anglican services. The rectors were paid by the Society for the Propagation of the Gospel, the Parliamentary grant, the Assembly, and, in at least Christ Church, by the parish itself—usually by a combination of these methods.

Besides the small number of clergy and Anglican laity, another problem was the personalities and abilities of the young and inexperienced clergymen usually sent to Georgia from England. Several of these men were contentious, bigoted, and doctrinaire; and they did not get along well with their parishioners or with the authorities. Perhaps the best Anglican minister in Georgia was Bartholomew Zouberbuhler, rector at Savannah from 1746 until his death in December 1766. Zouberbuhler combined a lively mind with a practical sense of what he could accomplish in his position. He worried at seeing "so many in this Colony destitute of divine worship." Still, he could not minister to the entire colony, and he never tried to do the impossible.

After Joseph Ottolenghe arrived in 1751 he was pressed to preach in the backcountry. Sensible of his ministerial shortcomings, he declined the request, sending books on religious instruction instead. Ottolenghe was faithful to his position as catechist to the slaves and did more for them than any clergyman in Georgia. In this he was encouraged by Zouberbuhler who left a part of his estate to finance this work. Ottolenghe built a small house in Savannah where, for more than a decade, he preached to and instructed any Negroes who came. His services, conducted at night, attracted ten to fifty blacks to each meeting. Ottolenghe usually opened with a prayer; taught reading through passages from the Bible; drilled the slaves in the catechism, the Lord's Prayer, and the Creed; and gave a simple talk based on the Bible and ideas of morality. A few Negroes responded, learning to read

imperfectly and to recite the Creed and brief prayers. For
Ottolenghe, there was a simple explanation for his failure:
"Slavery is certainly a great Depresser of the Mind."

Samuel Frink illustrated well the problems of Anglican priests
in Georgia. A 1758 graduate of Harvard and a former Congrega-
tionalist, Frink arrived at St. Paul's in 1765. He resented his
assignment to the frontier and used his pulpit to assail his
detractors, who soon became numerous. Frink moved to Savannah after Zouberbuhler's death in 1766, and there his youth and
personality continued to cause trouble. He claimed that he was
entitled to the prescribed fees for all weddings, christenings, and
funerals, even when the services were conducted by dissenting
ministers. This stand threatened the traditional tolerance between dissenters and Anglicans in Georgia. Always a minority,
Anglicans previously had never sought to challenge existing
dissenting groups under the 1758 law, preferring instead to share
authority with them. Frink's action undid in a few weeks the
conciliatory work of Zouberbuhler. Reaction came swiftly from
the most prominent dissenting minister in Savannah, John J.
Zubly.

Zubly had done temporary duty in Georgia before he moved
to the colony in 1760 as minister to the small and influential
congregation of Independent Presbyterians in Savannah who
described themselves as dissenters from the Church of England
and adherents to the doctrines of the Church of Scotland. The
congregation's membership included many of the colony's leading citizens, such as Jonathan Bryan, Robert Bolton, James
Edward Powell, Joseph and William Gibbons, William Wright,
Benjamin Farley, and John Fox.

Zubly and Zouberbuhler clearly had an understanding of each
other's place in Savannah's religious life, but Frink was less
cooperative. He refused to walk with Zubly in a funeral
procession; and, more tellingly, refused to conduct the funeral of
Zubly's child despite the father's request. Zubly entered into a
newspaper argument with Frink in 1769 when the latter claimed
the fee for tolling of the church bell during dissenting funerals.
This developed into an attempt in 1770 to create separate

dissenter and Jewish burial grounds in Savannah. Nothing came
of this but dissenters continued to use the public burial ground
and Jews to be buried on Jewish property in Savannah. Public
opinion backed Zubly, no mean antagonist especially when the
rights of dissenters were concerned. Governor Wright took no
action in the matter but probably deplored Frink's actions.
Georgia had seen no such religious arguments in its entire
history. Frink was finally removed from Georgia in 1771 by his
death.

When the Society for the Propagation of the Gospel sent
William Duncanson to Savannah in 1761 to replace the ailing
Zouberbuhler, the vestry and church wardens, with Governor
Wright's approval, rejected him as unsuitable. Duncanson then
went to St. Paul's at Augusta. Never was a ministry so ruinous.
In February 1762 Duncanson was convicted as a drunkard and a
profane swearer. Soon after he challenged a member of his
congregation to a duel. When the startled parishioner refused,
Duncanson sought him out, tried to horsewhip him, and
unsuccessfully attempted to discharge a pistol pointed at his
breast. In April, Duncanson was accused of seeking to debauch
his landlord's daughter. By the summer of 1762 he joined a
packhorse train bound for the interior of the Indian country and
vanished from Georgia's history. A better influence at Augusta
was James Seymour who came to St. Paul's in 1772 and was a
consistent defender of the king. Yet he was so well respected that
he was allowed to remain in Augusta unharmed until 1781 when
he finally went to British-held Savannah.

At Ebenezer and Bethany, the Lutherans stood apart from the
rest of the colony in their sincere religious practices. In 1752 the
churches at Ebenezer, Zion, Bethany, Goshen, and Savannah in
Georgia and Purrysburg in South Carolina were served by the
Reverends John Martin Bolzius, Herman Henry Lembke, and
the newly arrived Christian Rabenhorst. Bolzius continued to be
the spiritual and temporal leader of the now prosperous Salzburgers until his death in 1765. One sign of this prosperity was
the substantial brick church still standing at Ebenezer, built in
1767. Lembke lived only three years after Bolzius. In 1769

Christian Friedrich Triebner arrived from Germany to join Rabenhorst at Ebenezer and the other churches. With his coming the unity of the Salzburger ministry was destroyed.

Triebner and Rabenhorst quarreled over precedent, privilege, and procedures in the conduct of religious services and about church property and secular matters. Triebner's group was led by his brother-in-law, John Wertsch, while Rabenhorst's faction rallied around John Adam Treutlen. Possession of Jerusalem Church seemed the principal goal of both factions; and, in 1770, the church alternately was occupied, besieged, broken into, and reoccupied by both factions. Henry Muhlenberg, patriarch of the Lutheran church in America, traveled from Pennsylvania to Ebenezer in 1774 to settle the arguments. His judgment, which generally favored the Rabenhorst faction, accomplished little as the outbreak of revolt in 1775 revived the schism among the Salzburgers. Triebner, who came off second best, embraced the tory cause while Rabenhorst's followers mostly became whigs. On December 30, 1776, Rabenhorst died, but Triebner found it impossible to unite the Germans. The old unity at Ebenezer was gone, never to return.

At Wrightsborough, the Quakers established a thriving township and, by 1770, a monthly meeting as well. In 1773 they collectively reproved profanity, fornication, frolicking and dancing, excessive drinking, and other shameful offenses. Here on the Georgia frontier the Quakers were allowed to practice their brand of brotherly love until revolt broke out in 1775.

St. John's Parish was dominated religiously by the Congregational church at Midway with a branch at Sunbury. From 1752 to 1773, John Osgood, who had come from South Carolina with the original settlers, served the Midway Puritans as pastor. Osgood was a man of experience, wisdom, and integrity. A compromiser and a man "of moderate Principles, Sound in the Articles of Faith, and one who receives the Westminster Confession thereof, a moderate Calvinist," Osgood was a successful minister in every sense. The church prospered under his direction, having 150 members by 1771.

Georgia had long had a few Baptists, but in the 1760s more

came into the backcountry. In 1770 Daniel Marshall, a zealous Baptist minister, crossed the Savannah River near Augusta to carry his message to unchurched Georgians. The only record of a religious arrest in Georgia is that of Marshall who was apprehended in rural St. Paul's Parish for preaching without a license. At the trial when Marshall was ordered to preach no more in Georgia, he replied in the words of St. Peter and the apostles, "Whether it be right to obey God rather than man, judge ye." He continued to preach and was not molested further. He founded Georgia's first Baptist church on Kiokee Creek. By 1775 there may have been three Baptist churches in the up-country, but the records are inadequate.

In practice, few colonies had a more liberal religious policy than Georgia from 1752 to 1775. Except for the standard prohibitions against Roman Catholics, the arrest of Daniel Marshall, and occasional utterances against Savannah's few Jews, there was little that could be called religious persecution in the colony. The absence of religious harassment reflected not so much a deliberate policy on the part of Georgia's government as the general climate of opinion. Settlers were certainly more important than their religious beliefs.

In truth, most Georgians were unchurched, having little if any contact with organized religion. Outside Savannah, Augusta, Ebenezer, and Midway there was little chance to attend church or to have the services of a minister if they were desired. The great religious need in Georgia was missionary work, and only a small beginning was being made to fill this need by 1776. Clergymen and laity alike commented on the religious ignorance of many backcountry settlers who had often never seen a Bible nor participated in a religious service. For many this was not a matter of choice but was rather due to the absence of religious services within reach of their frontier homes.

Education in royal Georgia, like religion, was affected adversely by the frontier environment and favorably by the increased wealth and population of the colony from 1760 to 1775. Formal education existed in and around the colony's main towns, at Bethesda, and in a few plantation schools. In royal

Georgia schoolmaster's licenses were issued by the government to only eleven persons—Thomas Eastham, Valentine Bostick, Edmund Bermingham, Robert McClatchie, John Holmes, Alexander Findlay, James Seymour, John Gordon, Peter Gandy, Joseph Brooks, and Theobald Maighenaux; but this does not mean that they were the only teachers. At Bethesda, Augusta, Savannah, and Ebenezer ministers doubled as schoolmasters; and other people taught as well. On the whole, Georgia's teachers during the royal period seemed of indifferent quality and frequently ill-suited for their task. There were complaints of drunkenness, profanity, seduction, and of the transient nature of schoolmasters. In these complaints are reflected the low income and social status of the itinerant pedagogues of frontier America.

At Ebenezer, the Salzburgers endured a parade of unsatisfactory schoolmasters whose task was to teach the Germans English and other subjects. By far the best instructors at Ebenezer were the Germans themselves—their ministers, physicians, a lay teacher, John Adam Treutlen, and the colony's only recorded female teacher, Schoolmistress Heckin, who came in 1764. One of the best schoolmasters in royal Georgia was Treutlen, a precise, exacting individual whose self-assurance irritated Bolzius. Yet there were few complaints concerning Treutlen's classroom performance. By 1766 he left teaching to enter business, and in 1777 he became the state's first governor. Bolzius himself early learned English well and did some teaching, but he was too busy with many other things to devote much time to formal instruction.

Under royal control there were two schoolmasters paid £32 a year out of the Parliamentary grant. At least one of these officiated at Savannah, but the location of the other is not certain. These schoolmasters undoubtedly supplemented this meager income by collecting fees from their students.

Gone after 1752 were the benevolence and the public spirit of the Trustee school in Savannah, which had been ably served by such high-minded men as Charles Delamotte, James Habersham, and John Dobell. After several incompetent schoolmasters, Alexander Findlay and James Seymour, both educated at the

University of Aberdeen, set up a school in Savannah in 1768. In April 1770, their school was visited by Governor James Wright, the Anglican rector Samuel Frink, members of the Assembly, and several other gentlemen "favored with a liberal education." The scholarly declamations of the students impressed the visiting dignitaries. One of them said that if properly encouraged, Seymour and Findlay could "bring the rising generation in Georgia to great proficiency in the several branches of literature which they profess to teach." But the encouragement did not come; and, in 1771, both schoolmasters abandoned Savannah and went to London where they took holy orders. Seymour returned to Georgia in December 1771 as an Anglican priest at Augusta.

For the wealthier children in the coastal area, elementary education was sometimes conducted by teachers in schools supported by several neighboring planters. Joseph and William Gibbons alternated a boarding school between their plantations yearly, hiring John Portrees as its master from 1762 to 1765. He also taught children of nearby planters at this school. He emphasized grammar and practical mathematics such as geometry, arithmetic, plane and spherical trigonometry, navigation, and surveying. At Midway, John Baker sponsored a small school; and the Foxes, McLeans, and Bourquins at Little Ogeechee joined together to hire a master for their children.

There were more than thirty private schools operated in the province at some time during the royal period. At Augusta, John Hammerer kept a school for "young gentlemen" until he moved to Savannah. James Beverly operated one for ten pupils at Sunbury, and David Hughes in St. George's Parish. Reading, writing, mathematics of various types, Latin, Greek, and French were the favorite subjects offered, with variations according to the inclinations and abilities of the schoolmaster.

In Savannah, besides the schools to teach children the ordinary subjects, there were more specialized schools. Here one could study bookkeeping, writing, languages, the fine points of swordsmanship and military drill, painting, fancy needlework, dancing, and many other subjects according to advertisements in the *Georgia Gazette*. Classes were taught morning, afternoon, and evening to suit the convenience of the students. Private instruction in the home was also offered, especially for ladies. Thomas Lee's school most resembled a military academy and, in 1760, his cadets formed a juvenile company which greeted Governor James Wright upon his arrival in the colony. At John Revear's a gentleman could learn self-defense while either sex might learn the secrets of "all the celebrated dances that are used in polite assemblies" in Europe.

By far the best school in Georgia was Bethesda, operated under the supervision of the often absent George Whitefield. Here students were exposed to religion, the classics, and trades. Whitefield and James Habersham emphasized that one of the purposes of instruction at Bethesda was to ensure that students were "qualified to get their own living" and, thus, would be "useful to mankind." A succession of Methodist-inclined clergymen gave religious and classical instruction. The artisan "members of the family" taught trades to the orphans and boarding students. Bethesda produced sound scholars who impressed Governor Wright in 1771 when he visited it. In the royal period Bethesda tended to emphasize education more and care of orphans less.

In 1764 Whitefield sought aid to turn Bethesda into a college. He received the approval of the provincial authorities, the land grant requested, and a favorable recommendation to London. In England in 1767 when he sought a royal charter for his college, Whitefield refused to accept the recommendation of Archbishop Thomas Secker that the faculty and religious liturgy be Anglican, and so he did not receive a charter. Whitefield had not given up the idea of establishing a college at Bethesda when he died in 1770 in Newburyport, Massachusetts, but with him the idea died for the colonial period.

Whitefield willed Bethesda to Selina, Countess of Huntingdon, his friend and a patron of English Methodists. She administered the school through the Reverend William Piercy, its president. In

Selina, the Countess of Huntingdon.

The Reverend William Piercy.

1773 a fire destroyed the principal building, the library, and chapel and essentially ended Bethesda's colonial career. It would be rebuilt later, and it still functions today.

In spite of Bethesda and the efforts of schoolmasters in royal Georgia, many of the colonists remained untaught in formal schools. In 1768, the Reverend Edward Ellington, the Anglican priest at Augusta, observed that people in the backcountry were illiterate while those in town were not. The children of some frontiersmen and ordinary farmers undoubtedly learned their A B Cs and figures from their parents and neighbors and many learned much that was necessary to life in forest and farm by practical experience and not in schoolrooms. Georgia's schools enjoyed an unenviable reputation; and some who could afford the expense and thought education important enough sent their sons to Charles Town, to the northern colonies, or to England to be educated. Frontier areas have never been noted for the excellence of their schools, and Georgia was no exception before 1775. The Savannah area, which included Bethesda, offered the best and widest selection of schools, while Augusta undoubtedly came second by 1775. Elsewhere in the colony, distance from centers of settlement and the preoccupation of the residents with the daily business of living kept the amount of formal education to a minimum.

Informal education of many Georgians was helped by the *Georgia Gazette*, the colony's first newspaper, founded by James Johnston in 1763 and operated by him for the rest of the colonial period. Johnston, a twenty-five-year-old recent arrival from Scotland and an excellent printer and editor, believed that his first duty was to present the news. He printed freely on both sides of the growing revolutionary agitation after 1765. Personally Johnston was tory in his sentiments, but he never let his personal feelings interfere with news coverage.

Besides clergymen, the only professional people in Georgia were a few doctors and lawyers. There is little positive knowledge as to how the doctors received their training, but it was probably under the apprenticeship system used in the colonies. The most common public health problem was smallpox, and inoculations were given by some doctors. The colony created a "lazaretto" or quarantine station below Savannah for incoming ships, especially slave ships, in 1767. There were a few lawyers who had attended the Inns of Court in London, like the governor and chief justice, but most learned their law by apprenticeship in Savannah or Charles Town.

There were several civic organizations in Savannah. The best known was the Union Society, founded by 1750, which paid for the schooling of worthy poor, oversaw and bound out orphans, and made presentations to outstanding citizens in recognition of their civic endeavors. The Masonic lodge, founded in 1734, continued its usual activities. From 1763 or earlier the Georgia Library Society maintained a circulating library for the benefit of its members. Purely social clubs in and near Savannah included the St. Andrew's Club, the Thunderbolt Club, and the Ugly Club. There may have been similar clubs in other areas, but their existence has not been discovered.

The king's birthday was the most elaborately celebrated holiday, with a militia muster and a dinner for civilian and military officers. Gunpowder Plot Day, St. George's Day, St. Patrick's Day, and St. Andrew's Day were celebrated by at least some of the people. Cricket matches and other athletic contests were held, but by far the most popular sport was horse racing. Races were held at Savannah, Augusta, Sunbury, and throughout the colony. Purses were sometimes as high as £60, but there must have been many races for the sheer joy they afforded. For the more intellectually inclined, there were readings, plays, and musicals. Visiting musicians and actors sometimes performed in Savannah, but there was no regular theater establishment in the town. Public balls were a favorite social activity. Savannah and other towns had taverns which served food and drink to natives and visitors, and many people spent their evenings at some public house with friends over a bowl of punch or a bottle of wine. Beyond a doubt, the most common form of entertainment for Georgians was informal dining and drinking at home or in the taverns.

Savannah remained the social center of the colony, but by the

1770s Augusta increased in importance as it became the economic and social center for the rapidly expanding up-country. But it had not equaled Savannah in its shops, entertainments, or society by 1776. In Savannah there were enough of the "better sort of people" to give some of the tone to society so ardently wished for by Governor Wright, but Georgia was essentially a colony of yeomen farmers and frontiersmen who enjoyed a rough and tumble society. It is difficult to document in detail the daily lives, recreations, and hopes and ambitions of the more numerous "lesser folk" because they left so few personal records. While most Georgians naturally deferred to their "betters" in government and other matters, they were not dictated to by an aristocracy, as the events of the revolutionary years illustrate. Georgians were just beginning to feel able to take care of themselves materially. Greater cultural achievements would have to await the conquest of the frontier.

13

REVOLUTIONARY BACKGROUND, 1765–1775: THE PATTERN QUESTIONED

The disruption of Georgia's and the other colonies' prosperity by rebellion in 1775 was not something which came suddenly and without warning. In Georgia, the troubles developed hesitantly over the prior decade, while in some other colonies signs of dissatisfaction with their colonial status were older. In all colonies revolt came on more rapidly and more positively in the decade before 1775. The Proclamation of 1763 with its prohibition of settlement beyond the crest of the Appalachian Mountains is frequently taken as the act which set off concerted colonial opposition to British policy and action in some colonies. There was no opposition to the proclamation in Georgia because settlement had not yet reached the line specified in it. In fact the exit of the Spanish and the French as close neighbors, the extension of the colony's boundary to the St. Marys River, and the Indian land cession of that year all made for increased satisfaction and inspired hope for a better future among Georgians.

If the proclamation line aroused real objections in only some colonies, the Stamp Act of 1765 aroused universal colonial opposition, including that of Georgians. In September of 1765,

before the Stamp Act troubles, naturalist John Bartram, traveling through Georgia, recorded in his diary that Governor James
Wright was "universally respected by all the inhabitants. They
can hardly say enough in his praise." This was a good assessment
of Wright's position in 1765. Two months later, after the Stamp
Act troubles had begun, it was no longer true. Never again would
Georgia or Wright know the tranquility and mutual admiration
for each other which had existed during the governor's first five
years in the colony.

When the Sugar Act, a general customs law applicable to the
colonies, was passed by Parliament in April of 1764 the British
ministry announced that the next year a colonial stamp act
would be proposed. The Massachusetts House of Representatives
dispatched a circular letter to all colonial assemblies protesting
colonial taxation by Parliament. Five months later, in March
1765, the Georgia Assembly voted to instruct the Georgia agent
in London to protest the Sugar Act and the proposed Stamp Act
on economic grounds. The Assembly committee said that the
proposed stamp duty was "as equal as any" but that the manner
of imposing it was objectionable and the added financial burden
was too great for Georgians to bear. After the passage of the
Stamp Act in March of 1765 the Assembly further instructed its
agent to join other colonial agents in London in working for
repeal.

Again the Massachusetts House of Representatives issued a
circular letter, this time inviting the colonies to send delegates to
a congress called in New York for October to oppose the Stamp
Act. The Georgia Assembly was not in session when this
invitation arrived; but Alexander Wylly, the Speaker, invited all
members of the Commons House to meet him in Savannah to
discuss the matter. Sixteen of the twenty-five members responded, but Governor Wright opposed sending delegates to the
congress and refused to call the Assembly into session to permit
official action. Wylly wrote Massachusetts that no delegates
would be sent to the congress but that Georgia was concerned
with the welfare of the colonies and would support whatever
action the congress took.

Until late October objections to the Stamp Act remained verbal in Georgia, but through the *Georgia Gazette* Georgians learned of the many resolutions objecting to the Stamp Act being passed in other colonies. When the Assembly met on October 22, the Commons House thanked its Speaker for his response to the Massachusetts circular. On October 25, the anniversary of the accession of George III to the throne, and on November 5, Gunpowder Plot or Guy Fawkes Day, sailors and others carried effigies representing a stamp distributor about the streets of Savannah. Thus was the current opposition to the Stamp Act combined with the usual frivolity of the day. There was no trouble, but public opinion seemed clearly against the Stamp Act. With the law scheduled to go into effect on November 1, late October and early November were exciting. The Sons of Liberty, "Sons of Licentiousness" the governor labeled them, met at MacHenry's Tavern in Savannah and agreed when the stamp distributor appeared in Georgia to inform him of the unpopularity of his office.

Nowhere did Governor Wright record his own feelings about the Stamp Act, but he was undoubtedly too good a colonial to approve it, and there is considerable circumstantial evidence that he personally opposed the act or thought it unwise. James Habersham, the senior councilor, made his own opposition quite clear. Of course, for neither of these men would personal opposition to the Stamp Act interfere with its enforcement. Both considered themselves loyal servants to the king and bound to do his bidding.

On November 1, the day the Stamp Act went into effect, there were no stamps in Georgia, no stamp distributor, nor even a copy of the act. Wright and his Council decided to close the land office and suspend the courts but allow vessels to clear customs with endorsements on their papers that stamps were not available. In late November, Wright got a copy of the Stamp Act "in a Private way" and took the oaths required by it. On December 4 the port of Savannah was closed, and on December 5 the first stamps arrived in Georgia. Some sixty vessels were in the river, a number of them ready to sail, but no stamp distributor had yet arrived.

The governor and Council decided that a temporary distributor might be appointed upon a "general application" for one, and some merchants circulated a petition for such an appointment, but it does not appear to have been presented to the governor.

On the afternoon of January 2, 1766, the captain of the fifty-six rangers whom Wright had called into town to guard the stamps informed him that about two hundred liberty people had assembled. Afraid that they would destroy the stamps, Wright with musket in hand took personal charge of the rangers and confronted a crowd assembled at his own gate. They asked if he intended to appoint a temporary stamp distributor. He replied that their action was hardly "the manner to wait upon the governor" and that he would do his duty to the king if he received a request to make a temporary appointment. The crowd dispersed, vowing to reassemble whenever the governor took any action. Wright next led the rangers in the removal of the stamps from the storehouse at Fort Halifax on the outskirts of town to the guardhouse in the center of town where he thought they would be safer. The rangers guarded the stamps while a town patrol of merchants, clerks, and sailors was set up. The governor spent the several following nights fully clothed and ready for instant action.

The next day George Angus, an Englishman and the only non-American stamp distributor in the colonies, arrived at Tybee and was brought to Wright's house, without incident, where he began distributing stamped papers to the customs officers. On January 7, after an informal understanding between the merchants and the Liberty Boys, the port was opened and clearance of the waiting vessels with stamped paper carried out—the only stamps sold in any of the thirteen colonies which rebelled. After the clearance of the vessels, there seems to have been a general agreement not to buy any more stamps until the royal pleasure on repeal was known. Distributor Angus soon went "into the country to avoid the resentment of the people," and after a brief return to Savannah in late March he disappeared from Georgia's history.

After threats from the country in early January and efforts of

Wright to appeal to the "better sort" of people outside Savannah, there was peace until late January. There were rumors that several hundred people from the backcountry, stirred up by incendiaries from Charles Town, were marching on Savannah to prevent the further sale of stamps, prompting Wright to send the stamps for safekeeping with the rangers to Fort George on Cockspur Island below the town. The threatened "invasion" of Savannah did not take place on January 31. Governor Wright believed that with the help of "well disposed" gentlemen he had induced several hundred of the backcountrymen to turn back. Rumors were rife: the governor was to be shot if he was not amenable to the Liberty Boys; those who had supported the governor were in danger; and James Habersham was warned not to be at home for several nights. On February 2 H.M.S. *Speedwell*, which had brought the stamps to Savannah, returned, and Wright immediately had the stamps transferred from Fort George to the vessel by which they soon left Georgia.

On February 4 the liberty people from the country finally marched into Savannah with guns, flags, and drums; but they were too late. Wright had his rangers back in Savannah, along with twenty sailors from the *Speedwell* and other armed supporters from the citizens—nearly one hundred men in all. Faced with such opposition, the liberty people disputed among themselves as to their course of action and soon left, saying in parting that the four hundred to five hundred men promised from South Carolina had not arrived.

Throughout the Stamp Act excitement Wright and his Council worked together closely and were united in a determination to enforce the act. Wright's success lay in his having had a plan worked out beforehand which allowed him to take the initiative and to act decisively. He tried to work privately through influential colonists rather than through public statements and proclamations. He always insisted, with some truth, that things would have been much quieter in Georgia had it not been for the continual urgings from the Sons of Liberty in Charles Town. In fact, Wright tended to blame all of Georgia's troubles on Charles Town, hardly a correct assessment. The governor complained to London that his actions were limited by the absence of troops to keep order, but he insisted that had he called out the militia, he would have armed more against than for himself.

Membership of the Sons of Liberty in Georgia remains a mystery as none were ever identified by Wright, Habersham, or others who wrote of their activities. They were probably Savannah artisans and small merchants and perhaps the sons of some colonial leaders and certainly were known to Wright, Habersham, and others. Undoubtedly, as in other colonies, there was a small leadership cadre who influenced the mobs usually referred to as Liberty Boys by Wright and others who described their doings.

Interestingly enough, the Assembly was in session during most of the Stamp Act troubles. Its session began October 22, 1764, and lasted until March 6, 1766, with a Christmas recess from December 19 to January 14, the period when stamps were actually sold in Georgia. This was, from the records, a normal session in which the recommendations of the governor were generally carried out. The only mention of the Stamp Act was the adoption by the Commons House of the petitions and the memorial from the Stamp Act Congress. Their adoption and dispatch to England came just as the act went into effect in Georgia. At no time was there any communication between the Assembly and governor about the Stamp Act, a clear indication that many Georgians did not agree with the objections of the Liberty Boys and their mobs.

The colony's only newspaper, the *Georgia Gazette*, ceased publication when the Stamp Act went into effect because stamps were required for newspapers and did not resume publication until May 21, 1766, when it carried a notice that the repeal of the act was being considered in Parliament. When, in July, Wright called the Assembly into session to inform it officially that the Stamp Act had been repealed, he and the Commons House congratulated each other that there had been no violence or property damage and that the Assembly had not questioned the supremacy of Parliament or crown in America. Both houses thanked the king for repeal and for his consideration for the happiness of his American subjects. Wright was sure there were still Georgians with a "strange idea of liberty" not changed by the repeal, but he sincerely hoped and believed they were in a small minority. As a part of the celebration in Savannah, the Reverend John J. Zubly preached a special sermon, "The Stamp Act Repealed," acknowledging that American liberties had been upheld in repeal but careful to point out the difference between liberty and licentiousness.

One result of the Stamp Act was a controversy over Georgia's colonial agent in London who was William Knox, provost marshal of Georgia, former resident, plantation owner, and friend of Wright and Habersham. Knox was lukewarm in carrying out his instructions to object to the Sugar Act and the Stamp Act. Instead he published a pamphlet, *The Claim of the Colonies to an Exemption from Internal Taxes Imposed by Authority of Parliament Examined*, in which he defended the right of Parliamentary taxation. Part of his pamphlet was published anonymously in the *Georgia Gazette* in August of 1765 but soon was known to be Knox's work. This aroused considerable objection in Georgia, and on November 15 the Commons House resolved that Knox's services as agent were no longer needed. The Upper House, by contrast, voted its thanks to Knox for satisfactory services. The Commons House asked Charles Garth, South Carolina's agent in London, to present its petitions and memorial against the Stamp Act. Garth, a member of the House of Commons, had voted for the Stamp Act, but his vote must not have been known in Georgia.

When the Assembly met in the fall of 1766, the Commons House passed an ordinance appointing Garth as Georgia's agent. The Upper House refused to agree to this, pointing out that the same agent could not satisfactorily represent both Georgia and South Carolina in London where arguments between the two colonies frequently had to be adjudicated. The Commons House included Garth's salary in the tax bill and refused a conference requested by the Upper House on the principle that the Upper House could not amend money bills. The Upper House passed the tax bill under protest and thus lost its argument with the Commons House, but the Council refused to pass Garth's voucher when it was presented for payment.

The Stamp Act convinced Governor Wright more than ever of his own abilities and success as governor. He was the only governor of the thirteen colonies later to rebel who succeeded in enforcing the Stamp Act at all. This success may have led him to exercise less patience with future opposition in Georgia and thus hurt the British side in the rapidly developing argument.

On the other hand, the troubles also aroused an opposition, not yet organized or identifiable, which could be mustered to object to other unpopular British actions. This opposition would make life more unpleasant for the governor, and the principle of Parliamentary as against colonial rights raised by the Stamp Act crisis would haunt Wright, future legislatures, and many Georgians thereafter.

With the repeal of the Stamp Act in 1766, many hoped that peace and quiet would return; but it did not. In January of 1767 Wright transmitted to the Assembly a request for barracks necessities for the troops stationed in Georgia. Under the terms of the Parliamentary Mutiny Act of 1765, a colony must furnish troops stationed within its borders with light and heat, beds and bedding, cooking utensils, and rum or beer. The Commons House, influenced by the Stamp Act, promptly refused the request on the grounds that it would violate the trust of the people in the assemblymen and set a dangerous precedent. Two months later, when word arrived that the provincial rangers were to be disbanded, the Commons House asked Wright to request that General Gage send more troops to Georgia to replace the disbanded rangers. When Wright reminded the House that its refusal of barracks necessities would discourage the dispatch of any further troops, it passed a resolution making a daily allowance to every officer and soldier in the colony, but the House's refusal to send the resolution to the Upper House for concurrence resulted in no funds being paid to the troops.

Another argument involving Parliamentary authority concerned a statute of Queen Anne's reign that required postmen to be provided free passage on ferries. In the spring of 1767 the Commons House provided for two ferries without including free passage for postmen. The Upper House, at Wright's request, amended the bills to provide free passage. The Commons House objected that it could not submit to the enforcement of the Parliamentary statutes, and the ferry bill was lost.

The Commons House and the Upper House quarreled over the creation of a quarantine station on Tybee Island. The Commons House, which framed the bill in March of 1767, filled in the names of all the commissioners to supervise the installation, instead of leaving some vacant to be supplied by the Upper House as was the usual practice. The Commons House then refused any amendments of the Upper House on the grounds that this was a money bill. The Upper House, in turn, objected to this interpretation of a money bill and requested a conference to iron out the differences. The Commons House went along reluctantly and accepted the amendments of the Upper House, which included two of its members as commissioners. In this instance the Upper House's insistence on its prerogatives was sufficient to return the Commons House to its usual procedure, and the governor did not have to intercede in the argument.

In reviewing the actions of the Commons House after this session, Wright said that he feared the sovereignty of Britain had received a wound from which it would never recover. The Commons House, to thwart the sovereignty of Britain, had sought to reduce the weight of the Upper House and of the governor in the legislative process. Yet this Commons House had also carried out Wright's recommendations to the Assembly.

The contrast between the spring 1767 Assembly session, just narrated, and the spring 1768 session is very great. In the latter, the Commons House gave in on almost every point of contention, claiming to have been misunderstood by the governor in the former session, and making no recorded objections to his stern rebuke for its past actions. When the Upper House again objected to Garth as agent, the Commons House now agreed to Benjamin Franklin instead. It also agreed to a ferry bill which established five ferries with free passage for postmen. After

Dr Franklyn ——————— To Willm Pickett Dr

1770

Aprl 16 A Sett of Silver Buckles — 1.0.0

June 18 A Chased Mace 154 g 16 oz 9/1 d3 — 69.13.3

Gilding it all over at 2/3 d3 — 17.6.4

Red Leather Case to Ditto — 1.2.0

Graving Inscription — 0.2.0

Packing Box — 0.4.6

£ 89.8.1

Recd June 21. 1773 the Contents in full
of all Demands for Mr Pickett

P. Philip Purnell

A bill of Agent Benjamin Franklin for a mace for the Georgia Assembly.

General Gage's refusal to send additional troops without provision for barracks necessities and a specific command from the king to obey the Mutiny Act, the Commons House also included funds for this purpose in the appropriation bill. There are no recorded reasons for this change of position, but probably the Commons House decided that it could not dominate the governor and Upper House as it had tried to do in 1767 and get their cooperation or that of London in the necessary public business.

Undoubtedly much of the objection of the Commons House to Parliamentary legislation was a part of its fight for legislative superiority over the Upper House. Until the argument of Parliamentary authority arose, there had been little reason for the Commons House to assert its power at the expense of the Upper House. In fact, both houses had usually followed the governor's lead, and there had been little disagreement between them or the governor. Undoubtedly the Commons House attempted too much in 1767 and felt it necessary to make a strategic retreat the next year.

When he dissolved the Assembly at the request of the Commons House in April 1768, Governor Wright seemed to have won all his points of contention with that House. In reality, considerable damage had been done to his position and influence during the last three years. He would never again be the undisputed leader of the colony as he had been before the Stamp Act troubles, and as an astute politician, James Wright undoubtedly realized this. A new election, following the dissolution, was clearly a contest between Wright's supporters and the Liberty Boys. Two-thirds of the old Commons House was reelected; and eighteen out of the twenty-five were avowed Sons of Liberty. More than one-half of this Commons House was to sit in the Provincial Congress which met in July of 1775. Wright said that he was not surprised at the outcome of the election, but he must have been disappointed. The governor foresaw trouble over the old problem of Garth's salary, but none developed.

However, serious difficulties did arise over the Townshend Acts. At the time of the repeal of the Stamp Act in 1766 colonials had chosen to ignore the Declaratory Act which asserted Parliament's right to bind the colonies in all cases whatsoever, but Chancellor of the Exchequer Charles Townshend made clear with his new revenue act of 1767 that the declaration of Parliamentary sovereignty was not mere rhetoric. This act had caused some dissatisfaction in Georgia before the winter's legislative sessions but not enough to be a serious problem in the spring election of 1768. From January 27 through April 27, 1768, John Dickinson's *Letters of a Pennsylvania Farmer*, protesting the new trade measures, were published in the *Georgia Gazette*, along with considerable favorable comment. The Assembly, before its dissolution, instructed agent Franklin to work for repeal of the act.

The Massachusetts House of Representatives again distributed a circular letter against the Townshend Revenue Act, and Secretary of State Hillsborough instructed colonial governors to dissolve any assemblies which considered the Massachusetts circular. Wright relayed these instructions to the Commons House when it met in November of 1768, and the House assured him that no such letter had been laid before it and that it would proceed to its regular business. During the next month the Commons House considered routine matters, including the tax bill, a matter traditionally left until the end of the session. The Assembly also stayed in session longer into December than was usual. It finally requested the governor to approve the bills already passed on December 24 and adjourn it until January 9. Shortly before the scheduled meeting with the governor, the Commons House adopted a "dutiful and loyal address" to the king in which it avowed its readiness to acknowledge its constitutional subordination to Parliament but objected that Parliamentary taxation was a violation of the "indubitable right" of the colonists to grant away their own property. The House also considered the Massachusetts and Virginia circulars against the Townshend Act and declared them a very proper exercise of the right to petition the throne, a right of all British subjects.

These actions had all taken place so quickly that Wright was helpless to do anything to prevent them. He approved the acts passed and dissolved the Assembly as he had told the Commons House he would if it considered the circulars. In his dissolution speech, Wright placed all the blame for the trouble upon the Commons House, maintaining that it was impossible for Parliament to be the supreme legislature of the empire and not have the right to tax the colonists.

Throughout the first half of 1769 the protests and resolutions of other colonies against the Townshend duties were published in the *Georgia Gazette* but roused no vocal objections within the colony. Even the South Carolina nonimportation agreement published in July had no immediate effect, and Wright could say the next month that things were "quiet and happy." But on September 6, 1769, the *Gazette* carried an invitation to Georgians to uphold their rights as Englishmen by opposing the Townshend duties and called upon all to meet in Savannah to consider ways of obtaining relief from these burdens.

September 16 saw a meeting of some Savannah merchants who protested the act. They promised to cancel their orders to Britain and to purchase no more items taxed by the new duties. On September 19 a general mass meeting of the colony assembled in Savannah and passed resolutions objecting to the Townshend Act, providing for nonimportation of British goods with a considerable list of exceptions, and encouraging manufacturing. Georgia's nonimportation agreement followed the outline of South Carolina's, but it contained no enforcement machinery nor were there attempts to secure individual signatures of adherents. Jonathan Bryan, a member of the Governor's Council, presided at this meeting and was suspended from the Council for his action.

The fact that there was no attempted enforcement of the nonimportation agreement is explained by the irresolute feeling of most Georgians. Many, including a majority of the merchants, seem to have opposed nonimportation, and there was no evidence of concern outside Savannah. Certainly public opinion was much less vocal than it had been against the Stamp Act. There was no reason to object to the use of the income from the duties to pay colonial officials, as Georgia's royal officials had always been paid by Parliamentary grant. One disappointed Liberty Boy consoled himself with the prospect that Savannah might become the chief exporter of Carolina produce once the port of Charles Town was closed. Wright ignored the Savannah meetings, apparently believing that they would accomplish little and that objections from him might cause more trouble than they would prevent.

Wright was afraid that the new Assembly would enter into resolutions on the Townshend Acts when it met in October of 1769, but it contented itself with entering the Virginia resolutions upon its journal without comment. The Commons House began work upon the Governor's recommendations and the needs of the colony. Since a 1765 act had been disallowed, the Assembly had been trying to frame a slave code which would be approved in London. The delays in this needed legislation had become exasperating to the assemblymen. The Commons House now passed a bill without the required suspending clause and sent it to the Upper House. The Upper House refused to pass the bill, and the Commons House finally agreed to the clause from necessity only and "not from any Conviction" that such a clause ought to be required.

In considering the tax bill in November, the Commons House discovered that it had been practicing taxation without representation upon the four southern parishes created in 1765. Hence on November 15, 1769, the Commons House requested Governor Wright to issue writs of election for these parishes. Wright agreed on the desirability of representation but said he could not issue writs of election without specific permission from London, which he would request immediately. The Commons House objected to this reply and said that it dare not impose a tax unless the four parishes were represented. After a protracted argument between the two houses, a tax bill was passed which excused the four parishes, "they not being represented."

At the Assembly session in October 1770, the same argument with the governor was repeated. This time the Commons House refused even to enact a tax bill. During this argument, Thomas

Moodie, deputy secretary of the colony, declined to take an oath when giving testimony before a Commons House committee. Such oaths had not been required in the past, and Moodie insisted that he would not establish such a precedent. The House voted this a breach of its privilege and contempt of the committee and had Moodie arrested and imprisoned in the common jail during its pleasure.

Wright considered the refusal to pass a tax bill and the requirement of oaths for testimony to be improper actions of the Commons House, and he informed the Speaker that unless the two objectionable resolutions were removed from the House's journal, he would dissolve the Assembly. At the same time Wright told the Speaker that permission had just been received from London to allow representation to the southern parishes. When the Commons House did not reconsider its actions in its next business day, but talked of its rights instead, Wright dissolved the Assembly on February 22, 1771.

In future assemblies the southern parishes were represented and taxed. To prevent such trouble again, after the 1773 Indian cession, Wright requested permission to allow representation when there were a hundred families or voters in that area. This request was promptly approved in London, but no representatives were chosen from this area prior to the revolutionary troubles.

As no legislation had been enacted by the 1770-71 session, Wright immediately ordered new elections. Most of the members of the old Assembly were elected to the new one. When this Assembly met in April 1771, the Commons House unanimously elected Noble Wimberly Jones, a leading Son of Liberty, as its speaker. Wright rejected Jones, a privilege which his instructions gave him but which had never been exercised in Georgia before. The House thereupon elected Archibald Bulloch, fully as radical as Jones, and Wright accepted him. The next day the House declared the rejection of the Speaker "a high Breach of the Privilege of the House." When Wright's private efforts to get this resolution rescinded proved of no avail, he dissolved the Assembly upon its third day.

Noble W. Jones.

In July the governor departed for a leave of almost two years in England, and during his absence James Habersham, the senior councilor, served as acting governor. Habersham, like Wright, had grown wealthy and important in Georgia and was a true servant of the king. He had no political ambition and considered himself aged and infirm at fifty-eight. Habersham did not call a new election until the excitement of the dissolution had cooled. His instructions were to disapprove the Speaker of the Commons House when it met in order to establish the precedent of the governor's power.

When the Assembly met in April 1772, it unanimously elected Noble W. Jones its Speaker, and Habersham disapproved him. The Commons House elected Jones again and Habersham disapproved him. The Commons House elected Jones a third time, but this time he himself refused. The House then elected Archibald Bulloch, and Habersham approved him. Several days later, learning of the third election of Jones, Habersham informed the House that it must remove the minute of this last election from its journal or be dissolved. The House said that this last election was not intended as disrespectful to the king or to Habersham nor as an infringement of the prerogative, and it insisted upon letting the minute stand on its journal. Habersham thereupon dissolved the Assembly.

When a new Assembly met in December 1772, the Commons House elected Noble W. Jones as Speaker, but he declined and William Young was elected instead. Habersham said he told some of the assemblymen that he could not do business with Jones, who then declined in order to prevent a further dissolution. This Assembly passed the first legislation since 1769, and there was not another dissolution in colonial Georgia. The repeated dissolutions over the rights of the legislature as opposed to those of the crown and Parliament showed that neither side would surrender its position. The Commons House had made a strategic retreat, but it did not modify its stand. Still, in order to get on with the business of the colony, both sides seemed willing to compromise a little. All the Townshend duties except that on tea had been repealed and from 1771 through 1773 generally there was peace in the colonies.

Governor Wright, now Sir James Wright, Bart., returned to Georgia in mid-February of 1773 and was welcomed by committees of both houses of the Assembly. Wright's elevation to the nobility was the result of his actions as governor of Georgia. Rumor had it that he was soon to be appointed to the Board of Trade, a position that he undoubtedly would have liked; but nothing came of this. Wright found the Assembly likely to cooperate upon his return, as it did for the next two years.

Wright's great victory for the colony while he was in England was in securing approval for an Indian land cession north and west of the settled area which he and most Georgians were anxious to obtain to permit the continued growth of the colony. Movement towards this land cession had begun in 1771 when the traders to the Cherokees offered to cancel all Cherokee debts and furnish the Indians with additional goods for a cession of about sixty miles square north and west of Augusta. The Cherokees agreed to such a cession in early 1771, but it had yet to be made official, and to this end Wright and Indian Superintendent John Stuart met the Indians at Augusta in May of 1773. The Cherokee cession was complicated by the fact that part of the land was claimed by the Creeks, who were not anxious to cede it. They were offered similar terms to those given to the Cherokees, and agreed to the cession. The land involved comprised some 1,600,000 acres between the Savannah and the Ogeechee and Oconee north and west of the 1763 cession and about 500,000 acres between the Ogeechee and Altamaha ceded by the Creeks alone. Wright and the Assembly wanted more lands between the Ogeechee and Oconee, but the Indians would not agree.

The fact that many Creeks opposed this cession and that whites rushed in rapidly resulted in considerable Indian troubles during the next two years but not in the all-out Indian war which many expected. The northern part of this cession contained very fertile land and attracted many people from the Carolinas and Virginia until the revolutionary troubles erupted.

A problem which did not affect governor-Assembly relations

concerned the issuance of writs of assistance in 1772 and 1773. The attorney general applied for these general search warrants used to fight smuggling in both years. British-reared and educated Chief Justice Anthony Stokes favored the issuance of the writs, but the local assistant justices outvoted him, so no writs were issued.

When the Assembly met in late June of 1773, both houses thanked Wright for his endeavors in securing the recently ceded Indian lands; and this session was marked by harmony between the governor and the Commons House. When the Assembly reconvened in January 1774, Indian troubles resulting from the too-rapid settlement of the 1773 cession united the Assembly and governor in a request to London for troops to protect the settlers. Had troops been sent they might have helped to convince Georgians of the concern of the British government for their welfare, but none were.

In March the Commons House again sought to appoint Benjamin Franklin as the colony's agent in London, but the Upper House refused to agree on the grounds that Franklin had done nothing to earn his yearly salary since appointment. The Commons House on the last day of the session voted that it should have the appointment of the agent entirely in its hands, that he should obey its instructions, and that the agent should be Franklin. Wright requested London not to receive any agent appointed only by the Commons House, but no decision had been reached on this matter when the revolutionary troubles erupted the next year.

The recent harmony between Wright and the Commons House was shattered by the Boston Tea Party of December 1773 and the British reaction. The four Intolerable Acts passed by Parliament the following spring set off new protests in America. In May the dissolved Virginia House of Burgesses sent out invitations to an intercolonial congress to consider American-British relations. By July South Carolina was selecting delegates to the congress, and such activity in Charles Town prompted similar action in Savannah. An invitation signed by Noble W. Jones, Archibald Bulloch, John Houstoun, and George Walton invited Georgians to a meeting at the "liberty pole" at Tondee's Tavern in Savannah on July 27 to consider the critical situation in the colonies. At this meeting letters and resolutions from several other colonies were read and a committee appointed to draw up resolutions for consideration by a second meeting called for August 10 to which every parish was asked to send the same number of delegates that it had in the Commons House of Assembly.

Governor Wright issued a proclamation against such assemblages but every parish was represented when the August meeting was held. The main work of this body was the adoption of resolutions which constituted the first real statement of revolutionary sentiment in Georgia. Americans were affirmed to be entitled to all the rights, privileges, and immunities of Britons, especially the "clear and indisputable right" to petition the throne. The Boston Port Bill was denounced as "contrary to our idea of the British constitution" because it deprived people of property without judgment of their peers, because it was *ex post facto*, and because it punished the guilty and the innocent indiscriminately. The abolition of the Massachusetts charter was condemned as tending to subvert American rights. Parliament was criticized for attempting to tax Americans without representation and was urged to rely on requisitions upon colonial assemblies instead. The transportation of defendants for trial to England was criticized as contrary to natural justice and law. The meeting announced its concurrence with other colonies in all constitutional measures to obtain redress of grievances, and its membership was named a general committee to take further necessary action and to correspond with other colonies. These resolutions contained no new or startling ideas but were rather a statement of grievances by loyal subjects—a procedure which had a long and hallowed tradition in English history.

This meeting debated the sending of delegates to the First Continental Congress soon to meet in Philadelphia, but decided to send none, probably because too many Georgians were still undecided. This failure to act could not be blamed on Governor Wright, as had Georgia's absence from the Stamp Act Congress.

Wright did not think it advisable to oppose these resolutions publicly, but he did aid in securing petitions from at least four parishes objecting to the meeting, signed by 633 persons, including a number of future leaders in the revolutionary movement as well as future tories. When these petitions were published in the *Georgia Gazette* they inspired a series of counter petitions objecting to the way the signatures had been secured and pointing out that the number who signed was small when compared to the total voting strength of the colony. The one thing that this meeting and the opposing petitions made clear was how badly divided Georgians were over their rights and the issue of loyalty to Britain in 1774.

St. John's Parish, greatly disappointed in having no Georgians in attendance at the Continental Congress, made another effort about the end of August to send delegates in conjunction with St. George's, St. David's, and St. Andrew's parishes. Dr. Lyman Hall was chosen from St. John's, but he did not attend the Continental Congress probably because he felt that he could not speak for all of Georgia. Late in 1774 Wright reported that things were tolerably quiet, but he expected troubles again when something new excited the people. Wright, in a good analysis of American conditions a few months earlier, had said that America was now grown so large and strong that a constitutional settlement of the question of British authority, especially the matter of taxation, needed to be made. Otherwise colonial troubles would continue.

December saw the beginning of the troubles which Wright expected. There was much published in the *Gazette* for and against the Association adopted by the Continental Congress. A December 3 Savannah assemblage suggested that a provincial congress meet in January to consider the recommendations of the Continental Congress and American problems. Elections to this congress in at least some of the parishes followed the same procedure as those for members of the Commons House of Assembly.

St. John's Parish, at a parish meeting on December 6, adopted the Association and urged other parishes to do likewise. St.

Andrew's Parish did so in January. Objections to recent British actions and the Intolerable Acts were voiced with the statement that "such oppression neither we nor our fathers were able to bear, and it drove us to the wilderness." The gathering also resolved, "We hereby declare our disapprobation and abhorrence of the unnatural practice of Slavery in America, . . . founded in injustice and cruelty, and highly dangerous to our liberties (as well as lives,) debasing part of our fellow creatures below men, and corrupting the virtue and morals of the rest, and [it] is laying the basis of the liberty we contend for . . . upon a very wrong foundation. We therefore resolve, at all times to use our utmost endeavours for the manumission of our Slaves in this Colony, for the more safe and equitable footing for the masters and themselves."

Governor Wright informed London that he intended to make one more attempt to oppose the Liberty Boys and to keep Georgia out of rebellion. He was sure that two hundred troops and a sloop of war would facilitate his efforts. He believed that there would be a decision one way or the other soon, and he would welcome it.

The Assembly met in Savannah on January 17, 1775, and the Provincial Congress the next day. Five parishes—Christ Church, St. Paul, St. Matthew, St. Andrew, and St. George—sent delegates to the Congress. St. John would not join the Congress because it said the parish's acceptance of the Association prevented its joining with nonassociates. Six members of the Congress were also members of the Commons House and others had been former members. The Congress elected Archibald Bulloch, Noble W. Jones, and John Houstoun as delegates to the Second Continental Congress, and the Continental Association was adopted with some amendments. The Congress felt limited by its representation of only five parishes and by badly divided public opinion. Feeling that it had done all that it could do, it adjourned on January 25 hoping that the Assembly would endorse its actions.

Wright in his opening address to the Assembly showed the true concern of a man who believed in the complete powers of the British government and the rights of the colonists as well. He was, he said, an advocate of liberty in a legal and constitutional way. Both houses replied that they were worried over imperial relations and colonial rights, but they were not able to agree about how to safeguard these rights. The Commons House approved the resolves of the Continental Congress and agreed to elect delegates to the next Continental Congress. Wright prorogued the Assembly on February 10 to prevent its adoption of the resolutions of the Provincial Congress.

Georgia's delegates to the Second Continental Congress did not attend because they did not feel that they could speak for a majority of the colony's population. Instead they sent a report of recent happenings in Georgia and assured the Congress that there were men in Georgia who would prove their attachment to American liberties. A month later Noble W. Jones said he thought nine out of ten Georgians were in agreement with the other colonists, but this estimate was undoubtedly too high and did not accurately reflect the division still evident in Georgia.

Only St. John's and St. Andrew's parishes had adopted the Continental Association, leaving trade still open for the rest of Georgia. This traffic was stopped in May by South Carolina, some other provinces, and the Continental Congress. St. John's, highly indignant about the lukewarm stand of other Georgians, tried to become a part of South Carolina and to trade with Charles Town, but this was not allowed by that colony. St. John's elected Dr. Lyman Hall as its delegate to the Second Continental Congress and sent him to Philadelphia with two hundred barrels of rice and £50 in cash for the relief of the poor of Boston. Hall was joyfully received by the Congress.

Despite the difficulty of ardent whigs in getting Georgia to support the Continental Congress, royal officials were having even more trouble enforcing their authority during the first half of 1775. In mid-February attempts to seize illegal imports at Savannah resulted in the tarring and feathering of a tide waiter and the disappearance of the illegal goods. In spite of the special proclamation issued by Wright requiring the Assembly to meet in May, the Commons House refused, and the Assembly was prorogued until November 7.

News of the battles of Lexington and Concord arrived in Savannah on May 10. The next night the public powder magazine was opened by a mob and most of the powder stored there removed. This powder was used by Georgia and South Carolina whigs, and there is a tradition that some of it was sent to Boston and used at the Battle of Bunker Hill. On June 2 the twenty-one cannon on the battery in Savannah were spiked and thrown down the bluff to prevent their being used in the king's birthday celebration. Some of the cannon were recovered, drilled out, and fired in the celebrations. On June 5 the governor, his Council, and some gentlemen drank to the king's health under the flagpole. On the same day whigs erected a liberty pole and then retired to Tondee's long room for an "elegant dinner." There they spent the day in the "utmost harmony" concluding with toasts to the king, American liberty, no taxation without representation, and speedy reconciliation between Britain and America upon constitutional principles.

When word arrived in June that one small cruiser and one hundred soldiers requested by Wright to uphold his authority had been approved by London, Wright and his Council agreed that at least five hundred troops and two vessels would be necessary to do any good. Hence the orders for the transfer of the troops to Georgia were countermanded by Wright. In late June a vessel seized at Sunbury for illegal trading was freed by a mob. In June and July the public storehouse was entered and guns, shot, and other military stores were taken by the whigs. On July 10 when a vessel with gunpowder for the Indian trade arrived in Savannah, Georgia and South Carolina whigs removed the powder below the town and divided it between the two colonies. In June and July Wright's mail passing through Charles Town began to be opened by the Charles Town whig secret committee, and letters to General Thomas Gage and Admiral Thomas Graves saying things were well in Georgia were substituted for the ones telling of troubles.

By July Wright and leading whigs were agreed that Georgia was lost to the British and under the control of the whigs. Friends of royal government were falling off daily because they received no support. Wright said that he could not bear the daily insults and that a king's governor was now powerless in Georgia, hence he requested leave to return to England. Though he found his and Georgia's situation intolerable, he was forced to endure it six months longer.

During the summer of 1775, more people took sides for or against Britain. In their analysis, many Georgians still found adequate reasons to remain loyal to Britain. Georgia was a poor and young colony with only twenty years of self-government. She had numerous Indian neighbors still loyal to British Indian Superintendent John Stuart. Her undefended coastline and the British garrison at St. Augustine made her easily subject to military and naval attacks if a rupture came.

Georgia's diverse population also affected the division. The backbone of the population was English, but this made no appreciable difference in sentiment for or against the mother country. Recent immigrants from England tended to be tory. The Highland Scots in St. Andrew's Parish were mainly whig from the beginning, probably because of the length of time they had been in America. The Scotch-Irish on the frontier were somewhat slower in making up their mind, but most of them eventually became whig. The Scots most likely to be tories were the Indian traders, often recent immigrants who worked closely with the British Indian Department. The Ebenezer Germans, with no background of self-government and the beneficiaries of religious toleration and economic prosperity, were slow to rebel; but in the end they split, with probably the majority becoming whig. The small number of Jews were whigs from the beginning.

Religious divisions had some effect also. The Anglican laity was split, frequently including leaders on both sides. Anglican clergy tended to be tory. The strong religious bodies in Georgia were the Congregationalists in St. John's Parish, the Lutherans at Ebenezer, and Zubly's Presbyterian Meeting House in Savannah. The Congregationalists were whigs from the first and never changed. Lutherans tended to be tory at first and Zubly's congregation whig; but in the end both split. Quakers at Wrightsborough were pacifists and so were frequently classified as tories. Certainly the varied elements in the population, the language difference of the Germans, and the physical isolation of several groups made concerted effort to secure anti-British action difficult and probably delayed whig recruits. Revolutionists needed frequent contact and cross-fertilization of ideas—all difficult in a colony like Georgia.

The caliber and influence of leading officials was a reason why Georgia moved slower in early revolutionary activities than most other colonies. Governor Wright was by far the most important and influential royal official, and without him Georgia's actions and their timing undoubtedly would have been different. Wright was always a loyal servant of the king, even when he did not think British actions wise. His knowledge of the colonial mind, his personal stake in Georgia, the competent manner in which he performed, and the high regard in which he was held by the colonists helped him to keep ahead of his opposition and never to allow it to take leadership away from him until mid-1775. He certainly delayed the movement of many Georgians toward the whigs, even if he could not prevent it in the end.

Two important supporters of Wright were Noble Jones and James Habersham, leading Georgians who, like the governor, had achieved worldly success and political importance in the colony. Jones had come with the first settlers on the *Ann* and had been a militia officer, a councilor, assistant judge of the General Court, treasurer, and a man of considerable importance. Habersham had come in 1738 with Whitefield and had become a successful merchant and planter, secretary, and a senior councilor. Both backed Wright and the British, but they thoroughly understood the colonial viewpoint. Both died in 1775 before they had to make a final choice. Several other members of Wright's Council backed him, regardless of their natural interests. Georgia's political, economic, and social leaders were a relatively small and homogeneous group who lived in or near Savannah, knew each other personally, and had prospered under the existing government. Wright could easily influence such men through personal contacts.

The revolutionary leaders from Savannah, often the younger sons of the colony's leaders, must have found it difficult to break with their fathers and friends for whom they continued to retain high regard and personal friendship. Others among the revolutionary leadership were small merchants and artisans who became a new class of leaders in Georgia. Outside Savannah the most conspicuous whigs were the Midway Puritans. Arrivals in the 1760s and 1770s from the Carolinas and Virginia, especially in the up-country, had an undetermined effect but undoubtedly aided whig sentiment in Georgia.

From the time of the Stamp Act there was an opposition party in Georgia in essential agreement and communication with similar parties in other colonies. This group showed itself in every dispute between the mother country and the colonies from 1765 to 1775. It is impossible to identify many of its members except the leaders until 1774 or 1775, but there seemed to have been continuity of personnel throughout the decade. The fifteen years of rapid physical and economic expansion and growing political independence had given Georgians increased confidence in their abilities. Though many did not want to take sides in the growing argument, they were conscious of the fact that they were Americans; and this influenced them to become whigs. By 1775 they felt strong enough to assert their rights, with the encouragement of people from the other colonies. There can be little doubt that South Carolina, Virginia, and Massachusetts furnished much of the inspiration for the actions of Georgia's whigs; but basic decisions were made by Georgians. Georgia's measures often did not go as far as those of other colonies, and they always came later. But they did come, and they pointed more and more towards rebellion.

Ironically the very prosperity and increased population which Governor Wright had worked so hard to foster, made it possible for Georgians to rebel. The governor through his personal influence might delay Georgia's actions, but he could not change the basic character of its people. His hard line refusal to give in to colonial interests when they conflicted with his instructions from England helped to influence many to become whigs in the end. Georgians were Americans and realized it more and more as objections to British actions became increasingly common. If enough Americans rebelled, many Georgians would surely join them; and that is, in essence, what happened. Rapid growth, increasing power to the Commons House of Assembly, and the coming of settlers from the Carolinas and Virginia all had their effect. If "unfortunate poor" learned to ignore the Trustees long before 1752, then the "middling sort of people" learned to object strongly to unpopular British actions by 1775. In both instances the American environment and the love of English liberty were too powerful to be leashed by any leading strings from London.

14

GEORGIA AND THE AMERICAN REVOLUTION, 1775–1782: THE PATTERN DISRUPTED

Georgia whigs abolished the old royal colonial government and replaced it with an embryonic state government in the summer of 1775. On July 4, 1775, the Second Provincial Congress met at Tondee's Tavern in Savannah with delegates from all parishes except two small ones south of the Altamaha. The Congress first listened to a sermon by the Reverend John J. Zubly, one of its members, entitled "The Law of Liberty," an application of the ideas of Locke to religion. Next it sent a petition to the king and adopted a series of resolutions advocating American rights in much the same language of congresses in other colonies. This Congress aligned Georgia fully with the actions of the First Continental Congress by adopting the Continental Association and electing delegates to the Second Continental Congress—Archibald Bulloch, Lyman Hall, John Houstoun, Noble W. Jones, and the Reverend John J. Zubly. These delegates were instructed to work for the preservation of American rights and liberties and for the restoration of harmony with Britain upon constitutional principles.

All the delegates were planters, Hall and Jones were doctors, Bulloch and Houstoun were American-trained lawyers, and

Zubly was a clergyman. All but Hall lived in Savannah. Bulloch was born, reared, and educated in Charles Town and had moved to Georgia in 1750. His experience in the Georgia Commons House of Assembly and as its Speaker have been recounted earlier. Hall was born in Connecticut, educated at Yale, and moved to the Puritan settlement at Dorchester, South Carolina, about 1752 at the time of its removal to Midway, Georgia, where he accompanied his new neighbors. He was a leader at Midway and an early opponent to British measures. Houstoun, the son of Sir Patrick Houstoun, a leader in Georgia's colonial government, was the youngest of the five and the only one born in Georgia. He was also the last to become identified with the revolutionists in Georgia. Jones, born in England and an immigrant to Georgia on the *Ann* at an early age, was the son of Noble Jones, prominent in Georgia from its founding until his death in 1775. Noble W. was an early and consistent opponent of British measures. Zubly was born in Switzerland and lived in South Carolina before he came to Georgia in 1760. His position as pastor of Savannah's Independent Meeting House, defender of Georgia dissenters, and early opponent of British actions has been made clear. All remained prominent in political affairs in Georgia throughout the war except Bulloch who died in 1777 and Zubly who refused to go along with independence.

The Congress also provided for the issuance of £10,000 in certificates for expenses and allotted representation in future congresses. A Council of Safety, which became the executive arm of the Congress during its recesses, was created. Having taken Georgia down the path of the other rebellious colonies and created the first revolutionary government for the province, the Congress adjourned on July 17. It had been a momentous thirteen days for Georgia.

An immediate attempt was made to secure signatures to the Continental Association and to enforce it. There was, however, much difference of opinion about its enforcement which during the summer was sporadic at best. Georgia even applied to the Continental Congress for authority to export its 1775 crop and to import goods for the Indian trade.

Delegates Bulloch, Houstoun, and Zubly first attended the Continental Congress on September 5 and replaced Lyman Hall who had been representing St. John's Parish. Dr. Zubly initially created a favorable impression in Philadelphia, but he refused to go along with the increasing trend towards independence obvious by the fall, and left for Georgia under a cloud in mid-November still advocating American rights within the empire. Bulloch and Houstoun returned to Georgia a few weeks after Zubly.

During the latter half of 1775 the newly created whig organization took over more and more of the actual functions of government from the royal authorities in Savannah. The Council of Safety or the Provincial Congress began Indian negotiations, commissioned militia officers and assumed other defense activities, embargoed the export of needed provisions, and forbade the rector of Christ Church to preach after he refused to observe the whig day of fasting and prayer. As early as March 1775, the people of St. George's Parish had agreed to let no writs be served in the parish but reconsidered when Governor Wright objected strongly. In October the jurors called for the session of the General Court refused to be sworn; and, by now, none of the assistant judges would meet with the chief justice. Hence the work of the court effectively was ended. Governor Wright's Council continued to meet, but it had no power, and all royal officials were authorized to abandon their positions if they thought it necessary for their safety.

Besides beginning to set up their own government in the summer of 1775, Georgia whigs began to take action against obstreperous tories, and there were several tarring and featherings. Such overzealous action drove some neutrals into the tory camp and stored up resentment for the future.

After the whig capture of gunpowder intended for the Indians in July and September, Georgia whigs and royal officials worried about the effect of this event on Creek attitudes. Some of the gunpowder was sent to the Indians, but not as much as Governor Wright and Indian Superintendent John Stuart thought necessary. Stuart was genuinely afraid that whig actions would bring on frontier warfare, something which he dreaded and knew the whigs would blame upon him. Accordingly, he worked to keep peace among the Indians despite his orders from England to secure Creek friendship against the whigs.

Military action began in Georgia as a result of the arrival on January 18 of several British men-of-war hoping to purchase provisions. The Council of Safety refused to allow any dealing with the British, arrested Governor Wright and other leading tories, and called militia to duty. In February additional vessels and two hundred troops arrived. On the night of February 11–12 Wright and his Council broke their paroles and went down to Cockspur Island where they boarded one of the men-of-war.

The British wanted to secure the rice on several vessels in the river above Savannah. On the night of March 2 British troops boarded the ships and captured whigs sent out the next day to unrig the vessels. Shots were exchanged between the bluff at Savannah and the rice boats, but the distance was too great to do any damage. Several of the rice boats were burned by the whigs, but the British secured the rest by sailing them down the back river behind Hutchinson's Island. The British obtained some 1,600 barrels of rice; prisoners on both sides were released; and the battle of the rice boats was over. Governor Wright and several other tories left with the British, and royal authority was now completely gone from Georgia.

The ending of royal government emphasized the need to regularize the temporary whig government. While the British men-of-war were still off Cockspur, the Provincial Congress must have considered this question, for, on April 15, it issued Georgia's first temporary state constitution, a simple document of thirteen brief paragraphs called the Rules and Regulations of 1776. This document established in broad outline the form of the new government. To the one-house Provincial Congress it gave most of the real power. A plural executive was created consisting of a president and a Council of Safety elected by the Provincial Congress every six months. The executive was subject to the legislative control in almost all fields. The court structure was similar to the colonial system, and existing colonial laws and practices not in conflict with the changed conditions were to continue. Formal separation from England came with the Provincial Congress's statement on June 12 that henceforth justice should run in the name of the province instead of the king and with the adoption of the Declaration of Independence by the Continental Congress on July 4, 1776.

Button Gwinnett and Lyman Hall had arrived at the Continental Congress as new Georgia delegates on May 20, 1776, bringing broad instructions from the Assembly to work for the welfare of America as well as Georgia. They were in favor of independence, and Georgia was henceforth classified in this category in the growing debate in Congress. By the time the Declaration of Independence was voted, George Walton had arrived to give Georgia three signers. Gwinnett came from England to Georgia about 1765 and engaged first as a merchant, a calling he had followed in England, in Savannah. Soon he purchased on credit 6,200 acres on St. Catherines Island and became a planter. Walton, only twenty-seven years of age, had come to Savannah a few years earlier as a poor youth. There he read law under Henry Young, a leader in the colony, and soon began his rapid rise in the political life.

The Rules and Regulations went into effect on May 1, 1776, with no formal approval by the voters, and Archibald Bulloch became the first president under this document. He proved a capable executive until his mysterious death in February 1777. Bulloch was succeeded by Button Gwinnett, who remained in office until May.

The Continental Congress recommended in May 1776 that the colonies set up adequate governments. Georgia's Provincial Congress, sometimes called a convention, began work in the fall on a new and more complete constitution and adopted it on February 5, 1777. Those who wrote this constitution are not known, but they were obviously whigs of the more radical sort who were in control of Georgia's government of the day. The legislative, executive, and judicial departments were declared separate and distinct; but most actual power was given to the one-house legislature, called the House of Assembly, elected annually by the voters. Representation in the House was to be proportional to the number of electors in each county. Representatives must reside in the county they represented, be of the Protestant religion, twenty-one years of age, and own 250 acres of land or other property worth £250. Electors must be twenty-one years old, owners of property worth £10, or follow a "mechanic" trade. People qualified as electors were to be fined if they did not vote, but there is no evidence that this was ever done.

The executive consisted of the governor and Council to be elected by the Assembly on the first day of its session. The executive was given the usual powers except that it had no legislative veto, and the power to grant pardons or remit fines was reserved to the Assembly. The governor could hold office only one year out of three. There was to be a superior court in each county composed of the state's chief justice and three or more assistant justices from the county. Courts of conscience, or justice courts, were to continue as previously. Juries were made the judge of both fact and law, but they might apply to the bench for advice on legal matters. The fact that the same chief justice presided over all superior courts and that the same attorney general acted as prosecutor gave superior courts some uniformity of action.

This constitution created the first counties in Georgia. Beginning north of Augusta and coming down the river to Savannah and then down the coast, they were named Wilkes, Richmond, Burke, Effingham, Chatham, Liberty, Glynn, and Camden. All were named for English statesmen friendly to the American cause except Liberty, which included old St. John's, St. Andrew's, and St. James' parishes, and was considered by many the birthplace of liberty in Georgia. County officials who performed state functions were elected by the Assembly, but purely local ones were elected by the county voters.

Scattered throughout the constitution were several paragraphs which collectively made up a bill of rights. Free exercise of religion was guaranteed to all, no one was to be compelled to support any religion except his own, excessive fines and bail were forbidden, freedom of the press and trial by jury were to remain inviolate, and the principles of habeas corpus were declared a part of the constitution. In addition, schools were to be erected in every county and supported by the state, and intestate estates were to be divided equally between the widow and children.

This constitution had simplicity of style, brevity, and restricted itself to the bare fundamentals. It was divided into sixty-two paragraphs, most of which were short and easily understood by a layman. The political philosophy behind the document was based upon the theories of natural rights, separation of powers, consent of the governed, and guarantees of citizens against arbitrary government—typical beliefs of American whigs. The strong legislature and weak executive, common to most states, were reactions against strong colonial executives. The court structure kept judicial power in the hands of the citizens, and the relatively low voting and officeholding qualifications gave Georgia one of the more democratic state governments, usually listed with Pennsylvania and North Carolina as being leaders in this regard. While the old leaders and their sons were not all eliminated, politically the radicals had overthrown the old order with its aristocratic checks and had established a new order with no checks upon the will of the majority. This was their revolutionary victory.

In the Continental Congress, Georgia's delegates took little part in debates throughout 1776 and 1777 about the writing of the Articles of Confederation. Georgia ratified the proposed articles on February 26, 1778, before the congressional deadline of March 10, but no notice of this was sent to Congress before July. The Georgia Assembly proposed a few minor amendments to the articles, but Georgia's delegates were told to ratify if Congress would not consider the proposed amendments, and they were not considered.

The new state constitution, which went into effect in May 1777, made little difference in actual government. Though styled governor instead of president and elected for one year instead of six months, the chief executive was still weak and the Assembly strong. Legislation continued along similar lines as under the Rules and Regulations of 1776. One new subject was embraced in the confiscation and banishment acts of September 1777 and March 1778, which attainted 177 tories for high treason, banished them, and confiscated their estates. Before this act could be carried out fully, the British return to Georgia halted action under it.

Not only did Georgia whigs fight tories, they fought among themselves as well. Very soon after the whigs secured control of the government, they split into two factions. The merchant or low country conservative faction was opposed by the more radical or country party. Lachlan McIntosh, a Highland Scot who came to Georgia as a lad in 1736 and who had been a cadet in Oglethorpe's regiment and a leader of the conservatives, was elected colonel (later brigadier general) of the Georgia Continental forces, a job which radical Button Gwinnett desperately wanted. Gwinnett then became president of the state under the Rules and Regulations.

About mid-March 1777, McIntosh's brother, George, was arrested upon information from the Continental Congress accusing him of being pro-British. He was roughly treated by the Gwinnett-headed government, and this added to the animosity between Gwinnett and Lachlan McIntosh. Just after this the 1777 expedition against East Florida began. The lack of cooperation between McIntosh and Gwinnett was so complete that both were induced to leave active command to Colonel Samuel Elbert. After the expedition ended in failure, the Assembly investigated it and approved Gwinnett's actions. This was more than McIntosh could stand, and he called Gwinnett "a Scoundrell & lying Rascal" to his face on the floor of the Assembly. Gwinnett challenged McIntosh to a duel, subsequently fought on May 16, 1777. Both men were wounded, and Gwinnett died three days later. Feelings ran high against McIntosh, who was tried but acquitted by the next Assembly. He was removed from this explosive situation by orders to report to General Washington for reassignment.

Another cause of excitement in 1777 was South Carolina's proposal to unite Georgia and South Carolina into one state. William Henry Drayton, a bombastic Carolinian, appeared

Button Gwinnett.

Lachlan McIntosh.

before the Georgia Assembly with the offer and supported it by a long and involved argument to prove how much better off Georgia would be politically, militarily, and economically united with South Carolina. There were also threats of what South Carolina would do to harm Georgia if the union did not take place. The proposal was poorly handled by Drayton. If his purpose was to dissolve the long-standing jealousies between South Carolina and Georgia, the rather unrealistic proposal only raised these differences to a new pitch. Opposition was voiced by Georgia's political leaders and probably felt by most of her citizens, and nothing came of the proposal.

Georgia's first Continental Army troops were authorized by the Continental Congress on November 4, 1775, and consisted of one battalion or regiment—terms which seem to have been used interchangeably. In January the Georgia Provincial Congress elected Lachlan McIntosh, colonel; Samuel Elbert, lieutenant colonel; and Joseph Habersham, major. These troops might be enlisted in Georgia, the Carolinas, and Virginia. Georgia had possibly 2,500 to 4,000 men available for military duty, but if more than half of these were taken at once the economy would deteriorate badly. In early May 400 men were reported enlisted along with two troops of horsemen to guard the southern frontier against British Florida.

Georgians were very concerned with the state's defense but were certain they could not handle it alone. The Continental Congress agreed in February 1776, when Georgia was grouped with the Carolinas and Virginia into the Southern Military Department, commanded by Major General Charles Lee. Lee saw Georgia's needs but had no way of meeting them. Henceforth Georgia's military needs were usually considered in connection with those of the southern states, and South Carolina's Henry Laurens was frequently Georgia's best advocate in military matters in the Continental Congress.

In the summer of 1776 the Continental Congress authorized Georgia to raise two more battalions of foot troops, a regiment of rangers, two companies of artillery to garrison forts, and four row gallies for coastal defense. In the fall another battalion of foot was authorized. Recruiting for these Continental units could take place as far north as Pennsylvania as Georgia could furnish no more troops. Georgia also recruited state troops without much success.

The procurement of arms and munitions, food, and clothing was difficult. Some munitions were acquired in the West Indies, apparently from the British and Dutch islands. Thomas Young was discovered working as a double agent to secure clothing for Georgia troops in the West Indies and food for British West Indian islands in Georgia. By the fall of 1776 magazines of foodstuffs were being laid up in south Georgia and cattle removed from the sea islands to keep them out of British hands.

In the fall of 1775 before any troops were raised or supplied, there was talk of capturing St. Augustine and its garrison of about 150 men. East Florida became the refuge of southern tories in 1775 and 1776, and Indian Superintendent John Stuart made his headquarters there. British East Florida had never fed itself; and now with additional troops and tories it needed even more food. Much of this was taken in south Georgia by a tory partisan unit, the Florida Rangers, commanded by Thomas Brown.

On January 1, 1776, the Continental Congress recommended to the Carolinas and Georgia that they undertake the capture of St. Augustine, now reinforced with additional British troops. Border raids from both sides were soon being carried out by militia, rangers, and partisans. By August, General Lee, Continental commander in the South, was planning an expedition to break up the settlements and plantations between the St. Marys and St. Johns rivers but doubted that he could do more. Lee collected his troops, hopefully about a thousand, in Charles Town. Whig decisions and actions were usually known in St. Augustine almost as soon as in South Carolina and Georgia, relayed by tories and tory sympathizers to friends and relatives in East Florida. In early August Colonel McIntosh, Continental commander in Georgia, raided northern East Florida and broke up settlements, and General Lee thought this was all that could be accomplished. But the Georgia Council of Safety insisted upon pursuing the expedition further, so in September some American troops got as far as the St. Johns and laid waste the country. Most soldiers never got out of Georgia; none got as far as St. Augustine. The failure was blamed on hot weather, sickness among the troops, insufficient transportation, a recently reinforced St. Augustine garrison, hostilities of the Cherokees against back settlements, and the inability of civilian and military authorities to cooperate. Once the expedition ended, cattle stealing raids into south Georgia from East Florida resumed.

Almost as soon as the 1776 East Florida expedition was over, another was being planned. General Robert Howe, the new Continental commander in the South, came to Savannah in March of 1777 to confer with President Button Gwinnett and his Council of Safety. There were only the four hundred troops of the First Georgia Battalion available for duty, but Gwinnett was sure that Howe could furnish sufficient additional troops to capture St. Augustine, something that Howe refused to attempt. Howe soon returned to Charles Town, and Gwinnett was left to plan his own expedition, which he did without consulting General McIntosh.

Militia and Continental troops reached Sunbury by mid-April where cooperation between McIntosh and Gwinnett proved impossible. Upon the advice of the Council of Safety, both returned to Savannah and left Colonel Samuel Elbert in command of the troops. Elbert's Continental troops proceeded down the inland passage while militia went overland. The militia reached the St. Johns sooner than the Continentals and had to fight British regulars and Florida Rangers. Most of the Georgia militia fled northward. The Continentals' provisions ran short, sickness developed, and the boats could not be got through Amelia Narrows, just below the St. Marys River. On May 26 Elbert decided to abandon the expedition, and he and his troops were back in Savannah by June 15. The only material result of this action was the collection of some one thousand cattle by the Georgia troops, hardly worth the effort. The end of the expedition was the signal for renewed raiding parties of Florida Rangers whom Governor Patrick Tonyn reported got to within five miles of Savannah and to Augusta.

After the St. Augustine expedition, Henry Laurens persuaded the Continental Congress to consider Georgia's defense, to vote $600,000 for back pay and expenses, and to appoint Joseph Clay of Savannah as the state's paymaster. Clay, a Savannah merchant and nephew of James Habersham, was trusted by Laurens and would hopefully give some stability to the Georgia military establishment. In the fall when General McIntosh left Georgia for a new command in the north, Colonel Samuel Elbert became commander of Georgia's Continental brigade.

The new year of 1778 had hardly begun when Georgians began planning their annual St. Augustine expedition. In January the Assembly recommended it, but General Howe was sure that there were insufficient troops and supplies and that an attack should not be undertaken during the planting season when militiamen were needed at home. The Assembly was certain that none of these objections were valid. In March Georgia offered five hundred acres of East Florida land to anyone who would operate north of the St. Johns River for three months. Governor Patrick Tonyn of East Florida tried to get Georgia Germans to desert to East Florida and was confident that Georgia could be captured if Colonel Augustine Prevost, the East Florida British commander, would but implement Tonyn's plans.

By the end of April there were about two thousand troops ready to descend upon St. Augustine. They consisted of Continentals under Howe, Georgia militia under Governor John Houstoun, South Carolina militia under Colonel Andrew Williamson, and the Georgia navy under Commodore Oliver Bowen. Howe and Houstoun immediately differed over which should command, and Bowen refused to take orders from either of them since it was not clear whether his navy was a Continental or a state unit. As the expedition approached the St. Marys on June 29 the Florida Rangers destroyed their rendezvous, Fort Tonyn, and retreated to the south. Howe now received approval from the Continental officers to end the expedition, so the Continentals started north in mid-July. Houstoun and Williamson wanted to continue operations but decided they could not do so alone, so they returned to Savannah.

Thus the third attempt to capture St. Augustine ended without any enemy contact. This expedition had more whig troops involved than any of the previous ones and should have had the best chance of the three for success, but the hot weather impaired operations almost as much as the inability of the commanders to agree upon a common policy.

These three expeditions against St. Augustine were Georgia's major military effort in the first three years of the war. Both British and whig military leaders were lukewarm about direct action because they were not optimistic about success. Civilian leaders were more insistent that action was necessary and that success was possible. Perhaps Governor Tonyn's Florida Rangers were the key to British success. Though a small partisan unit, the Rangers were made up of tories who knew what they were fighting for and who were ready to fight whenever there was any chance of success. Had Georgia possessed a similar dedicated unit, she might have achieved greater success. Tonyn was obviously a superior administrator who supported and encouraged the Rangers, and a large share of the British success is owed to him. Georgia, by contrast, had a succession of chief executives, each of whom repeated his predecessor's mistakes.

Another military problem for Georgia was the Creek Indians. Both the British and whigs tried to keep Creek friendship throughout the war to prevent their helping the other side. Initially the British had the advantage in that the Indians were accustomed to dealing with Indian Superintendent John Stuart and respected him. The Indian demand of presents at stated intervals could be met more easily by the British than by the whigs. But the whigs realized the importance of Creek friendship, and both the Continental and state governments undertook to secure it. George Galphin, an important Augusta Indian trader, became a Continental Indian commissioner and was always able to find whig adherents among the Creeks. In fact, the Indians returned to their earlier policy of playing one group of whites against the other to their own advantage. The main British trouble was that they had no troops with whom the Indians could cooperate in Georgia. Since the whigs were in control of the state, the Creeks must of necessity deal with them.

Although there was talk of another St. Augustine expedition for 1779, Georgia was invaded by the British instead. Governor Wright and Governor Lord William Campbell of South Carolina began agitation to recapture their colonies almost as soon as they arrived in England early in 1776. The governors and lieutenant governors of both colonies presented a memorial in August 1777, in which they expressed their belief that many loyalists and Indians in these colonies were anxious to reassert their loyalty to Britain if they had military support. The memorial insisted that many valuable exports from these colonies were helping the economy of the United States and could just as well help Britain's. In March 1778, when Sir Henry Clinton was appointed commander in chief of the British army in America, London suggested that he might begin operations to recapture South Carolina and Georgia, where campaigning could be carried on during the winter.

Clinton decided to proceed against Savannah in the winter of 1778, hoping to contact loyalists and friendly Indians in the backcountry before moving against Charles Town. An expedition of 2,500 to 3,500 British, German, and loyalist troops was collected in New York under the command of Lieutenant Colonel Archibald Campbell. General Augustine Prevost, British commander in St. Augustine, was ordered to march into Georgia and to cooperate with Campbell upon his arrival. The army was to be used to capture Georgia and to back the loyalists whom it was hoped would restore British control and set up a colonial government again. Any punishment of rebels was to be meted out by the restored civil government. Clearly this expedition was intended to have the psychological effect of returning the colonies of Georgia and Carolina to their "natural" condition in hopes that this would set an example for other colonies to follow.

Because of delays in the sailing of the expedition from New York, Prevost sent his troops into Georgia in late November before Campbell arrived. Lieutenant Colonel L. V. Fuser, the commander of part of the expedition, demanded the surrender of Fort Morris, at Sunbury. Lieutenant Colonel John McIntosh, the whig commander of the fort, replied, "Come and Take it." When Fuser discovered that the other troops from St. Augustine had not arrived to cooperate with him, he returned to Florida with no attempt to take Fort Morris. The Georgia Assembly voted McIntosh a sword with his reply engraved upon it. The other British troops from Florida, under the command of Lieutenant Colonel James Mark Prevost, met Georgia troops under Colonel John White and burned the meeting house at Midway before returning to Florida.

Although Georgians had been warned of a possible invasion of their state from New York, they did not connect the invasions from Florida with this warning and took no special precautions. After repeated delays, the New York expedition sailed on November 27 and arrived off Tybee Island on December 23. The invading troops landed unopposed below Savannah on December 29, marched into the city over a little-known path through the swamps, and had it captured before many whigs knew what was happening. While the British had from two to three times as many troops as the whigs, a proper defense of the town might have offset this. Continental General Robert Howe, Governor John Houstoun, and militia Colonel George Walton did not coordinate their defense activities. Each tried to blame the other for the capture of the city, and responsibility cannot now be properly placed. Any British delay might have resulted in General Benjamin Lincoln bringing troops from South Carolina and a different outcome. The whigs lost 450 troops captured and 100 killed or drowned in the swamps while trying to escape. British losses were 7 killed and 19 wounded.

On January 4, 1779, Colonel Campbell and Commodore Hyde Parker, the naval commander of the expedition from New York, issued a proclamation inviting Georgians to take an oath of loyalty to the king within three months and receive full pardon for past disloyalty. General Prevost now returned to Georgia, capturing Sunbury and its garrison on January 10 on his way to

Savannah. Campbell proceeded to Augusta to be the first officer "to take a stripe and star from the rebel flag of Congress." He arrived in Augusta on January 31 with little whig opposition on the way. He scoured the countryside for sixty miles around Augusta to make his presence known. About fourteen hundred men submitted, took the oath to the king, and allowed themselves to be formed into royal militia. Others left Georgia instead.

The return of the British to Georgia in December of 1778 caused considerable confusion in the state government. A new Assembly had been elected and was to meet in January of 1779, but the British invasion prevented this. Governor John Houstoun made no further claim on the office he had occupied during 1778. An attempt to convene the Assembly in Augusta on the first Tuesday in January brought only representatives from Wilkes, Richmond, and Burke counties—inadequate for a quorum. This meeting, which did not call itself an Assembly, elected an executive Council to keep the government in operation if possible.

Once the whigs realized what had happened, they set about to see what they could do to repair the damages. General Benjamin Lincoln, who was replacing Howe as Continental Commander in the South just as Savannah fell, collected troops from the Carolinas and Virginia to see if he could drive the British out of Georgia or at least confine them to the Savannah area. Some Georgians rendezvoused at Burke Jail, above Savannah, to cooperate with Lincoln and harry the British. In backcountry Wilkes County, Colonels Elijah Clarke, John Twiggs, and John Dooly collected whigs. By mid-February it was obvious that all of up-country Georgia had not submitted as Campbell hoped it would.

Anticipated help from loyalists and Indians did not materialize when Campbell arrived in Augusta. The number of loyalists in the backcountry had been overestimated by governors Wright and Campbell, and Superintendent Stuart had not been informed of the invasion in time to raise Indians to cooperate. Soon after Campbell reached Augusta, General John Ashe arrived opposite the town with twelve hundred North Carolina whig

Elijah Clarke.

troops, and Campbell discovered that his newly formed militia was of extremely doubtful loyalty. He was now outnumbered and saw no chance for reinforcements. Hence on February 14 he marched out of Augusta and took station at Hudson's Ferry, about twenty-four miles above Ebenezer. The same day whig militia under colonels Andrew Pickens, John Dooly, and Elijah Clarke surprised about seven hundred tories under tory Colonel Boyd at Kettle Creek, in Wilkes County. Boyd and many of his followers were killed, and others captured. This ended the efforts to raise tories in the up-country to cooperate with Campbell. The defeat of Boyd and the withdrawal of Campbell from Augusta insured whig predominance in the up-country. Kettle Creek illustrated how well properly led militia could fight.

Throughout February General Lincoln pushed the collection of troops. General Ashe on March 3 was surprised and defeated by Lieutenant Colonel James Mark Prevost at Ashe's camp at Briar Creek and the Savannah River. This hurt whig morale and effectively ended Lincoln's hopes for any immediate action against the British. On the same day that Prevost defeated Ashe at Briar Creek, he was made lieutenant governor of Georgia in the reinstituted colonial government. Other officials were appointed, and loyalists from other southern colonies were invited to settle in Georgia. Governor Wright, Lieutenant Governor John Graham, and Chief Justice Anthony Stokes arrived in Savannah from England in July and replaced the military officers who had been acting for four months. The British government suggested that Wright call an Assembly soon after his return to Georgia, but he delayed because he believed, correctly, that many had taken the oath to the king expediently because they thought the whig cause was dead or in great danger for the present. These people, Wright knew, would reinstate their loyalty to the United States if it seemed to be winning. Wright wanted more troops to protect the tories and to ensure Georgia's loyalty, and he refused to call an Assembly because he believed that people of doubtful loyalty could control it.

In March and April 1779, Georgia was uneasily divided between whigs and tories. Savannah and an area of twenty-five to forty miles around it was tory, while the up-country and a part of the lower coast was whig. Neither side had enough strength to mount a serious attack against the other, but there were continual raids from one area into the other, and the no-man's-land between the two was badly devastated. Whigs moved easily back and forth across the upper Savannah River between South Carolina and Georgia.

By the end of April, Lincoln, with five thousand men under his command, believed himself strong enough to attack Savannah. He crossed into Georgia at Augusta and marched toward Savannah. General Prevost in that city, discovering the weak defenses of South Carolina, crossed into that state and advanced towards Charles Town. Lincoln now abandoned operations in Georgia and rushed back to save Charles Town from the British. Hence neither side profited from their invasions, and both returned to the uneasy truce and raids against the other.

Whig attempts to regularize the state government resulted in the meeting in Augusta on July 24 of a body calling itself "the Representatives of the Counties of Wilkes, Richmond, Burke, Effingham, Chatham, Liberty, Glynn and Camden and other free men of the State." It never claimed any legal authority for itself but created a Supreme Executive Council to which it gave full executive powers, subject to the approval of the people, in an effort to keep the government as close as possible to the constitution. John Wereat became the president of this Council and the chief executive of the state government. This government operated in Wilkes and Richmond counties but was very weak and had no funds. It ordered the election of an Assembly the first Tuesday in December, the day specified by the constitution.

After the British capture of Savannah, there was little hope of whig reconquest, as General Washington said he could spare no troops and few could be found elsewhere for this task. But in early September 1779, the French naval commander Count Charles Henri d'Estaing arrived unexpectedly at Savannah with four thousand troops and twenty-two vessels of the line. He came in response to the request of Governor John Rutledge of South Carolina for help in recapturing Savannah. General Lincoln

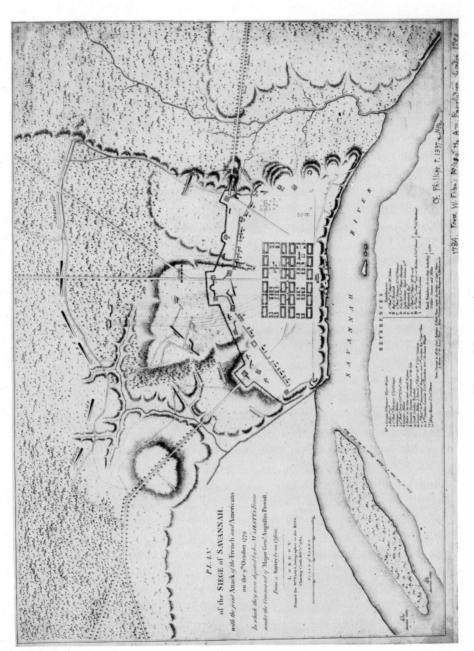

Siege of Savannah, 1779.

began collecting what whig troops he could in South Carolina, and General Prevost and Governor Wright worked feverishly on the defenses of Savannah.

On September 16 d'Estaing demanded Savannah's surrender, but Prevost asked for and was granted a twenty-four hour delay to consider the matter. The "consideration" consisted of getting Lieutenant Colonel John Maitland's eight hundred troops from Beaufort, South Carolina, into Savannah and strengthening the defenses of the town by four hundred to five hundred Negroes brought in to do the labor. Soon after the demand for surrender had been made, General Lincoln joined d'Estaing with fifteen hundred troops. The allies now outnumbered the British about two to one; but they were never able to cooperate effectively, probably because of d'Estaing's superiority complex. He maintained that he understood that the British would surrender upon his arrival at Savannah, hence his granting of the delay which the British used to such good advantage.

After entrenching operations and a bombardment commenced on October 4 did considerable damage to the town, d'Estaing personally led an attack upon the lines on October 9. After its failure, d'Estaing said he could remain no longer. The French were gone by October 20, and the whigs recrossed into South Carolina. The siege of Savannah was over. Had the French stormed Savannah upon landing, they undoubtedly could have taken it, but they took no action until it was too late. Any real liaison between the French and the Americans should have prevented Maitland's return to Savannah and might have produced a different outcome.

Despite the failure at Savannah, the whigs still controlled the up-country. Late in December a group calling itself an assembly, but apparently considerably short of a quorum, met in Augusta. There is no knowledge of how this body came into existence or how many counties were represented. A Richmond County grand jury in March of 1780 objected that this group assumed powers contrary to the constitution. This Assembly elected George Walton as governor and an executive Council with delegates from five counties (Liberty, Effingham, Burke, Richmond, and Wilkes). Walton, characteristically aggressive, began operating as governor. The Supreme Executive Council, which did not recognize the new government and continued to claim authority, was called the "Tory Council" by Walton and his group, though they had no better legal basis. Neither was paid the $500,000 voted by the Continental Congress for the use of Georgia. Thus were Georgia's whigs divided into two factions, both claiming to be the state government, when neither had the power to carry on effective government. The colonial government in Savannah exercised more power over more of Georgia than did both the whig governments combined.

The Assembly elected at the call of the Supreme Executive Council met in Augusta in January 1780. It was controlled by the Walton faction, but it did bring back a unified constitutional state government. Richard Howley was elected governor, and Walton a delegate to the Continental Congress. This Assembly elected a full slate of state officials and declared the acts of the Supreme Executive Council illegal. Congressional funds were now turned over to it.

With the British firmly entrenched in coastal Georgia, only the up-country was left to the state government. Hence the 1780 state Assembly, the first not dominated by the coast, concerned itself with the rich piedmont as the key to Georgia's future. Augusta became the capital and provisions were made to lay out the town again, regularize its streets, and sell town lots for the anticipated growth. Public lots and land for churches, schools, and a burying ground were ordered reserved. A town of a hundred lots was to be laid out adjacent to the Wilkes County courthouse and named Washington. New settlers in the state were offered two hundred acres of land plus fifty acres for each additional member of their family.

Before the arrival of d'Estaing at Savannah, Sir Henry Clinton, the British commander in chief in America, was already preparing an expedition in New York for the capture of Charles Town. Once the siege of Savannah was known to have failed, Clinton could resume his plans. The expedition arrived at the mouth of the Savannah River at the end of January 1780 and

Clinton set up an operating base on Tybee Island. Both Clinton and Lincoln stripped Georgia of troops for use in the Charles Town campaign. On May 12 Clinton captured Charles Town, Lincoln, and his entire army. Clinton soon returned to New York, leaving the Earl of Cornwallis to complete the conquest and occupation of South Carolina and Georgia.

On March 3, 1780, Clinton, to help in his efforts in South Carolina, promised pardon to all rebels who would swear allegiance to the king. To prevent more ex-rebels from gaining the right to vote in Georgia, Wright now called an election. The new Assembly met from May 9 to July 10 and worked hard to restore Georgia to her prerevolutionary status. All the acts of the whig state government were declared illegal, and 151 prominent rebels plus any others who had occupied official position under the state government were disqualified politically. By this time Charles Town had fallen and most of Georgia, except the 1773 Indian cession, was in British hands.

In May, Augusta was occupied by tory troops under Colonels Thomas Brown and James Grierson, both of whom were anxious for revenge for rough treatment received earlier from whigs. Throughout the summer Wright and his officials worked hard at extending the colonial government throughout all of Georgia and hoped vainly that all Georgians would submit to the king's government. But this did not happen.

One of the most noteworthy actions of the royal Assembly in the spring of 1781 was the provision it made for the growing up-country. The 1773 Indian cession and the western part of St. Paul's Parish were made into two new parishes, St. Peter and St. Mark. A western circuit court was also established for the parishes of St. Paul, St. Peter, and St. Mark. As this act was passed only a little over a month before the recapture of Augusta by the whigs it is doubtful that the new parishes ever operated. Certainly the circuit court never did.

Financially the restored colonial government lived off the bounty of the British government, which voted additional funds for its support. Since Parliament had agreed to give up colonial taxation, it urged that the colonies grant to the king a permanent revenue as their share of imperial expenses. In March of 1781 the Georgia Assembly voted a 2 1/2 percent duty on all exports produced in the colony. For this action the governor and Assembly were complimented by the Board of Trade.

At the first session of the restored colonial Assembly, bills were passed by both houses to attaint 112 prominent rebels for treason and to confiscate their property, but the two houses could never agree on a single bill so nothing was done except to disqualify 151 rebels politically. The April 1781 Assembly did pass a bill to attaint for treason 24 rebels and all others who occupied civil or military office under the state government and to confiscate their property. This bill was not to go into effect until it received royal approval, and there is no indication that it was ever considered by the Privy Council.

Under Georgia's restored colonial government Governor Wright continued to be the leader as he had been before 1776. He had the support of his Council and had no real disputes with the Assembly even though it often did not do all that he wanted. His biggest trouble was with the British army which could never see Georgia or its importance the way that Wright did. There were never enough troops to ensure Georgia's complete protection from the whigs, and Wright always insisted that this was necessary to create an example which might influence other colonies to return to colonial status. But neither the military commanders in America nor the ministry in London would agree.

If the colonial government's support was inadequate, that of the state government was even worse. On February 5, 1780, with Georgia stripped of whig troops to fight at Charles Town, the state executive resolved to adjourn to Heard's Fort, in Wilkes County, but it is not clear whether the move actually took place then. Governor Howley called upon Georgians to stand firm against the British and did not go to the Continental Congress as his Council urged him to do. After Charles Town fell to the British on May 12 there was immediate danger that they would overrun up-country Georgia. Hence when the Council again on

May 25 urged Howley to repair to Congress, he did so, leaving Stephen Heard, the president of the Council, as chief executive.

With Augusta back under British control, the only part of Georgia left to the whigs was Wilkes County and the upper part of Richmond County. In July Wright reported that all Georgians had submitted except eight or nine hundred in Wilkes County, but this was probably overly optimistic. Many Georgia whigs did abandon the state, but others stayed and fought it out. From the end of May 1780 until July 1781, the whereabouts or existence of a state government is unknown. Augusta was in British hands for most of this period. Tradition has it that the government moved about in Wilkes County and even into South Carolina, and it may have done so. But the absence of any evidence of a state government makes it clear that such a government was in default for most of that period.

From mid-1780 to mid-1781 there was as savage guerrilla fighting in the Georgia-Carolina backcountry as anywhere during the war. Whig Colonel John Dooly was reported murdered in his bed by tories in the summer of 1780, and Nancy Hart had the pleasure of revenge upon the murderers, if legends about Nancy can be believed. Partisan leaders for the whigs— Elijah Clarke, John Twiggs, Benjamin and William Few, James Jackson, and John Dooly—matched the exploits of tories James and Daniel McGirth, Thomas Brown, and James Grierson. Anyone who fell into the hands of the other side expected, and probably received, the worst possible treatment. Neither side got much help, supplies or otherwise, from outside Georgia or Carolina. The tories fared somewhat better in this regard than the whigs. These partisan groups assembled if there were any chance of success against the enemy, took any action possible, and then dispersed to their homes. Elijah Clarke made an attack upon the tories in Augusta in mid-September, but Thomas Brown and his garrison were reinforced by Colonel John H. Cruger. The whigs retreated leaving some of their wounded whom they could not transport. From these wounded whigs, according to tradition, Colonel Brown selected twelve to be hanged from the staircase of the Indian trading house, the White House, and watched the death agonies from the bed to which he was confined by wounds.

After Clarke's failure at Augusta, the British and tories made a new and determined effort to overrun and subdue all of up-country Georgia, but they were no more successful this time than earlier. Wright's pleas for a few more troops to bring all Georgia under his control went unheeded by the British military commanders.

By April of 1781, General Nathanael Greene, the Continental commander in the South, began an offensive against the British with the few troops at his disposal. Frequently this was as much a psychological attack as a military one. Georgia and South Carolina state militia under colonels Elijah Clarke and Micajah Williamson began a siege against Augusta in April, and about May 20 some Continental troops under General Andrew Pickens joined them. The forts guarding the town were captured on May 25 and June 5, and up-country Georgia was now free of British and tory troops. Throughout May up-country posts in South Carolina surrendered to the whigs. Finally, on July 3, the British abandoned Ninety Six because of difficulties of communication, and the up-country was now free of British and tories, except for occasional raids. Many tories fled to the British-controlled areas closer to the coast and were formed into militia, but they could do little without regulars to give them backbone and supplies.

After the whig capture of Augusta in June, General Greene sent Joseph Clay, his paymaster general, to Augusta to try and form a state government where apparently there was none. Dr. Nathan Brownson, head of Continental hospitals in the South, came in August to attempt to unite the Georgia militia. An Assembly met in Augusta on August 17 with representatives from every county except Camden. It elected Brownson governor and a full slate of state officials, county officers from most counties, and Congressional delegates. All state laws expired or near expiring were extended. This Assembly also began to reclaim citizens who had taken the oath of loyalty to the king and to try and secure the return of citizens who had fled the state since the British return.

The Assembly which met at Augusta on January 1, 1782, contained representatives from every county. The majority of the state was now in whig hands, the British being confined to the Savannah area. Finances were the main concern of this Assembly which lasted only twelve days. Salaries were reduced and assemblymen voted to serve gratis. An attempt was made to begin settling the state's accounts for the last three years. No tax bill was considered, probably because there was so much chaos and confusion that most Georgians could not pay taxes if they were levied.

By December General Alexander Leslie, the British commander in Charles Town, had been authorized to abandon Georgia if he thought it best. In truth, the whigs were little better off and in constant fear that British reinforcements might result in whig losses. Their requests for more troops met with no success. Since the spring of 1780 there had been six hundred to a thousand British troops in Georgia—loyalists, Hessians, and British regulars. Wright continually complained of Georgia's neglect and asked for more troops to subdue the province completely, but the troops never came. In late 1780 the colonial Assembly agreed to draft slaves to work on fortifications and to arm Negroes in time of extreme danger.

Whig troops were even harder to come by than were British. In 1779 the Continental Congress had ordered a reduction of Georgia's Continental line from four battalions of infantry and one regiment of light dragoons to one battalion of infantry and one regiment of horse, but there were hardly enough men available to fill even these two units. A suggestion the next year that a battalion of Negroes be authorized was never approved. From the time of the British capture of Savannah in late 1778 until mid-1781 the state government was too weak to be of any help in troop supply. After the up-country was freed of British and tories, the revived state government began to secure some militia and a few state troops, especially the Georgia State

Legion commanded by Lieutenant Colonel James Jackson, raised in the summer of 1781. Such state units were usually composed of people who wished to reinstate their loyalty to the United States now that it seemed to be winning. They were paid whatever the state had available from confiscated tory estates, a precarious source at best.

After the surrender of Lord Cornwallis at Yorktown in October 1781, the southern Continental army received more consideration and a few additional troops. In early January 1782, Brigadier General Anthony Wayne arrived in Georgia as Continental commander, bringing some dragoons and artillery with him. British troop strength was now about a thousand and whig five hundred. But Wayne immediately took the offensive wherever possible and forced the British to give up several points near Savannah and confine themselves to the town itself. Governor John Martin cooperated fully with Wayne and was able to furnish him with several hundred militia. Wayne said that his tasks were more difficult than those of the children of Israel in Egypt, who only had to make bricks without straw. He had to secure food and other supplies wherever they could be found and make whigs out of the ex-tories who joined his forces. Nevertheless he persevered. Throughout the winter of 1781–82 more ex-tories joined the whigs, and so many of the Hessians stationed in Savannah deserted that the British offered a reward to Negroes and Indians of two guineas for each deserted Hessian they brought to army headquarters dead or alive. Wayne was not in a position to make any advances against the British, but neither were they against the Americans.

Because of the progress of the peace negotiations in Paris by May, the British commanders in Charles Town and in Savannah proposed to Greene and Wayne a cessation of hostilities, but neither whig general felt himself authorized to accept. When in April General Clinton called on General Leslie for two thousand of the six thousand British troops in South Carolina, Georgia, and East Florida, Leslie suggested that Georgia be evacuated. Governor Wright still insisted that only a few more troops would make Georgia completely loyal to the king—something which obviously was not true.

During the first six months of 1782, there was no great change in the condition of the state government. The executive spent considerable time in trying to secure food and other supplies for itself, the militia on active duty, and for many people who could not support themselves until a crop could be harvested. Efforts to convert those who had taken the oath of loyalty to the king continued with considerable success. In May the executive undoubtedly moved to Ebenezer, where General Wayne had his headquarters, but the Assembly session called to meet there on July 3 to consider the imminent British evacuation of the state failed to secure a quorum.

On July 10 and 11 the last of the British troops left Savannah, and the whigs moved in, Lieutenant Colonel James Jackson of the Georgia troops receiving the surrender of the city. By the end of July the last of the British troops had left Tybee Island, and Thomas Brown's loyalists had headed for St. Augustine. Merchants were allowed to remain in Savannah for six months, probably because the supplies they had were needed by the whigs. Tories who wished to remain in Georgia could reinstate their loyalty to the state by joining the Georgia Continental battalion for two years. Two hundred joined by July 12.

The promised transportation for loyalists who wanted to leave Georgia proved inadequate, and many had to get to St. Augustine as best they could. The slaves of large planters like Governor Wright and several others went mainly to Jamaica, where as many as two thousand ex-Georgia slaves may have found a new home. East Florida received at least five thousand ex-Georgians. While the total number of exiles cannot be determined, it could hardly have been more than two thousand to twenty-five hundred whites and thirty-five hundred to five thousand Negroes. Slaves who had served in the British army were considered loyalists and entitled to the same treatment as whites. Of the five thousand exiles in East Florida an undetermined number, free and slave, returned to Georgia by the time

Florida was turned over to Spain in 1785. Tradition has undoubtedly exaggerated the number of Georgians who left permanently with the end of the war.

A state Assembly met in Savannah on July 13 and the executive on July 14. Thus did the state government return to the capital from which it had been driven by the British on December 28, 1778. Georgians were now free to begin recovering from the ravages of seven long war years. Well might they be thankful and look forward to better days.

The evacuation of Savannah by the British ended the war so far as Georgians were concerned. Some results of independence and separation from England were obvious in July of 1782, while others revealed themselves over the next several years.

Several political changes had become evident during the war years. First in the thinking of many Georgians was the end of English control and the greater ability of Georgians to determine their own destiny. In the governmental framework there had been a weakening of the executive and a strengthening of the legislature, which was now the dominant element of the state's government. Georgia had one of the more democratic early state constitutions, allowing practically all adult free men to vote and reducing considerably the property qualification for office-holding.

With the return of the British to Savannah in 1778, the up-country became the principal part of the state under whig control. This made for faster development of up-country political leadership than might have come if the older coastal leaders had remained free to exercise control. By the time the British left in July 1782, the up-country leaders were used to running the state government. Many of the older coastal leaders were tainted with toryism, had left Georgia, or had died. Hence up-country control of the state government continued after peace came. The apportionment of the legislature was fairer to the up-country than it was in many of the older states.

Typical leaders before and after the war also indicate important changes. Among the colonial leaders were Governor James Wright, James Habersham, and Noble Jones. Wright was a professionally trained lawyer with good connections in London who climbed the ladder of colonial officeholding in South Carolina, London, and in Georgia, where he was one of the largest planters and wealthiest men in the colony. Habersham and Jones had both come to Georgia early and had grown economically, politically, and socially with the colony until they were patriarchs by the 1760s. These men had risen slowly within the existing system.

During and after the Revolution, Elijah Clarke and George Walton were typical leaders. Clarke was a North Carolina Regulator and illiterate frontiersman who came to Georgia in the 1770s with no material goods but with an ability to succeed in the rough-and-tumble frontier society. He was a leader in the severe guerrilla backcountry fighting of the war years and an Indian fighter afterwards. In the decade after the war he was usually a member of the Assembly, often a member of the Council, and a militia brigadier general. Yet his biographer does not think that he ever learned to write his name.

Walton was a Virginia orphan apprenticed to a carpenter who came to Georgia, obviously hoping for better things, at about the age of twenty. He read law and was a militia colonel during the war. But his political offices were of more importance. He was governor, chief justice, member of the Continental Congress and of the Constitutional Convention, and a United States Senator. His aggressive leadership especially appealed to frontiersmen and small farmers. Walton would undoubtedly have risen in colonial society but not as rapidly as he did because of the War for Independence. That Clarke could have achieved such success as he did in a colonial society seems totally unlikely. Clarke and Walton were in several respects products of the Revolution, and they profited from it as did many others.

In economic affairs the most obvious change of the war and postwar years was growth. Much of this growth would have come regardless of revolt or revolution, but land was easier to acquire from the state of Georgia than it had ever been from the colony of Georgia. With soldier land bounties, confiscated tory lands, and the desire of the new state to acquire more population, land acquisition was made easier than ever before; and land was the economic base for most Georgians, whether poor frontiersmen or wealthier planters. Of course independence brought increased freedom of trade, but this was a two-edged sword. The benefits of membership in the British economic system were now gone, and trade with Britain and the British West Indies became more difficult than it had been in the colonial period.

In social affairs several changes became apparent. Perhaps the most obvious was the disestablishment of the Church of England in the Constitution of 1777. Now that it had lost its favored position and because of its tory taint, the Anglican church declined to two active parishes in the postwar decade. Methodist and Baptist churches, by contrast, began an impressive growth in the up-country in the immediate postwar years and have remained the leading denominations in the state since. In addition, every person was now free to support the church of his choice, or no church if he so chose.

In education, the Revolution brought the creation of what amounted to a statewide public school system, topped by a state university. This development, which could not have come in the colonial period, resulted from a combination of eighteenth-century enlightenment and the optimism of the frontier, rein-forced by the successful war against Britain. True, only a half-dozen county academies were founded in the postwar decade, and it took sixteen years for the university to begin operation, but there was a dream of a better future through education for the common man.

Certainly the war brought an end to Governor Wright's hoped-for growth of "tone" to society and the creation of an aristocracy after the English model. In the new social order there was greater equality between free men than ever before. The common man was the greatest beneficiary of the changes of the war and immediate postwar years. He could now participate more fully in a government which was more receptive to his ideas and desires than ever before. He had a firmer economic base, as land was more easily acquired. Education was much easier for those who were interested in obtaining it. While these changes might well have come in time without independence, they would not have been as rapid and might not have gone as far as they did.

Many of the older upper class did not favor these changes, but many common men who saw the possibilities of a better day for themselves and their children did approve. Governor Wright must have gone home to London in 1782 a tired and embittered man convinced that his superiors had not done enough to bolster his own valiant efforts to save Georgia for the empire. Already the colony that he loved and understood had fallen apart before his eyes. He did not live long enough to see the new state which was to take its place emerge clearly. It may have been just as well; from the distance of London and with his vision blurred by a longing for a past that could never again be, he probably would not have approved the changed Georgia. Yet it was a Georgia he should have been able to predict to a considerable degree from his intimate knowledge of its earlier development.

In bringing this account to a close, it is interesting to note that James Edward Oglethorpe and Sir James Wright, Georgia's two most outstanding leaders in the colonial period, died only five months apart in 1785. Both had made major contributions to Georgia's colonial development, but their views of her present status and future development were considerably different. Oglethorpe, only a few weeks before his death in June, called on John Adams, the first United States minister to England, to express his esteem for America and his regret at the recent troubles between her and Britain. Wright could harbor no such views because he had only recently returned from his greatest failure in the Empire's loss of Georgia. Oglethorpe's career in Georgia had ended forty years earlier, and he could now view his accomplishments and failures there in perspective and with the softening effect of time. James Wright did not live long enough to achieve the same detachment in his views of Georgia's development and rebellion.

BIBLIOGRAPHY

This is a working bibliography, but by no means an exhaustive one. Many periodical articles are omitted when the subject is covered adequately by a book cited.

Where two places or dates for the publication of a single work are given, the second refers to a reprint edition.

BIBLIOGRAPHIES

Arthur Ray Rowland, *A Bibliography of the Writings on Georgia History* (Hamden, Conn., 1966); John Wyatt Bonner, *Bibliography of Georgia Authors, 1949–1965* (Athens, 1966); and *Catalogue of the Wymberly Jones DeRenne Georgia Library* (3 vols. Wormsloe, Georgia, 1931). (The DeRenne Library, one of the best on early books, pamphlets, and maps on Georgia, is now at the University of Georgia.) More specialized bibliographies are found in many of the recent secondary works cited later.

PRIMARY SOURCES

By far the greatest collection of primary source material on colonial Georgia is the records in the British Public Record Office, Colonial Office Papers, Class 5, vols. 636–712. Many other Georgia items are scattered through the Treasury Papers, War Office Papers, Audit Office Papers, etc. The best guide to the Public Record Office is Charles M. Andrews, *Guide to the Materials for American History, to 1783, in the Public Record Office of Great Britain* (2 vols. Washington, 1912; New York, 1965).

Copies of part of the Georgia volumes have been published in Allen D. Candler and Lucian Lamar Knight, eds., *The Colonial Records of the State of Georgia* (26 vols. Atlanta, 1904–1916). Volumes 27–39 are available in transcript from the State Archives, Atlanta, and publication of additional volumes is scheduled to begin in 1975. The principal materials included in these volumes are legislative and Council journals, official correspondence, and colonial laws. A similar but less ambitious publication is Allen D. Candler, *The Revolutionary Records of the State of Georgia* (3 vols. Atlanta, 1908). In 1968 further search of Georgia materials in the Public Record Office was made by Kenneth Coleman, and copies of many more documents are now deposited in the University of Georgia Library.

The oldest publication of Georgia sources is in the *Collections of the Georgia Historical Society* (15 vols. to date. Savannah, 1840 to date). Much of this material is from the colonial period. George White, *Historical Collections of Georgia* (New York, 1854) published official and nonofficial materials. Various documents have been published in the *Georgia Historical Quarterly*.

For the voyage to Georgia and the early settlement, the following should be consulted. Robert G. McPherson, ed., "The Voyage of the *Anne*—A Daily Record," *Georgia Historical Quarterly*, XLIV (1960), 220-30; E. Merton Coulter, "A List of the First Shipload of Georgia Settlers," *Georgia Historical Quarterly*, XXXI (1947), 282-88; E. Merton Coulter and Albert B. Saye, eds., *A List of the Early Settlers of Georgia* (Athens, 1949); E. Merton Coulter, ed., *The Journal of Peter Gordon, 1732-1735* (Athens, 1963).

The Trustee period is further illuminated in *Diary of Viscount Percival, Afterwards First Earl of Egmont, 1730-1749* (3 vols. London, 1920-1923); Robert G. McPherson, ed., *The Journal of the Earl of Egmont, 1732-1738* (Athens, 1962); E. Merton Coulter, ed., *The Journal of William Stephens, 1741-1745* (2 vols. Athens, 1958-1959); Malcolm H. Stern, "The Sheftall Diaries: Vital Records of Savannah Jewry (1733-1808)," *American Jewish Historical Quarterly*, LIV (1965), 243-77; John Tate Lanning, ed., *The St. Augustine Expedition of 1740: A Report to the South Carolina General Assembly* (Columbia, 1954); and "Oglethorpe's Treaty with the Lower Creek Indians," *Georgia Historical Quarterly*, IV (1920), 3-16.

The Salzburgers come in for special consideration in George Fenwick Jones, ed., *Henry Newman's Salzburger Letterbooks* (Athens, 1966); George Fenwick Jones and Marie Hahn, eds., *Detailed Reports of the Salzburger Emigrants who Settled in America . . . Edited by Samuel Urlsperger* (3 vols to date. Athens, 1968-1972); George Fenwick Jones, translator and ed., "John Martin Bolzius Reports on Georgia in 1739," *Georgia Historical Quarterly*, XLVII (1963), 216-19; George Fenwick Jones, "The Secret Diary of Pastor Johann Martin Bolzius," *Georgia Historical Quarterly*, LIII (1969), 78-110; Lothar L. Tresp, translator and annotator, "August, 1748, in Georgia, from the Diary of John Martin Bolzius," and "September, 1748, in Georgia, from the Diary of John Martin Bolzius," *Georgia Historical Quarterly*, XLVII (1963), 204-16, 320-32; George Fenwick Jones, translator, "Commissary Von Reck's Report on Georgia," *Georgia Historical Quarterly*, XLVII (1963), 94-111; George Fenwick Jones, "Von Reck's

Second Report from Georgia," *William and Mary Quarterly*, 3rd Series, XXII (1965), 319–33; Klaus G. Loewald, Beverly Starika, and Paul S. Taylor, eds. and translators, "Johann Martin Bolzius Answers a Questionnaire on Carolina and Georgia," *William and Mary Quarterly*, 3rd Series, XIV (1957), 218–61, and XV (1958), 228–52; and Andrew W. Lewis, ed., "Henry Muhlenburg's Georgia Correspondence," *Georgia Historical Quarterly*, XLIX (1965), 424–54.

For the royal and revolutionary periods there are *Minutes of the Union Society: being an Abstract of Existing Records, from 1750 to 1858* (Savannah, 1860); Lilla M. Hawes, ed., "Letters to the Georgia Colonial Agent, July, 1762, to January, 1771," *Georgia Historical Quarterly*, XXXVI (1952), 250–86; Alexander A. Lawrence, "Journal of Major Raymond Demere," *Georgia Historical Quarterly*, LII (1968), 333–47; Heard Robertson, "Georgia's Banishment and Expulsion Act of September 16, 1777," *Georgia Historical Quarterly*, LV (1971), 274–82; and Charles C. Jones, Jr., ed., *The Siege of Savannah in 1779, as Described in Two Contemporaneous Journals of French Officers* (Albany, N.Y., 1874).

MANUSCRIPTS

While many colonial records have been lost except for those sent to England, the State Archives in Atlanta has various colonial records and more for the Revolutionary period, including legislative and Council journals, military and pension records, Indian records, etc. Land records from 1754 are fairly complete and are located in the Surveyor General's Office, Atlanta. Crown grants, 1755–1775, have been published in nine mimeograph volumes (Atlanta, 1972–1974), compiled by Pat Bryan and Marion R. Hemperley.

At the University of Georgia Library the largest single collection on colonial Georgia is the Egmont Papers which give many intimate details as well as official records of the Trustee period. The Telamon Cuyler Collection, a collection of miscellaneous papers from colonial times to 1860, contains many colonial and revolutionary items. Besides there are similar collections of individuals and areas.

The Georgia Historical Society, Savannah, has many miscellaneous collections and several larger ones. The papers of Joseph Habersham, Joseph Clay, Clay and Telfair, James Jackson, Noble Jones, Lachlan McIntosh, W. B. Stevens, and Joseph V. Bevan are perhaps the most valuable. Some of these have been published in full or in part in the *Collections* of the Society.

The Library of Congress, Manuscripts Division, has the Force Transcripts (including Indian papers and Council correspondence, governor's proclamations, James Habersham correspondence, 1738–1775), miscellaneous personal papers, many transcripts from the British Public Record Office and Fulham Palace, and much Florida material of value to Georgia historians.

The South Carolina Archives Department, Columbia, has transcripts from the Public Record Office which throw much light upon Georgia history, especially *Records in the British Public Record Office Relating to South Carolina*, 36 vols.

The William L. Clements Library, University of Michigan, Ann Arbor, has the William Henry Lyttelton Papers, the Sir Henry Clinton Papers, Thomas Gage Papers, Earl of Shelburne Papers, Lord George Germain Papers, Von Jungkenn Mss., Nathanael Greene Papers, and many valuable colonial and revolutionary maps.

Duke University, at Durham, has a number of collections with some Georgia materials. Among the most useful are collections of the papers of Henry Ellis, the Telfairs, John Gibbons, Levi and Mordecai Sheftall, and Georgia Miscellaneous.

SECONDARY WORKS

A. GENERAL

References in this section cover the entire colonial period and sometimes the revolutionary period also.

While the writing about Georgia began before its founding, little attempt was made to write a history of the colony before the Reverend Alexander Hewatt published his *Historical Account of the Rise and Progress of the Colonies of South Carolina and Georgia* (London, 1779; Spartanburg, 1962). Edward Langworthy announced in 1791 the early publication of *A Political History of the State of Georgia from its First Settlement with Memoirs of the Principal Transactions which Happened Therein During the Late Revolution*, but there is no evidence that the book was ever written. Three general histories of Georgia during the colonial and revolutionary eras were published in the nineteenth century. Hugh McCall, *History of Georgia* (2 vols., Savannah, 1811–1816; Atlanta, 1909), shows inadequate research. William Bacon Stevens, *History of Georgia* (2 vols., New York and Philadelphia, 1847 and 1859; Savannah, 1972), reflects his abilities in writing history and in using documents. So does Charles C. Jones, Jr., *The History of Georgia* (2 vols., Boston, 1883; Spartanburg, 1965). Both these works are of value to historians today and give the most detailed treatment of the colonial period available in single works. A recent overall view of Georgia's colonial historiography is in Kenneth Coleman, "Colonial Georgia: Needs and Opportunities," *Georgia Historical Quarterly*, LIII (1969), 184–91.

Several more specialized works are Trevor R. Reese, *Colonial Georgia: A Study in British Imperial Policy in the Eighteenth Century* (Athens, 1963); Albert Berry Saye, *A Constitutional History of Georgia, 1732–1945* (Athens, 1948); and Albert B. Saye, *New Viewpoints in Georgia History* (Athens, 1943). John G. W. DeBrahm's *History of the Province of Georgia* (Wormsloe, Ga., 1849) has been edited with scholarly apparatus in Louis DeVorsey, Jr., *DeBrahm's Report of the General Survey in the Southern District of North America* (Columbia, S.C., 1971). Reba C. Strickland, *Religion and the State in Georgia in the Eighteenth Century* (New York, 1939), is the best treatment of religion in colonial Georgia. It may be supplemented by the journals of John and Charles Wesley and George Whitefield and various denominational histories.

Economic history has received little consideration except in Milton Sydney Heath, *Constructive Liberalism: the Role of the State in Economic Development in Georgia, from 1733 to 1860* (Cambridge, 1954), and a yet uncompleted general economic history of colonial Georgia by Milton L. Ready, the first part of which is included in An Economic History of Colonial Georgia, 1732–1754 (Ph.D. diss., University of Georgia, 1970). Other works are James C. Bonner, *A History of Georgia Agriculture, 1732–1860* (Athens, 1964); Lewis Cecil Gray, *History of Agriculture in the Southern United States to 1860* (2 vols. Washington, 1935); Mary Thomas McKinstry, "Silk Culture in the Colony of Georgia," *Georgia Historical Quarterly*, XIV (1930), 225–35; Reba C. Strickland, "The Mercantile System as Applied to Georgia," *Georgia Historical Quarterly*, XXII (1938), 160–68; William E. Heath, "The Early Colonial Money System of Georgia," *Georgia Historical Quarterly*, XIX (1935), 145–60; and Louis DeVorsey, Jr., "Indian Boundaries in Colonial Georgia," *Georgia Historical Quarterly*, LIV (1970), 63–78.

Various national, racial, and religious elements are treated in John P. Corry, "Racial Elements in Colonial Georgia," *Georgia Historical Quarterly*, XX (1936), 30–40; P. A. Strobel, *The Salzburgers and Their Descendants* (Baltimore, 1855; Athens, 1953); Hester W. Newton, "The Industrial and Social Influences of the Salzburgers in Colonial Georgia," and "The Agricultural Activities of the Salzburgers in Colonial Georgia," *Georgia Historical Quarterly*, XVIII (1934), 248–63, 335–53; Adelaide L. Fries, *The Moravians in Georgia, 1735–1740* (Raleigh, 1905); Leon Huhner, "The Jews of Georgia in Colonial Times," *American Jewish Historical Society Publications*, X (1902), 65–95; David T. Morgan, "Judaism in Eighteenth-Century Georgia," *Georgia Historical Quarterly*, LVIII (1974), 41–54; Jacob R. Marcus, *Early American Jewry* (2 vols., Philadelphia, 1951) and *The Colonial American Jew* (3 vols., Detroit, 1960); Leo Shpall, "The Sheftalls of Georgia," *Georgia Historical Quarterly*, XXVII (1943), 339–49; Darold D. Wax, "Georgia and the Negro Before the American Revolution," *Georgia Historical Quarterly*, LI (1967), 63–77; and Ruth Scarborough, *The Opposition to Slavery in Georgia Prior to 1860* (Nashville, 1933).

Miscellaneous social subjects are included in Hortense S. Cochrane, "Early Treatment of the Mentally Ill in Georgia," *Georgia Historical Quarterly*, XXXII (1948), 105–18; Joseph Krafka, Jr., "Medicine in Colonial Georgia," *Georgia Historical Quarterly*, XX (1936), 326–44, and "Notes on Medical Practice in Colonial Georgia," XXIII (1939), 351–61; and John P. Corry, "The Houses of Colonial Georgia," *Georgia Historical Quarterly*, XIV (1930), 181–201. Harold Earl Davis' forthcoming *The Fledgling Province: A Social and Cultural History of Colonial Georgia* (Chapel Hill, 1976) is badly needed.

B. PRE-ENGLISH SETTLEMENT

The Spanish period in Georgia has received little intensive study. The most complete work is John Tate Lanning, *The Spanish Missions of Georgia* (Chapel Hill, 1935). A view of the entire English-Spanish contest in the southeast is Herbert E. Bolton and Mary Ross, *The Debatable Land* (Berkeley, 1925). Several more specialized studies are Herbert E. Bolton, "Spanish Resistance to the Carolina Traders in Western Georgia," *Georgia Historical Quarterly*, IX (1925), 115-30; Mary Ross, "The French on the Savannah, 1605," *Georgia Historical Quarterly*, VIII (1924), 167-94; J. G. Johnson, "The Yamassee Revolt of 1597 and the Destruction of the Georgia Missions," *Georgia Historical Quarterly*, VII (1923), 44-53, and "The Spaniards in Northern Georgia during the Sixteenth Century," *Georgia Historical Quarterly*, IX (1925), 159-68; and Charles W. Arnade, "The English Invasion of Spanish Florida, 1700-1706," *Florida Historical Quarterly*, XLI (1962), 29-37; and E. Merton Coulter, ed., *Georgia's Disputed Ruins* (Chapel Hill, 1937).

Early English interest in the Georgia area is best treated in Verner W. Crane, *The Southern Frontier, 1670-1732* (Durham, N.C., 1928; Ann Arbor, 1929, 1956). Other treatments of this same topic are Kenneth Coleman, "The Southern Frontier: Georgia's Founding and the Expansion of South Carolina," *Georgia Historical Quarterly*, LVI (1972), 163-74; Sir Robert Montgomery, *The Most Delightful Golden Islands* (Atlanta, 1969); Richard P. Sherman, *Robert Johnson, Proprietary and Royal Governor of South Carolina* (Columbia, 1966); Verner W. Crane, "Dr. Thomas Bray and the Charitable Colony Project, 1730," *William and Mary Quarterly*, 3rd Series, XIX (1962), 49-63; and several works cited in the general section of this bibliography.

C. THE TRUSTEESHIP

Good coverages of the proprietary period are included in Jones, Stevens, Saye, Strickland, Heath, and Ready cited earlier in the general section. Of books limited to this period James Ross McCain, *Georgia as a Proprietary Province* (Boston, 1917; Spartanburg, 1972), is the best and most complete.

James Edward Oglethorpe looms large in any account of Georgia's first decade. The best biographies are Amos A. Ettinger, *James Edward Oglethorpe: Imperial Idealist* (Oxford, 1936), and Leslie F. Church, *Oglethorpe: A Study of Philanthropy in England and Georgia* (London, 1932). B. Phinizy Spalding's *Oglethorpe's American Career* should be in print soon. See also his "James Edward Oglethorpe: A Biographical Survey," *Georgia Historical Quarterly*, LVI (1972), 332-48.

On other individuals the following may be consulted: Thomas Stephens, *The Castle-Builders: or the History of William Stephens* (London, 1759); Ann Elizabeth O'Quinn, Thomas Causton's Career in Georgia, (M.A. thesis, University of Georgia, 1961); Trevor R. Reese, "Harman Verelst, Accountant to the

Trustees," *Georgia Historical Quarterly*, XXXIX (1955), 348–52, and "Benjamin Martyn, Secretary to the Trustees of Georgia," *Georgia Historical Quarterly*, XXXVIII (1954), 142–47; Edith D. Johnston, "Dr. William Houstoun, Botanist," *Georgia Historical Quarterly*, XXV (1941), 325–39; Charles C. Jones, Jr., *Historical Sketch of Tomo-Chi-Chi* (Albany, N.Y., 1868); E. Merton Coulter, "Mary Musgrove, 'Queen of the Creeks,' " *Georgia Historical Quarterly*, XI (1927), 1–30; H. B. Fant, "Picturesque Thomas Coram, Projector of Two Georgias and Father of the London Foundling Hospital," *Georgia Historical Quarterly*, XXXII (1948), 77–104; E. D. Wells, "Duche, the Potter," *Georgia Historical Quarterly*, XLI (1957), 381–90; and Knox Mellon, Jr., "Christian Priber's Cherokee 'Kingdom of Paradise,' " *Georgia Historical Quarterly*, LVII (1973), 319–31.

The best and most complete treatment of the origin and development of the Trustees' plan for the founding of Georgia is in Saye, *New Viewpoints*, and more recently "The Genesis of Georgia Reviewed," *Georgia Historical Quarterly*, L (1966), 153–61. All the standard histories include something about the origin of the Georgia plan. See also Milton Ready, "The Georgia Concept: An Eighteenth Century Experiment in Colonization," and Kenneth Coleman, "A Rebuttal to 'The Georgia Concept,' " *Georgia Historical Quarterly*, LV (1971), 157–72, 172–76. Randall M. Miller, "The Failure of the Colony of Georgia Under the Trustees," *Georgia Historical Quarterly*, LIII (1969), 1–17, concurs with the views of numerous historians about the Trustee plan. A more detailed analysis is in Paul S. Taylor, *Georgia Plan: 1732–1752* (Berkeley, 1972), and "Colonizing Georgia, 1732–1752: A Statistical Note," *William and Mary Quarterly*, 3rd Series, XXII (1965), 119–27. Other aspects of the early period are treated in Edgar L. Pennington, "Anglican Influences in the Establishment of Georgia," *Georgia Historical Quarterly*, XVI (1932), 292–97; H. B. Fant, "Financing the Colonization of Georgia," *Georgia Historical Quarterly*, XX (1936), 1–29; H. B. Fant, "The Indian Trade Policy of the Trustees for Establishing the Colony of Georgia in America," *Georgia Historical Quarterly*, XV (1931), 207–22; H. B. Fant, "The Labor Policy of the Trustees," *Georgia Historical Quarterly*, XVI (1932), 1–16; Geraldine Meroney, "The London Entrepot Merchants and the Georgia Colony," *William and Mary Quarterly*, 3rd Series, XXV (1968), 230–44.

The social history of the Trusteeship is covered, in part, in McCain, Stevens, Jones, Strickland, and others. For a view of life and ordinary people see Sarah Gober Temple and Kenneth Coleman, *Georgia Journeys: Being an Account of the Lives of Georgia's Original Settlers . . . from . . . 1732 until . . . 1754* (Athens, 1961). Other references are Bertha S. Hart, "The First Garden of Georgia," *Georgia Historical Quarterly*, XIX (1935), 325–32; Laura P. Bell, "A New Theory on the Plan of Savannah," *Georgia Historical Quarterly*, XLVIII (1964), 146–75; Margaret D. Cate, "The Original Houses of Frederica, Georgia: The Hawkins-Davison Houses," *Georgia Historical Quarterly*, XL (1956), 203–12; Charles H. Fairbanks, "The Excavation of the Hawkins-Davison Houses, Frederica National Monument, St. Simons Island, Georgia," *Georgia Historical Quarterly*,

XL (1956), 213–29; Betty Wood, "Thomas Stephens and the Introduction of Black Slavery into Georgia," *Georgia Historical Quarterly*, LVIII (1974), 24–40; Neil J. O'Connell, "George Whitefield and Bethesda Orphan-House," *Georgia Historical Quarterly*, LIV (1970), 41–62; Lothar L. Tresp, "The Salzburger Orphanage at Ebenezer in Colonial Georgia," *Americana-Austriaca*, III (1974), 190–234; David T. Morgan, Jr., "The Consequences of George Whitefield's Ministry in the Carolinas and Georgia, 1739–1740," *Georgia Historical Quarterly*, LV (1971), 62–82; David T. Morgan, Jr., "George Whitefield and the Great Awakening in the Carolinas and Georgia, 1739–1740," *Georgia Historical Quarterly*, LIV (1970), 517–39; and E. Merton Coulter, "The Acadians in Georgia," *Georgia Historical Quarterly*, XLVII (1963), 68–75.

Military and Indian activities are included in Ettinger, Jones, Stevens, Reese, and other standard accounts. Larry E. Ivers, *British Drums on the Southern Frontier: The Military Colonization of Georgia, 1733–1749* (Chapel Hill, 1974), gives complete detail on the Spanish War. John Tate Lanning has done "The American Colonies in the Preliminaries of the War of Jenkins' Ear," and "American Participation in the War of Jenkins' Ear," *Georgia Historical Quarterly*, XI (1927), 129–55, 191–215; and the whole problem of Spanish-English relations in *The Diplomatic History of Georgia: A Study of the Epoch of Jenkins' Ear* (Chapel Hill, 1936). Other aspects of diplomatic history during this period appear in Margaret Davis Cate, "Fort Frederica and the Battle of Bloody Marsh," *Georgia Historical Quarterly*, XXVII (1943), 111–74; and Billups Phinizy Spalding, *Georgia and South Carolina During the Oglethorpe Period* (dissertation, University of North Carolina, 1963). John Pitts Corry, *Indian Affairs in Georgia, 1732–1756* (Philadelphia, 1936), is the best and most complete treatment on Indian affairs.

The problem of the malcontents who dissented from the Trustee plan is treated in David M. Potter, Jr., "The Rise of the Plantation System in Georgia," *Georgia Historical Quarterly*, XVI (1932), 114–35; Benjamin Martyn, *Reasons for Establishing the Colony of Georgia* (London, 1733; Savannah, 1840); Benjamin Martyn, *An Account Showing the Progress of the Colony of Georgia* (London, 1741); Benjamin Martyn, *An Impartial Inquiry into the State and Utility of the Province of Georgia* (London, 1741); Patrick Tailfer, et. al., *A True and Historical Narrative of the Colony of Georgia in America* (Charles-Town, 1741; Athens, 1960, edited by Clarence L. Ver Steeg); and Thomas Stephens, *A Brief Account of the Causes that Have Retarded the Progress of the Colony of Georgia* (London, 1743). Malcontent writings are reprinted in *The Clamorous Malcontents: Criticisms and Defenses of the Colony of Georgia, 1741–1743* (Savannah, 1973).

D. ROYAL PERIOD

The royal period has not aroused as much interest as the Trustee period. The works cited in the general section are useful with Jones, and Stevens, and Saye probably the best.

In political history there is, in addition, Percy S. Flippin, "The Royal Government in Georgia," *Georgia Historical Quarterly*, VIII–XIII (1924–1929); W. W. Abbot, *The Royal Governors of Georgia 1754–1775* (Chapel Hill, 1959); Albert B. Saye, "Commission and Instructions of Governor John Reynolds, August 6, 1754," *Georgia Historical Quarterly*, XXX (1946), 125–62; John P. Corry, "Procedure in the Commons House of Assembly," *Georgia Historical Quarterly*, XIII (1929), 110–27; Jack P. Greene, "The Georgia Commons House of Assembly and the Power of Appointment to Executive Office, 1765–1775," *Georgia Historical Quarterly*, XLVI (1962), 151–61; and Jack P. Greene, *The Quest for Power: The Lower House of Assembly in the Southern Royal Colonies, 1689–1776* (Chapel Hill, 1963). Several works covering pre-revolutionary political activities are cited in the next section of this bibliography. Military and frontier problems are covered in John R. Alden, *John Stuart and the Southern Colonial Frontier* (Ann Arbor, 1944), and Robert L. Meriwether, *The Expansion of South Carolina, 1729–1765* (Kingsport, Tenn., 1940).

Economic matters are covered in the works cited in the general section. In addition consult G. Melvin Herndon, "Naval Stores in Colonial Georgia," *Georgia Historical Quarterly*, LII (1968), 426–33; and G. Melvin Herndon, "Timber Products of Colonial Georgia," *Georgia Historical Quarterly*, LVII (1973), 56–62. More research is needed in this area.

Social affairs are covered in James B. Lawrence, "Religious Education of the Negro in the Colony of Georgia," *Georgia Historical Quarterly*, XIV (1930), 31–57; Robert L. McCaul, "Education in Georgia During the Period of Royal Government, 1752–1776," *Georgia Historical Quarterly*, XL (1956), 103–13, 248–60; Robert L. McCaul, "Whitefield's Bethesda College Projects and Other Attempts to Found Colonial Colleges," *Georgia Historical Quarterly*, XLIV (1960), 263–77, 381–98; Mollie C. Davis, "Whitefield's Attempt to Establish a College in Georgia," *Georgia Historical Quarterly*, LV (1971), 459–70, and "The Countess of Huntingdon and Whitefield's Bethesda," *Georgia Historical Quarterly*, LVI (1972), 72–82; Douglas C. McMurtrie, "Pioneer Printing in Georgia," *Georgia Historical Quarterly*, XVI (1932), 77–113; Alexander A. Lawrence, *James Johnston: Georgia's First Printer* (Savannah, 1956); Ralph C. Scott, Jr., "The Quaker Settlement of Wrightsborough, Georgia," *Georgia Historical Quarterly*, LVI (1972), 210–23; and E. R. R. Green, "Queensborough Township: Scotch-Irish Emigration and the Expansion of Georgia, 1763–1776," *William and Mary Quarterly*, 3rd Series, XVII (1960), 183–99.

E. THE REVOLUTION

This period is covered in the general works by Stevens, Jones, and Saye. John Richard Alden, *The South in the Revolution, 1763–1789* (Baton Rouge, 1957), may be consulted for the entire South.

The only general study of the revolution alone is Kenneth Coleman, *The American Revolution in Georgia, 1763–1789* (Athens, 1958). Most of the background of revolt in Georgia is covered in the preceding section. A few other works may be cited. Barratt Wilkins, "A View of Savannah on the Eve of the Revolution," *Georgia Historical Quarterly*, LIV (1970), 577–84; Marjorie Daniel, "John Joachim Zubly—Georgia Pamphleteer of the Revolution," *Georgia Historical Quarterly*, XIX (1935), 1–16.

On military matters see Alexander A. Lawrence, "General Robert Howe and the British Capture of Savannah in 1778," *Georgia Historical Quarterly*, XXXVI (1952), 303–27; Alexander A. Lawrence, "General Lachlan McIntosh and His Suspension from the Continental Command During the Revolution," *Georgia Historical Quarterly*, XXXVIII (1954), 101–41; Alexander A. Lawrence, *Storm Over Savannah: The Story of Count d'Estaing and the Siege of the Town in 1779* (Athens, 1951); W. S. Murphy, "The Irish Brigade of France at the Siege of Savannah, 1779," *Georgia Historical Quarterly*, XXXVIII (1954), 307–21; Otis Ashmore and C. H. Olmstead, "The Battles of Kettle Creek and Brier Creek," *Georgia Historical Quarterly*, X (1926), 85–125; and William E. Cox, ed., "Brigadier-General John Ashe's Defeat at the Battle of Brier Creek," *Georgia Historical Quarterly*, LVII (1973), 295–302.

Biographical treatments include E. Merton Coulter, "Nancy Hart, Georgia Heroine of the Revolution: The Story of the Growth of a Tradition," *Georgia Historical Quarterly*, XXXIX (1955), 118–51; William O. Foster, *James Jackson* (Athens, 1960); Louise F. Hays, *Hero of Hornet's Nest: A Biography of Elijah Clark* (New York, 1946); Charles F. Jenkins, *Button Gwinnett* (New York, 1926); and Charles C. Jones, Jr., *Biographical Sketches of the Delegates from Georgia to the Continental Congress* (Boston, 1891; Spartanburg, 1972).

On political matters see Homer Bast, "Creek Indian Affairs, 1775–1778," *Georgia Historical Quarterly*, XXXIII (1949), 1–25; Kenneth Coleman, "Restored Colonial Georgia, 1779–1782," *Georgia Historical Quarterly*, XL (1956), 1–20; Lucien E. Roberts, "Sectional Problems in Georgia During the Formative Period, 1776–1798," *Georgia Historical Quarterly*, XVIII (1934), 207–27; and William Frank Zornow, "Georgia Tariff Policies, 1775 to 1789," *Georgia Historical Quarterly*, XXXVIII (1954), 1–10.

On confiscation and banishment see Robert S. Lambert, "The Confiscation of Loyalist Property in Georgia, 1782–1786," *William and Mary Quarterly*, 3rd Series, XX (1963), 80–94; William I. Roberts, "The Losses of a Loyalist Merchant in Georgia During the Revolution," *Georgia Historical Quarterly*, LII (1968), 270–76; Gary D. Olson, "Thomas Brown, Loyalist Partisan, and the Revolutionary War in Georgia, 1777–1782," *Georgia Historical Quarterly*, LIV (1970), 1–19, 183–208; and Alex M. Hitz, "Georgia Bounty Land Grants," *Georgia Historical Quarterly*, XXXVIII (1954), 337–48.

INDEX

Abercorn, settlement of, 39, 40
Acadians, arrival of, 224–25
Acton, settlement of, 39
Adams, John, Oglethorpe calls on in London, 307
Agent, colonial: in London, 198; and controversy resulting from Stamp Act, 251–52; controversy revived in 1774, 263
Agriculture: Trustee fund to improve, 112; in Trustee period, 111–28; affected by land grant pattern, 123–24, 127–28; and indentured servants, 137; in royal period, 209–13
Aix-la-Chapelle, Treaty of, 74–75
Altamaha River: mission on, 4; settlement on, 9, 10
Altamirano, Bishop Fray de las Cabezas, visits Guale, 3
Amatis, Nicholas, silk expert, 114–15
Amatis, Paul, silk expert, 115
Amelia Island, named by Oglethorpe, 56
Anderson, Hugh: as malcontent, 99; as inspector of public garden, 113
Anglican church: in Trustee Georgia, 145–55; in royal period, 230–34
Angus, George, stamp distributor, 248
Ann, brings first colonists to Georgia, 22–24
Apalache missions, 4, 6
Articles of Confederation, Georgia ratifies, 279
Artisans: in Trustee period, 141; at Bethesda, 168; in royal period, 229–30
Arrendondo, Antonio de, Spanish negotiator, 56
Ashe, Gen. John: at Augusta, 290; defeated at Briar Creek, 292
Assembly: called by Trustees, 104–5; operation of, 105–7; in royal period, 177–78;

and arguments between two houses, 251–55; state, 295–96
Assembly-governor relations, 259, 263
Association, Continental, 265–67, 274
Attorney general, in royal period, 179
Augusta: location and settlement of, 50–51; as Indian trade center, 50–51, 215–16; and neglect of government, 92; and Indian trade, 134; and Anglican church, 153–54; and lack of education, 161; as social center of up-country, 244; Treaty of (1773), 262; capture of, by Lt. Col. Campbell, 290; occupation of, by tories, 297; capture of, by whigs, 299–300
Aviles, Pedro Mendez de: settles St. Augustine, 2; plants Spanish in Guale, 2–3
Azilia, Margravate of, advocated by Sir Robert Montgomery, 8–9

Bailiffs, 32, 91, 92, 94–95
Baptists, in backcountry, 235–36
Barber, Rev. Jonathan, at Bethesda, 166, 168
Barnwell, Col. John, erects Fort King George, 10
Bartram, John, opinion of Gov. Wright, 246
Bathurst, Sir Francis, titled resident of Trustee Georgia, 173
Beaufort, S.C., French settlement at, 1–2
Beef: import of, 121; export of, 213
Bethany: as German settlement, 53, 224; church at, 157
Bethesda: supplies dairy products, 121; artisans at, 141; origin of idea, 162–63; in Trustee period, 160, 162–69; in royal period, 239–42